Performing Politics

Performing Politics

Media Interviews, Debates and Press Conferences

Geoffrey Craig

polity

First published in 2016 by Polity Press

Polity Press
65 Bridge Street
Cambridge CB2 1UR, UK

Polity Press
350 Main Street
Malden, MA 02148, USA

ISBN-13: 978-0-7456-8961-6
ISBN-13: 978-0-7456-8962-3 (pb)

A catalogue record for this book is available from the British Library.

Library of Congress Cataloging-in-Publication Data

Names: Craig, Geoffrey.
Title: Performing politics : media interviews, debates and press conferences / Geoffrey Craig.
Description: Malden, MA : Polity Press, 2016. | Includes bibliographical references and index.
Identifiers: LCCN 2015038690| ISBN 9780745689616 (hardback : alk. paper) | ISBN 9780745689623 (papeback : alk. paper)
Subjects: LCSH: Communication in politics. | Mass media–Political aspects.
Classification: LCC JA85 .C73 2016 | DDC 320.01/4–dc23 LC record available at http://lccn.loc.gov/2015038690

Typeset in 10.5 on 12 pt Sabon
by Toppan Best-set Premedia Limited
Printed and bound in the UK by CPI Group (UK) Ltd, Croydon, CRO 4YY

For further information on Polity, visit our website: politybooks.com

Contents

Preface and Acknowledgements

The public performance of politics is significantly practised through interrogative exchanges in the media. Whether this consists of extended critical questioning in a political interview, prime ministerial posturing in a leaders' debate during the height of an election campaign, or the relaxed, jovial banter in an interview on a daytime chat show, political success is predicated on the ability to perform across a variety of such exchanges. These encounters are a vital means by which politicians promote themselves and are subject to scrutiny. Political leaders must express in a dramatic yet authentic way an individual identity or subjectivity, and their performances are realized by the successful negotiation of the power struggles that occur between the politicians themselves and the journalists they encounter.

This book will highlight broadcast interviews, leaders' debates and press conferences as fundamentally contestable encounters and argue that this 'dialogical' (Bakhtin 1981, 1986) and 'agonistic' (Mouffe 1993, 2000) quality is integral to political subject formation and democratic process. This argument is in contrast to research and public discourse that assesses how the conventions of interaction across types of mediated political interrogative exchanges fail to facilitate ideals of mutual understanding and truth production. In this sense, the book argues that public consternation over the 'games' of contemporary political communication must be reoriented to appreciate how interviews, debates and press conferences represent necessary struggles over the meanings of important public issues. It does not offer a 'solution' to the crisis of political communication: rather, it argues that we should understand that the 'games' that are played in interviews, debates and press conferences are the necessary 'play' of politics. This is not to be blind to the limitations of modern interactions between politicians and journalists or closed to seeking more constructive relations between the two, but it is to argue that we need to develop greater media and political literacy about such interrogative exchanges specifically, and political and media relations more generally.

It has been claimed that we live in an 'interview society' (Atkinson and Silverman 1997) and that the interview is 'the fundamental act' of contemporary journalism (Schudson 1994). Journalism researchers identify the importance of interviews, but such discussion is usually limited to the practice and mechanics of interviewing (Conley and Lamble 2006; Sedorkin 2011). Much existing scholarly research on political interviews, debates and press conferences has been dominated by linguistic studies that have focused at a textual level on the nature of exchanges between the participants (Clayman and Heritage 2002a; Tolson 2006). While these kinds of studies are vital in understanding the communicative effects of interviews, debates and press conferences, we are also concerned with locating such interactions in the contexts of a broader struggle between journalism and politics that can be illuminated with reference to media and political theory.

The first two chapters will outline the theoretical framework of the book. The opening chapter will provide a comprehensive theorization of the mediated and televisual contexts of interviews, debates and press conferences and the importance of individual performance and style in political and journalistic practice, in contrast to political communication research which sees media and public focus on image and performance as a distraction from more substantive political realities. It will begin by outlining the mediated basis of public life and then discuss both how disciplined bodily performance is integral to journalistic and political professionalism and why the reading of bodies is an important feature of the meanings of interviews, debates and press conferences. Bourdieu's concept of habitus will be introduced, and the chapter will conclude by offering a theorization of performance and, specifically, note the centrality of televisual performance to the production of political and journalistic identity.

The second chapter discusses the idea of the 'game' that accounts for the discursive and institutional struggles between journalists and politicians in interrogative encounters. It introduces political interviews, leaders' debates and press conferences as communicative events, briefly accounting for their similar and different features and describing their significance as both face-to-face and highly mediated exchanges. The role of the public in such interactions is also considered. The chapter then explains how the political games that occur in political talk television formats derive from the contestable nature of both language and politics. The dialogical basis of language and the agonistic nature of politics will be outlined, and it will be argued that politics is concerned primarily with persuasion and trust and that the main task of journalists in interviews, debates and press conferences is not to discover the truth but to engage in a constant scrutiny that keeps the political open. Finally, the chapter will set out the methodological approaches that inform the analyses in the book.

The succeeding chapters will offer a textual analysis of a range of interview genres, leaders' debates and press conferences. This will be supplemented with discussion of how such interactions are manifestations of broader struggles between the media and political fields for public authority (Bourdieu 1991, 1998). The textual analysis will be informed by critical discourse analysis theory, and the resulting thick descriptions will reveal how language use expresses the power relations between interview participants and their struggles to represent the nature of their relations with other social actors, including the public. In addition, the bodily performance of both interviewers and interviewees will be analysed.

The book argues that the essential communicative form of interviews, debates and press conferences facilitates the interrogation and the promotion of the interviewee, as well as the promotion of the interviewer. These functions are necessarily fused in these interactive exchanges, but the relationship between interrogation and promotion varies across different formats, initiating different power relations between participants, generating different kinds of knowledge, values and emotions, and establishing various representations of social actors, institutions and public life. Political interviews on current affairs programmes, for example, are characterized by greater degrees of interrogation than interviews in so-called soft media, where the interactions between interviewer and interviewee can function more collaboratively in the construction of personal narratives. In contrast to dyadic interview structures, the dynamics of press conferences usually enable politicians to exert more control over the interactions, and there is usually less sustained and direct interrogation.

The case studies in chapters 3 to 7 draw on interrogative exchanges with high-profile political leaders across the United States, the United Kingdom and Australia. Chapter 3 offers analyses of political interviews with the UK prime minister David Cameron on *The Andrew Marr Show* and the former Australian prime minister Kevin Rudd on *Insiders* and the *7.30 Report*. It prefaces such discussion with a brief overview of the history of political interviews and an examination of the nature of the dialogue of political interviews as well as their public dissemination. Chapter 4 provides analyses of leaders' debates in the 2010 United Kingdom election campaign and the debates between Barack Obama and Mitt Romney in the 2012 US presidential campaign. It outlines the formats and structures of leaders' debates and considers their functions and effects in election campaigns. Chapter 5 examines press conferences through case studies involving US President Barack Obama, both a solo press conference and a joint press conference between Obama and the former Russian president Dmitry Medvedev. It also details the history and dissects the significance of different types of press conferences. Chapter 6 examines current affairs forum television, where politicians appear on a panel of public figures and are questioned by members of the studio audience. The case study involves the high-profile Australian programme *Q&A*. The chapter first defines the genre of current affairs forum television before examining the roles of the programme host, panelists and audience members. Chapter 7 deals with political celebrity interviews and features an analysis of Barack Obama's performances (including with his wife, Michelle) on the daytime talk television programme *The View*. It offers a theorization of the concept of political celebrity – in particular the celebrity status of the American president – and the engagement of such individuals with 'non-political' media. A conclusion brings together these analyses of different interrogative exchanges and offers some judgements about the nature of the political games that take place between politicians and journalists, including the production of identity and the power struggles that occur between the journalistic and political fields.

It is important here both to acknowledge the basis of the selection of case studies and the limitations of the comparative basis of the analyses and to provide some perspective on the strength of the overall conclusions that are offered. The individual case studies have been chosen because they feature current or recent national political leaders who will be familiar to students and other readers across a range of countries, most notably the United States, the United Kingdom and Australia. Their selection also derives partly from my own political interests and previous research, most notably the inclusion of the former Australian prime minister Kevin Rudd, who generated considerable public discussion about the nature of contemporary political performance during his tenure as a political leader. It is acknowledged that there is not a strict uniformity to the approaches in each of the chapters. With the exception of the press conferences, the case studies involve interrogative exchanges that are also part of televisual programming. There is a greater degree of scrutiny of news media coverage of the interactions in some chapters than others, and the extent of the interactions between politicians and journalists varies. The chapter on leaders' debates, for example, sees journalists in the more limited role of moderator, and the emphasis is more on the interactions between politicians, their engagement with the audience, and the reactions from the public on social media. In this sense, as the title of the book suggests, the focus is on the nature of political performance across a range of interrogative formats that primarily feature journalists but also include questions from the public in different communicative contexts. In three of the chapters there are two case studies, and the final two address a single programme. These selections have been made to enable a more in-depth textual analysis that would not have been possible had there been a study of fragments across a greater range of programmes. The book adopts a synchronic approach, examining instances of contemporary political performance, rather than a diachronic approach to explain the historical evolution of the interrogative encounters. The analysis chapters do, however, provide the historical contexts of each of the studied formats, revealing how and why they have assumed their present-day shape and significance.

It must be acknowledged that we are providing examples of political leaders who are working in different political systems. While there is considerable uniformity in the nature of the performances of contemporary political leaders across modern Western democracies, and although there has been a general trend towards 'presidentialization' in national politics, we should note, for example, that the president of the United States has a different orientation towards the media and journalists than prime ministers, who regularly perform and experience scrutiny in parliamentary chambers. In addition, the significance of political performance is influenced by a range of factors, such as whether there are compulsory or voluntary voting systems, and the character of the media industry, including the distribution and cultural significances of public and private broadcasters.

This book has been prompted partly by the belief that, while political communication has been well served by research into individual respective areas, such as political interviews and political talk shows, there has been less research that has considered the character of political performance and the interactive relationships between politicians and journalists across the range of interrogative encounters examined here. In this way, it is hoped that one advantage of the book is that readers can observe the contrasts and similarities of political performance across the communicative genres. It is acknowledged that is difficult for systematic conclusions about political interviews, leaders' debates, press conferences, current affairs forum television, and political celebrity interviews to be derived from a study that is limited to one or two case studies in each chapter, and this volume in a more modest way seeks to highlight the range and flexibility of political performances. This task has been facilitated by examining the performances of individuals such as Barack Obama and David Cameron across a number of the chapters. As always, then, the book is but a contribution to the field of political communication, and it is certainly hoped that it will encourage further research on political performance across these communicative genres.

Performing Politics is the culmination of research and teaching on the topics of political interviews, leaders' debates and press conferences over several years, and I have benefited greatly from feedback from colleagues and students. My interest in political interviews was initially provoked many years ago as an honours student at Macquarie University in Sydney, where I was fortunate enough to be supervised by Philip Bell and Theo van Leeuwen and to have been taught by other outstanding scholars, including John Tulloch and Warwick Blood. Later, my investigations into the nature of journalism were facilitated by great support from my PhD supervisor John Hartley. More recently, research that has informed the book has been presented at a number of conferences and seminars: the 2010 Australian and New Zealand Communication Association conference in Canberra; the 2011 International Communication Association conference in Boston; the 2012 conference on Identity, Culture and Communication in Madrid; the 2012 Celebrity Studies conference in Melbourne; and the 2014 Media, Communication and Cultural Studies Association conference in Bournemouth. I have also presented seminars at the University of Canberra and the University of Otago. I am grateful for the support I have received from many colleagues across a number of institutions over recent years, among them Lance Bennett, Libby Lester, Cathy Greenfield, Peter Putnis, Kerry McCallum, Jason Wilson, Stephen Harrington, Marian Simms, Philip Nel, Chris Rudd, Janine Hayward, Vijay Devadas, Olivier Jutel, Tim Luckhurst and Alex Frame. I have also enjoyed exploring ideas with students across different courses, including 'Political Talk' and 'Theory of Communication Studies' at the University of Otago. I appreciated the feedback from three anonymous reviewers of the manuscript. And I am grateful, as always, for the love and support of my family: Wendy Parkins, Maddy Parkins-Craig and Gabriel Parkins-Craig.

Parts of this book have been previously published in article form, and I am grateful for permission from the journals and editors to reproduce them here: 'How does a prime minister speak? Kevin Rudd's discourse, habitus and negotiation of the journalistic and political fields', *Journal of Language and Politics*, 12/44 (2013), pp. 485–507, with kind permission of John Benjamins Publishing Company, Amsterdam/Philadelphia, www.benjamins.com; and 'Kevin's predicaments: power and celebrity across the political and media fields', *International Journal of Press/Politics*, 19/1 (2014), pp. 24–41, with kind permission of the publishers.

1

Mediated Political Performance

Introduction

There is often a widespread uneasiness about the performances of politicians in contemporary times, and yet public performance is necessary for the practice of politics; it generates legitimacy for politics, and occasionally it can even provide inspiration. Politics is a communicative practice, requiring embodied subjects who can perform and engage in speech acts in a domain that is public, where others can witness and freely respond to those performances and speech acts. Our uneasiness, and sometimes cynicism, about modern political performance is at odds with perceptions about political performance in ancient Greece, where the public realm, in contrast to the necessary strictures of work and household duties in the private realm, was associated with freedom and civic virtue (Arendt 1958). We must be wary about idealizing earlier epochs (Keane 2010), and the ancient Greeks were certainly aware of manipulative or empty rhetoric, encapsulated in the criticisms of the Sophists, but there was also a fundamental appreciation of the process of communicating ideas and persuading others in a dialogical context. The performative skills associated with oratory were taught, keenly observed and held in esteem. Here were the means to realize political change in a non-coercive manner and also to express excellence in character and leadership. By contrast, the modern era tends to sever the 'performance' of politics from its substance, its perceived 'real' status. We are sceptical that performance is a necessary and legitimate vehicle for the transmission of information and the persuasive power of ideas.

Performance carries negative connotations of superficiality and a unidirectional rather than a dialogic orientation. The public domain has assumed a greater theatrical character and political activity aligned more with a kind of show business, where behavioural appeal – a winning smile, pleasant personality and populist manner – becomes more integral to political success than the communication of the merit of ideas and policies. Such a perspective is encapsulated in Habermas's claim that the contemporary public sphere represents a process of 'refeudalization', where contemporary political presence resembles the representative publicity of the king in the High Middle Ages; there publicness was 'something like a status attribute' (Habermas 1989, p. 7), *displayed before* the populace, rather than the site of a 'social realm' where the open exercise of reason could be conducted.

This chapter outlines an understanding of political performance that informs our subsequent analyses of media interviews, debates and press conferences. It attempts to reclaim performance as intrinsic to political communication, noting the significance of embodied political communication and the legitimate functions of performance in political rhetoric. This reclamation of political performance is based upon a broader recognition of the dramatic basis of mediated public life and the centrality of performance to identity and meaning. In this chapter we will firstly discuss the mediated character of the contemporary public domain, examining how the televisual contexts influence the performances of politicians and journalists in their interrogative encounters. We will then consider how we can conceptualize the bodies and subjectivity of politicians and journalists as they are engaged in political performance. Contrary to popular dismissals of 'talking heads', it will be argued that a disciplined bodily deportment is integral to a performance of professionalism and successful political persuasion. We will also argue that any substantive analysis of political performance must extend beyond scrutiny of the 'cut and thrust' of the interrogative encounter to an appreciation of how the habitus of politicians and journalists informs the skills and resources they bring to acts of political communication. We will then apply theorizations of performance and performativity in discussion of the dramatic basis of journalism, the visual character of television, and the particular performative requirements for both politicians and journalists in acts of contemporary political communication.

Mediated Public Life

The disparity in appreciation of political performance between the ancient Greeks and ourselves is perhaps partly due to the *mediated* status of contemporary political performance. Public political performance in earlier times occurred in contexts of co-presence: the Pynx, for example, was a place where assembled citizens could directly see and hear public oratory. The desirability of this unmediated context of political performance is underlined by Aristotle's famous comment that the ideal size of a state should be limited to an assemblage that could be easily surveyed in a single view (Aristotle 1981; see also Hartley 1992, p. 35). By contrast, modern public life is a profoundly mediated phenomenon. The public realm is now located in media texts rather than on a rocky hilltop. Our experience of our political representatives is primarily through representations of their performances rather than via direct encounters. It is difficult to grasp the significance of this character of modern public life given it is such a naturalized feature of our everyday experience. The significance is realized not only in the recognition that we are deluged each day with an array of journalistic stories, media programmes and online sites, where our public life is visualized, presented and interrogated, but by the more fundamental observation that media in contemporary times constitute public life (Craig 2004; Hartley 1992; Thompson 1995; Washbourne 2010). The issues, debates, spectacles, scandals, contests, protests and ceremonies that give shape to our public life continue, of course, to have a material reality in the real world, but they assume a general public significance when they are subject to media representation and diffusion.

Public discontent about contemporary political performance derives partly from the alienation people feel from such performances, given the mediated character of the communication, and also because the performances seem to be oriented primarily towards the journalistic encounter and the contest of the political sphere rather than towards the viewing populace. The performances in media interviews, while ostensibly held for the benefit of the public, seem to exclude them, and the performances are highly disciplined and predictable. As Habermas noted with reference to modern media: 'today the conversation itself is administered' (1989, p. 164). Modern politicians are highly professional figures who carefully position themselves vis-à-vis their opponents, and this strategic positioning is often prompted and foregrounded by the journalistic framing of issues. Consternation about political performance in this way derives from perceptions that the politician's performance is not so much an expression of their individual self but more of a generalized professional performance, and also that the performance does not reflect the true thoughts of the individual but is more pragmatically oriented towards political differentiation and advantage.

There may be feelings of alienation from contemporary political performances but, paradoxically, our experiences of such performances are also remarkably intimate. Earlier historical experiences of political performance, before the introduction of audio-visual media, may have been more dialogical, but they were also usually quite a distanced interaction: hearing a local MP speak at a community hall, for example. As John Thompson (1995, p. 98) has noted, the experience of contemporary publicness is determined by a condition of 'tele-visibility', where audio-visual presence is combined with spatial-temporal distance. This condition allows politicians to be presented on a more equal level with viewers and to identify with them more easily, but at the same time such intimacy robs them of the aura of distinction and power that is associated with more aloof communicative contexts. The minutiae of bodily performance is amplified in a television interview – we can see a prime minister sweating during a tough interrogation – but at the same time we are substantially distanced from the interview, which is probably taking place far removed from the place and time of our viewing, and this, in turn, prevents interaction on the part of the viewer. This communicative context thus both elevates and estranges political performance. Further, political performance across mediated political interrogative exchanges is complicated by the simultaneous occurrence of different forms of interaction, as this kind of 'mediated quasi-interaction' (Thompson 1995) enables the viewing of the face-to-face interaction of the interrogative encounter. The 'media-constituted field of interaction' (ibid., pp. 117–18), which also includes forms of dialogical mediated interaction such as a telephone call, and the particular interactions of online and social media, therefore render a layeredness, plurality and complexity to forms of modern political performance.

More broadly, we also need to consider the context of the image-saturated public realm, which significantly affects our witnessing and evaluation of modern political performance. DeLuca and Peeples (2002), in their attempt to account for the roles of visually dominant, screen-based media and their modes of perception in processes of public formation, posit the metaphor of the 'public screen' in contrast to the 'public sphere'. They note that, 'in comparison to the public sphere's privileging of rationality, embodied conversations, consensus and civility, the public screen highlights dissemination, images, hyper-mediacy, publicity, distraction and dissent' (ibid., p. 125). Significantly, the public screen is not a replacement but a supplement for the public sphere. Such work points not only to the iconicity and spectacle of modern politics; it also has ramifications for the complexity and difficulty of assessing political performance in interviews, debates and press conferences. These conventional forms of inter-rogative exchanges are variously viewed and reported in terms of the ideals of dialogue, the machinations of political contestation, and also the demands of public screen culture, where dramatic, visual moments and sound bites dominate. The singularity of these interrogative exchanges is thus undermined, and they are largely understood pub-licly as texts of dissemination, segments of which circulate and are reworked in media commentary and reportage. In addition, the char-acter of public and political discourse is changing in the contexts of mediated public life. Dominique Mehl (2005), for example, talks about a 'public sphere of exhibition' where the rise of reality shows and other televisual genres associated with private life create a more fluid relationship between the public and private spheres and alter the dynamics between experts and ordinary people; the nature of political and public discourse subsequently changes from an emphasis on confrontation and argument to one on narrative and conviction.

Disciplined Bodies

Interviews, debates and press conferences are representations in medi-ated public life, but they are also specific instances of embodied com-munication. We tend not to dwell on the significance of the bodies of journalists and politicians even though everyday media display a plethora of bodies that are highly stylized and obviously attributed with cultural value. When there is focus on the body of a politician, it is often presented as *inappropriate*, as we saw in misogynistic com-ments about the body of the former Australian prime minister Julia Gillard (Martinson 2013). Of course, the career of a television jour-nalist is helped if they are televisual (and this is a highly gendered phenomenon), but generally politicians and political reporters are differentiated from other public figures, such as celebrities, who are distinguished (in both senses of the word) partly by their bodily fea-tures: the good looks of a film star, the honed body of an Olympic athlete, etc. The performance of politics is thus in one way judged not to be dependent upon bodily attributes, but equally embodiment is not only necessary but privileged in evaluations of political per-formance in public life. Political ideas and rhetoric are conveyed through speech acts, and the mastery of voice, gesture and general bodily deportment is crucial in successful political communication.

The body has been subject to comprehensive and widespread theo-rization that we are not able to explore fully here. Suffice to say, prominent theorists, such as Bourdieu (1977, 1990, 1991), Butler

(1990, 1999), Foucault (1991, 1988), Goffman (1959) and Merleau-Ponty (1962), among others, have in different ways challenged the mind–body split of Cartesian dualism and sought to retrieve and explain the importance of the body in the exercise of power, the production of identity, and the structural organization of institutions and societies. Much of the struggle across this research resides in expressing how and when power is exercised on and through the body and, alternatively, how and when the body exerts its power. The narrative of Foucault's (1991, 1988) work, for example, saw a transition from an emphasis on the way the body is subject to the techniques, practices and calculations of institutional regimes to later investigations of the 'technologies of the self' and the reflexive and ethical potential that resides in forms of self-fashioning.

This struggle between structure and agency – acknowledging that we are both socially constituted as subjects and able to use our bodies in particular expressions of identity – also crucially informs the analysis here of the political games that are played between politicians and journalists. The significance of the body in journalistic practice and political performance, has, however, not received the level of scrutiny that might have been expected, given this broad disciplinary spread of research. Certainly Habermas's influential theorizations of both the public sphere (1989, 1992) and communicative action (1984, 1987) downplay the status of publicly communicating subjects as *embodied* subjects (Alway 1999; Crossley 1997; Gardiner 2004; Young 1987). This study, however, also argues that we need to do more than merely address this deficiency; we must in addition emphasize the centrality of corporeal *intersubjective* relations (Crossley 1995). That is, the significance of the bodies of politicians and journalists in interrogative encounters does not dwell solely in their individual expressions but also intrinsically in their generic and interpersonal contexts. As Nick Crossley (ibid., p. 142) has argued: 'the exercise of body techniques is...acting-towards-others; it is [also] acting-towards-others in a way that is acceptable to others...by virtue of its reliance upon commonly held rules and resources, and its observance of ritual considerations.'

The bodies that are scrutinized in the case studies, with the exception of the female panelists on the *The View* in chapter 7, are *male* bodies; most of the journalists who question these political leaders are also men. Both professions, politics and journalism, have traditionally been male-dominated occupations. While women now have a stronger presence on the front benches and in front of the camera, they are still under-represented and encounter undue, critical scrutiny when they do succeed in positions of power, as we have just noted above. It is significant, though, that the 'serious' public affairs communicative genres we examine feature men and that, across the 'hierarchy' of political talk formats we analyse, women dominate only in the programme that would be deemed 'less' political and more entertainment oriented.

Both journalism and politics are profoundly embodied practices, a point often overlooked because of the ubiquity of unruly and spectacular bodies that populate media screens. Journalists and politicians practise their craft through the performance of professional and disciplined bodies. Journalistic professionalism, informed by ideas of 'objectivity', does not render the journalistic body invisible but, rather, creates disciplined bodies that are governed by occupational codes of values and behaviour. Similarly, the credibility and authority of politicians in interrogative encounters is in no small way expressed through a disciplined mastery of the body. As Bourdieu (1990, p. 58) has noted, institutions require their objectified logic to be realized in the practices of bodies. It also follows from noting the importance of corporeal intersubjective relations that both journalism and politics involve the reading of bodies. Assignation of value and meaning derives from the reading of bodily deportment and the embodied performance of utterances. Often in interviews, debates and press conferences a disciplined performance is in accord with discursive control, but nonetheless it is necessary that the disciplined body is produced and its power made visible. It is also the case that the disciplined body is 'never totally fixed and self-contained' (Craig 1999, p. 118). The disciplined body of the journalist and the politician is not a mechanistic, inflexible entity but one who is able to read another body in a forensic manner and is sensitive to the exigencies of the political moment. The disciplined bodies of journalists and politicians are not dehumanized actors; rather, they are efficient and comprehensive bodies, where there is an appropriate melding of personality and knowledge, deference and authority, adherence to generic dictates and expressions of individual authenticity.

Habitus

The subjectivity of political leaders undergoes extraordinary, fine-detailed public scrutiny: their character and personality, their way of speaking, their style of dress, their upbringing and professional background – all realize a concatenation of values around issues such as class, gender, ethnicity and aesthetics. We saw this profoundly in the fascination with, and dissection of, Barack Obama's background during the 2008 US presidential election campaign. In the 2010 British election there was a detailed comparison of the privileged backgrounds of the Conservative leader David Cameron and the Liberal Democrat leader Nick Clegg. Asking who was 'posher', the media coverage contrasted not only their respective family back-grounds but also the type of schools they had attended (Byrnes 2010). These matters of background and personal style are not incidental features of political subjectivity but, rather, cumulatively inform rep-ertoires of political action and modes of relating that are integral to political success.

That is to say, there is a profound 'layeredness' to political interac-tive encounters. It is tempting in an analysis of political games to focus on the surface of the interaction – the immediate cut and thrust, the verbal twists and turns. We do need to focus on these actions, but such interactions are also based upon a more deep-set structuring of professional roles as well as the durable set of dispositions and character of individual politicians and journalists. As Bourdieu reminds us, 'the truth of the interaction never lies entirely in the interaction' (1990, p. 291). The weight of the past, objectified in social structures and embodied in individual behaviour and character, very much informs the encounters of the moment. This is something that is sometimes forgotten in the analyses of the journalistic present.

We can capture this sense of subjectivity through Pierre Bourdieu's concept of habitus, which refers to our 'embodied history' (Bourdieu 1990, p. 56) – the ways the sedimentation of social contexts inform our sense of self, comprehensively manifested in the way we speak, the way we look and present ourselves, the way we conduct ourselves in the world and interact with others. Bourdieu (2002, p. 27; original emphasis) refers to habitus as 'a system of *dispositions*, that is of permanent manners of being, seeing, acting and thinking, or a system of *long-lasting* (rather than permanent) schemes or schemata or struc-tures of perception, conception and action.' The idea that we are creatures of our own upbringing may not be controversial, but habitus seeks in a more subtle and comprehensive way to account for how the power of social structures and institutions is exercised through individual bodies, both in processes of formative socialization and in our subsequent encounters with particular social fields. This power does not create a static sense of identity but variously equips individu-als with the resources and skills that are necessary in the access to, and engagement with, a range of social institutions. Habitus, then, is a more generalized and structural account of subjectivity than the 'persona' of a politician, which can give more emphasis to the self-conscious strategy of the presentation of an individual self.

Habitus, as a theory of subjectivity, seeks to account for the struggle between structure and agency that was outlined above in the discussion of disciplined bodies. As Crossley (2001, p. 83) has noted, habitus 'emerges out of...the need for a conception of human action or practice that can account for its regularity, coherence, and order without ignoring its negotiated and strategic nature.' Bourdieu writes that habitus is similar to what has been traditionally called character but with an important difference: the habitus is 'a set of *acquired* characteristics which are the product of social conditions' (2002, p. 29; original emphasis). As such, we can refer to the habitus of an individual, but it will always be framed primarily as an individual variant of a more generalized collective or group identity (Bourdieu 1977, p. 86; see also Crossley 2001, pp. 84–5). The example of Cameron and Clegg highlights that, for all the high-profile scrutiny of their individual and political differences, there is a fundamental commonality to their social constitution as subjects that accounts in no small way for their advancement in politics, their outlook on the world, and their capacity to manage everyday exigencies. The structured basis of habitus is crucial, but Bourdieu is also at pains to emphasize that habitus does not offer a monolithic, mechanistic and unchanging account of subjectivity: 'As a dynamic system of dispositions that interact with one another, [habitus]...has, as such, a generative capacity; it is a structured principle of invention, similar to a generative grammar able to produce an infinite number of new sentences according to determinate patterns and within determinate limits' (Bourdieu 2002, p. 30). There is a dialectical relationship between the way that social fields such as politics and journalism (to be discussed in chapter 2) structure the habitus and the way in which 'habitus contributes to constituting the field as a meaningful world, a world endowed with sense and value, in which it is worth investing' (Bourdieu and Wacquant 1992, p. 127). Habitus, then, facilitates a sense of agency, or 'regulated liberties' (Bourdieu 1991, p. 102), where subjects can engage with the world and act in a flexible manner, evolving over time, although it can be also argued that, with its emphasis on the habitual and regularized contexts of actions, habitus does not fully capture the creative and innovative basis of human agency (Crossley 2001, pp. 94–6).

Habitus accounts for the constancy of subject formation in particular socio-economic contexts and the continuities of the exercise of those subjectivities, but it is also the case that increasingly we live in an age of what Beck and Beck-Gernsheim (2002) have termed 'individualization'. Such a concept refers to the way that individual life trajectories have become less structured by institutional and generational continuities and are increasingly determined by individual calculations and decisions that yield both new opportunities and possibilities for failure. 'Individualization', in a rather confusing way, is not an account of the individual of liberal political theory; Beck and Beck-Gernsheim stress that it refers to a form of '*institutionalized individualism*' (ibid., p. xxi; original emphasis). Contemporary processes of biography formation, in this sense, are not freely chosen but become a 'task' that is imposed upon subjects. There is, then, a productive tension between the concepts of habitus and individualization that is further complicated by the rich semiotic environment in which people are immersed in everyday life. Of course, our degrees of 'choice' are still very much variously circumscribed in an age of individualization, and an array of representations of other lives does not equate necessarily with people adopting different life pathways, but these points should not distract us from the observation that there are greater degrees of flexibility and complexity in the contemporary functioning of habitus.

Habitus provides an account of structured and structuring embodied practice that is useful for our understanding of political and journalistic performances, but we also need to consider the mediated contexts within which these exercises of habitus occur. It could be argued that Bourdieu's account of habitus does not sufficiently incorporate the significance of the media (Calhoun 1995; Couldry 2004; Wynne and O'Connor 1998). As Couldry (2004, p. 359; see also Bourdieu 1990, p. 108) points out, Bourdieu is open to the role of representations in expressions of habitus, but nonetheless the crucial role of media, both in the physical places of our formative socialization and in their offering of an extraordinary array of representations of events, people, lifestyles and values, means that it 'is difficult to capture the sheer breadth and complexity of how media might work as habitus'. Bourdieu's account of habitus, in this sense, needs to be enhanced with an appreciation of how the range of contemporary media forms and the blizzard of media and popular culture representations that individuals encounter provide a greater porousness to traditional class and taste boundaries.

In the next chapter we will discuss how politicians develop as they learn and negotiate the conventions, knowledge base, and networks that cumulatively structure the governance of the political field. Politicians must display great flexibility as they adapt to such institutional rigours, but this flexibility also extends to responding to the *representations of themselves* that they encounter following media performances. As I have noted previously (Craig 2004, p. 57), individuals undergo a tremendous transformative process when they become public figures, as their performances and utterances are subject to readings by journalists and the public. There is often a sense of disjuncture between self-perceptions and public perceptions, and politicians must learn to respond appropriately to their political 'images'. Of course, this is not simply a 'responsive' phenomenon: intrinsic to successful contemporary political practice is the cultivation of a subjectivity that is attuned to the requirements of the media field. The habitus of contemporary public figures is, then, a profoundly mediated phenomenon.

The habitus of both politicians and journalists is also crucially manifested in the manner of their language use, a point of particular interest given our scrutiny of the interrogative encounters of media interviews, debates and press conferences. Drawing on a tradition that includes the work of Mauss, Bourdieu (Bourdieu and Wacquant 1992, p. 149) notes both that language is a bodily technique and that societal power relations are expressed through the language and verbal competency of particular bodies. As such, we can refer to the notion of a linguistic habitus as a

> set of socially constituted dispositions that imply a propensity to speak in certain ways and to utter determinate things (an expressive interest), as well as a competence to speak defined inseparably as the linguistic ability to engender an infinite array of discourses that are grammatically conforming, and as the social ability to adequately utilize this competence in a given situation. (Ibid., p. 145)

For Bourdieu, every speech act is a product of a conjuncture between a linguistic habitus and a linguistic market: the mobilization of a linguistic habitus occurs in contexts where there is recognition of the accord between a linguistic habitus and a particular communicative encounter and also the capital at stake in that particular communicative encounter. Capital is anything that has an exchange value, and it can be manifested variously: financial capital, symbolic capital (i.e., status), social capital (i.e., social contacts) and cultural capital (i.e., educational qualifications, aesthetic style and taste) (Crossley 2001, p. 87). The importance of the idea of a linguistic habitus (and the idea of habitus more generally) is that it forces us to acknowledge the extent to which the discursive struggles between politicians and journalists are determined by the pre-existing social status and authority of the participants (Bourdieu and Wacquant 1992, p. 148). That said, and as will be discussed in the next chapter, this argument is not sufficient because, on account of discursive struggle, it does not also account for both the negotiations of a habitus that have been identified here and the changing authority of respective fields over time. Our analysis of political talk formats, then, needs to offer a balance between an appreciation of the sociological significance of political and journalistic professionalism and an acknowledgement of the discursive significance of the interrogative encounters that animate and justify those positions.

Performance

Our discussion of the disciplined bodies of journalists and politicians, their habitus, and the contexts of mediated public life points to the fundamental importance of performance in political communication. This evaluation of performance is based upon a broader understanding of politics as an 'expressive' phenomenon that foregrounds both the 'values, perspectives and emotional attachments people have to politics' and the way such attachments and meanings are embodied in political leaders (Washbourne 2010, p. 43). But how are we to understand the performance of politicians and journalists? Performance is a physical phenomenon that extends to the verbal performance or 'voice'. To what extent are such performances expressive solely of the individual's opinions and intentions and to what extent do they speak for others, including us, the public? And how are we to evaluate the merits of political performances and decide whether they effectively and sincerely communicate opinions, sentiments and policies, or whether they are merely slick and shallow expressions designed to evade scrutiny and further self-interest? Moving beyond the performances of individuals, we also need to consider the role of journalism as the stage upon which performances are enacted. Finally, what particular features of political performance are manifested in the interrogative exchanges of interviews, debates and press conferences? How are the performances of both journalists and politicians determined by the nature of their interactions in different communicative genres?

The act of performance, or performativity, enables the construction and expression of identity. Theorists across a number of fields have offered critiques of the idea of the self as a pre-existing and independent entity and argued instead that the self is generated through the iteration of behaviour as a response to particular everyday and institutional social contexts and interactions with others. Goffman (1959), for example, highlighted the 'plastic' nature of the self, demonstrating how people adapted both their appearance and their behaviour to certain interactive social frameworks. He observed

how, across and within particular communicative events, the performative self differentiates between a 'front region' and a 'back region'.
The front region of communicative encounters is governed by more
public standards of behaviour – Goffman talks of manners, decorum
and 'make-work', where workers give the appearance of fulfilling
their duties (1959, pp. 106–9) – and also where positive aspects of
ourselves, relative to the communicative encounter, are highlighted
and negative aspects are suppressed. The back stage, alternatively,
consists of the places where such public conventions apply less strictly
and where people can be more 'themselves', or, as Goffman (ibid., p.
114) puts it, where 'individuals attempt to buffer themselves from
the deterministic demands that surround them.' Such a division,
however, should not be a means of ushering in a sense of a singular,
true identity when we drop the 'public mask' of the front region. A
young man, for example, may be independently expressing various
facets of his 'genuine self' as he behaves very differently with a girl-
friend, his male friends and his parents. Some communicative encounters, such as a public concert, will be defined more by a front region
between the performer and an audience, while other events, such as
a drinks reception, will be comprised of a series of verbal interactions
where people may shift between front and back regions. Some sites
are physically demarcated between front and back regions: Goffman
gives the example of an undertakers, where the bereaved are sepa-
rated from the work of the preparation of the body, but more relevant
for us might be the news studio, where we can see the journalists
working at their computers behind the glass partition that divides
them from the newsreader. As part of his broader theory of practice,
Bourdieu's account of habitus, with the stress on its 'generative capacity', outlines how the logic of institutions and social norms is incorporated in embodied performances. In feminist theory, Judith Butler's
account of performativity demonstrates how apparently natural
forms of gender identity have in fact 'no ontological status apart from
the various acts which constitute … [their] reality' (1990, p. 136).
That is, Butler argues that gendered performance does not *express*
an identity that is behind or gives rise to the performance; rather, the
gendered performance *constitutes* the identity: 'Gender is the repeated
stylization of the body, a set of repeated acts within a highly rigid
regulatory frame that congeal over time to produce the appearance
of substance, of a natural sort of being' (ibid., p. 33).

Both Bourdieu and Butler draw on J. L. Austin's (1975) famous
account of speech acts in their understandings of performance. Austin
highlighted that language itself has a performative dimension; that it
not only describes the world but sometimes has the power to bring

into being and change a state of affairs and social status. For Austin, while constative utterances merely describe a state of affairs, performative utterances enable action through language. Famous and well-known examples of performative utterances are a presidential oath or a wedding vow. Subsequent theorists, most notably Searle (1969), extended Austin's account of language to emphasize the performative nature of language in general.

We have ascertained that performance is intrinsic to the production of identity, that the performances of the self are shaped by their social contexts, and that language itself is performative. In addition, we need to highlight how the voices of politicians and journalists are always informed by their orientation towards others, and that successful political and journalistic discursive performances involve the adept collation and management of different voices. We tend to think verbal discourse expresses the consciousness of an individual regardless of intended recipients, but this profoundly misunderstands the very nature of language. All speech (and indeed all texts) has a *dialogic* character. That is to say, there is always at least one other voice implicit in an utterance, and that other voice influences the utterance in some way. This implication of others in our language use reflects the fact that our employment of words is always cognizant of the way those words have been used by others. Words and concepts may be more or less contestable, but such a point highlights not only how our utterances have a social context but also that social context informs the very constitution of the utterances (see chapter 2).

Both journalism and public life more broadly are *dramatic* and *performative* phenomena. The uneasiness with contemporary individual political performances that we noted at the outset of this chapter perhaps blinds us to the recognition that society generally, and journalism more specifically, is reliant on performance and dramatic conventions to convey meaning. Drama and theatrical process have always been fundamental to communication *per se*, but, particularly in modernity, drama has ceased to be a mainly distinctive or ritualistic activity and now structures and pervades everyday and public life (Carlson 2004; Chaney 1993; Eldridge 1997; Kershaw 1999; Williams 1975). Both the political demands of democracy, which require the display and negotiation of authority, and the economic demands of capitalism, where the market must have a fundamental public presence, cumulatively inform this 'performative society' (Kershaw 1999, p. 13). Journalism expresses its performative power through its presentation of content and also its form and style. As Broersma (2010, p. 19) has stated: 'Performative power is essential for journalism's status and position in society. Every day, journalism stages the social world in language. Every day its authority has to be reconfirmed.' It is readily apparent that forms of broadcast journalism are performances, and those performances express a professional authority that also gives credence to the information they provide, but the presentation of all forms of journalism involves the performance of such professional authority. Journalism provides the stage or setting for public life, and the news is a cultural form that facilitates performance (Broersma 2010; Chaney 1993; Craig 1999). David Chaney has argued that the news offers a 'mode of ceremonialization' (1993, p. 138), and that dramatic conventions expressed through the order of the news 'govern the space or the stage within which the cast of public life can act and give...their actions a plausibility and dramatic verisimilitude' (ibid., p. 139).

The dramatic and performative character of journalism and public life is, of course, highlighted in its televisual representations. Television, as a medium, has profoundly influenced the practice of political communication. As we will note in chapter 4, President Nixon's inability to master the visual demands of television in his leaders' debate with John Kennedy has now passed into televisual folklore. Television offers a high degree of realism – the perception of an authentic portrayal of reality – and this persists even in contemporary media platforms which incorporate televisual representation in more articulated modes of representation that enable greater user manipulation of images. As John Corner (1995, p. 13) has noted, the visual character of television enables it to

> give to viewers a sense of independent surveillance and evidence ('see it for yourself') which is both a mode of communicative engagement and a primary point of (relative) trust between the television industry and its audiences. In respect of the former, the television 'message' brings with it...an expanded sensory/informational field...as well as distinctive kinds of satisfaction and pleasure.

Television privileges notions of drama, 'liveness', interaction and authenticity, and these features of the medium have shaped the evolution of a form of 'performance journalism' (Liebes and Kampf 2009). Liebes and Kampf outline this type of journalism in an account of the changing styles of conflict reporting, but it has also influenced television presentation, reportage and genres more pervasively. The ubiquity of live crosses in television news, the interactive banter between presenters and reporters, and the dominance of forms of reality television, for example, all arise partly from the representational features of the medium. The dominance of performance in television, however, is also linked to the commercial demands to maximize audiences. Television has been integral to the rise of info-tainment genres (Thussu 2007) and, specifically with regard to televi-sion news, there has been a trend away from monological, authoritative news bulletins and stories to more conversational and looser forms of presentation that are deemed to be more viewer friendly (Ben-Porath 2007). These points have relevance to the kinds of political or 'public affairs' programming that we will be examining here in this volume. Various forms of interactive political talk shows are fundamental to formations of political knowledge and public debate, but they are also attractive to broadcasters because they 'are inex-pensive to produce,…they embody qualities of "eventfulness," "spontaneity," and "liveliness" that are regarded as intrinsically tele-visual and popular with audiences' (Clayman 2004, p. 30).

The dramatic and visual basis of televisual representations of jour-nalism and politics may well be acknowledged, but we also need to consider how to evaluate the performances of contemporary political communication in this context. Both journalism and politics have received criticism in recent years precisely because they have been *too* concerned with performance at the expense of substance. In politics, it has been argued the criteria for political leadership now prioritize image-conscious, media-savvy politicians, and the rise of a culture of 'spin' unduly elevates the importance of the presentation of informa-tion. The increased focus on individual political leaders, and a cor-responding lesser focus on political parties and institutions, has been captured in the concept of 'presidentialization' (Mughan 2000; Poguntke and Webb 2005) and the related but broader concept of 'personalization' (Van Aelst et al. 2012). The prominence of indi-vidual leadership in politics has arisen partly because of an historical erosion of traditional class divisions and reliable electoral support and a lessening of ideological differences between major parties. As Thompson has noted (2000, p. 111), this has meant a shift from a traditional emphasis given to policy towards what might be termed the 'politics of trust'. The kinds of interrogative encounters that we are examining here are primary vehicles through which this 'presi-dentialization' occurs, and, while a focus on the performative skills of individual leaders at the expense of more substantive policy scru-tiny is an obvious concern, we also need to be cautious about the establishment of a binary between 'image' and 'substance' that equates political image with ideas of 'falseness' or 'manipulation' and instead recognize the legitimacy of performance in political commu-nication. A focus on expressions of political style or a more aesthetic form of politics (Ankersmit 2003; Pels 2003; Street 2003) can lead us to understand the ways in which successful political subjectivity requires the complex coexistence of substantive forms of expertise and communicative skills. As Pels (2003, p. 45) has noted, political style is a 'heterogeneous ensemble of ways of speaking, acting, looking, displaying, and handling things, which merge into a symbolic whole that immediately fuses matter and manner, message and package, argument and ritual.' Successful mediated political performances must not only combine style and substance but also address the symbolic dimensions of political representation that are always negotiated through relations of distinction and identification (see Ankersmit 2002, 2003; Pels 2003; Street 2004). We will investigate this point further in chapter 7 in our discussion of political celebrity interviews, but here we simply note that the performances of politicians in media interviews, debates and press conferences are crucial in the constitution of their relations with the public: politicians must simultaneously demonstrate the basis of their distinction, manifested in expertise, character and argumentative skills, and their identification with the interests and concerns of their constituents, manifested in knowledge about real-life issues, appropriate expressions of affect and uses of everyday language.

As the analysis in a number of the following chapters demonstrates, the cultivation and expression of an affective subjectivity is an important component of a successful political performance. The importance of affect has been insufficiently recognized in much political communication research and particularly in considerations of interrogative exchanges, where there is a focus on the ways that modes of rationality are facilitated and limited by the interpersonal dynamics. Affect is a complex concept, but for our purposes here we can simply note that it includes, but extends beyond, emotions and feeling; it relates in a more substantive way to the driving forces that give rise to emotions and feelings and also compels people to act (or to refrain from action). As Zizi Papacharissi (2015) has noted in her overview of the history of the theoretical understanding of the concept, affect is produced within the body through interactions with other bodies, and it is also facilitated by, and channelled through, institution and technologies. Affect is integral to the immaterial labour that is performed in contemporary capitalism, across service industries and more professional work (Hardt and Negri 2004). Papacharissi (2015, p. 21) notes that 'media typically invite audiences to consume content via affective relationships developed with particular media genres and media personas', and in particular she explores how affect is vital in public formations and the networks of emergent political movements, such as the Arab Spring and Occupy.

Ultimately, then, affect is not only an integral feature of individual political performance but also crucial in the expressions of a productive everyday life, the enactment of contemporary labour, and manifestations of civic life.

The performance of journalists in television is also complex given the tension between the performative demands of the medium and the normative demands of the discipline that has conventionally downplayed individualism, opinion and exhibitionism in professional practice. Televisual journalistic performances are complex phenomena because they must embody a range of interests or positions: the interviewer or reporter must portray the values and style of the particular media outlet for which they work; they reproduce more generalized journalistic standards and principles; they must work to attract and sustain the interest of their audience and also represent their interests; and they must mobilize their individual personalities and bodily attributes to fashion a professional and engaging performance. The noted changes in recent decades in television news presentation and reportage has prompted criticisms that news bulletins are now driven less by a quest for quality reporting and more by the visual appeal of the sets and graphics and the charm of newsreaders, and equally that the more conversational style of reportage unduly foregrounds the personality of the journalist rather than the substance of the story. Traditionally, journalists have negotiated the tension between inquiring into the truth while remaining neutral or impartial by assuming the role of the 'honest-broker' (Kumar 1977) of opinion, where the interviewer speaks on behalf of the public, although such an orientation tends to render public opinion as a unified and depoliticized, or at least a conservative, phenomenon (Craig 2004, p. 102). The speaking roles of interviewers and presenters are also complicated by the various modes of address throughout a programme, as they move between opening addresses direct to camera, introducing and then interrogating guests, throwing to commercial breaks, and closing a programme. These different performative roles, relating to both the production demands of the programme and the modes of interaction with interviewees, can be captured in Goffman's (1981) 'footing shift' concept, where he distinguishes between the person who produces an utterance (animator), the person who composed the words that are being uttered (author) and the person whose ideas are being expressed (principal). Often such roles are embodied in the one person. However, in the example of a political speech, the politician may be the animator and the principal, but the author is a speechwriter, and in a news bulletin the newsreader will be the animator, a journalist will be the author, and the principal would be the editor-in-chief and/or the proprietor (Bell 1991). Individual journalists can shift footing at various stages of an interview – introducing a topic, engaging in aggressive questioning and defending criticism – as they negotiate varying levels of 'ownership' of the ideas they are raising and attempt to balance the competing needs of neutralism and interrogation.

We have demonstrated why and how performance is fundamental to the practice of both politicians and journalists, and why it is integral to public life, but we also need to consider the particular performative requirements of politicians and journalists in the interrogative encounters that are the object of inquiry for us here. Interviews, debates and press conferences are not obviously performative events, particularly when contrasted with the theatrical stunts of election campaigns or solemn national rituals. We have already noted nonetheless that the disciplined deportment of politicians and journalists is crucial for successful contemporary political communication. Unlike more singular and exceptional 'media events' (Dayan and Katz 1994) that aim to foster national unity, interviews, debates and press conferences are everyday, more prosaic political encounters that are marked by contestation and conflict. While we have established that all language use and performances are oriented towards others, interviews, debates and press conferences are, of course, explicitly interactive performances, and their drama and meaning derive largely from these interactions. As we will see in later chapters, the nature of the interactions and subsequent performances differ across various forms of interviews, debates and press conferences. Politicians must exhibit sensitivity as they move between the performative conventions of the adversarial political interview, the friendly banter of a political celebrity interview, the complexity of a leaders' debate – where they must counter their political opponent while also appealing to the electorate – and the diplomacy required in international press conferences with other political leaders. The analyses in the following chapters illustrate that the structural positions that politicians and journalists occupy in the political and media fields provide them with access to, and authority in, these encounters, but equally that their respective performances determine who wins out in the machinations of political games.

Conclusion

In this chapter we have retrieved an understanding of the important and legitimate functions of performance in contemporary political communication. The groundwork for this understanding has been laid by discussing the mediated nature of public life and highlighting how our perceptions and evaluations of political performances are very much influenced by the televisual form of representation, which provides both an intimacy and a distance from the on-screen protagonists. While understandings of performance are shaped by the representations of those performances, the significance of the material bodies of journalists and politicians was also discussed, noting that individual bodily performances and their intersubjective relations are intrinsic to identity, and also that journalists and politicians are engaged in acts of disciplined bodily deportment that are central to their professionalism. We further argued that the performances of politicians and journalists in interviews, debates and press conferences are determined not only by the immediate contexts of interaction but also by the deep-set and long-lasting competencies and resources that individuals bring to such encounters. It was noted that Bourdieu's account of habitus captures this phenomenon but equally that the theory of habitus needs to incorporate the increasingly mediated and individualized social contexts in which habitus is generated. We concluded our discussion by highlighting how performances constitute identity and by noting that journalism is a fundamentally dramatic and performative phenomenon that enables the staging of public life. The increasing importance attributed to the televisual performative skills of politicians was considered, but it was also observed that 'political style' is an amalgam of expertise and communicative skills. We saw that the demands of modern television have contributed to the rise of a form of 'performance journalism' and demonstrated the flexibility and shifts in footing that television journalists exhibit in their performances as they negotiate competing demands involved in the presentation of the programme and the forms of reportage, including the questioning of politicians.

2

Political Games

Introduction

We are confronted every day with the game of politics as political opponents wrestle with each other, as journalists report on politics, and journalists and politicians interact with each other. These games involve arguments, rational explanations, challenges, exclamations, jokes and whatever other resources participants can muster to persuade others and bring about desired actions. The resources drawn on by politicians and journalists are linguistic resources, and this underlines how the practice of politics is a profoundly discursive phenomenon (Chilton and Schaffner 2002; Lakoff 1990). It also underlines the centrality of the media to the practice of politics and to the constitution of public life more generally (Bennett and Entman 2001; Corner and Pels 2003; Craig 2004; Hartley 1992; Thompson 1995; Washbourne 2010). Politics and the media are individual institutional sites, or fields of action (Benson and Neveu 2005; Bourdieu 1991), governed by their own regulations, conventions, practices and values. The tensions and clashes between journalists and politicians, then, derive partly from their different subject positions as representatives of particular institutions. Political and media games, however, are also contested by individual personalities, and success as a politician, and also as a journalist, depends partly on the character and style that the individual can bring to communicative encounters (Pels 2003; Street 2003). There are, of course, many different communicative events where politicians encounter journalists in order to convey information to the public, but the focus here is on interrogative encounters in interviews, debates and press conferences. It is here that the game of political communication is cast in sharp relief, where issues of subjectivity and performance are highlighted as integral to successful communicative outcomes.

The invocation of the 'game' of political communication can be seen to allude to the common belief that there is a lack of authenticity and seriousness to the interactions. There is the view that, as they seek to persuade others, politicians do not offer full disclosure of relevant information and are not interested in engaging with alternative points of view. Similarly, there is the belief that journalists are motivated primarily by a desire to 'catch out' politicians and that they focus unduly on the images of politicians and political strategies at the expense of the issues under consideration. Such a portrayal of the game of political communication is a long way from rational, exploratory dialogues in the best sense of the term (Anderson et al. 2004; Wierzbicka 2006), where people fully disclose all relevant information, set aside their own interests and are responsive to other points of view as they seek the truth, or at least a substantive consensus.

Political communication scholars recognize the distinction between news media reportage of the political game or 'strategy' and more substantive coverage of issues, and studies have used this distinction to evaluate journalistic reportage in election campaigns and the effects of such framing on levels of political engagement (Cappella and Jamieson 1997; Lawrence 2000; Rudd et al. 2009). The historical shift in increasing focus on political strategy at the expense of reportage of issues has been analysed (Esser et al. 2001; Kerbel 1999; Patterson 1993), with more recent scrutiny being given to 'meta-coverage' in political reportage, where journalists concentrate not only on strategy but also on their own involvement in political processes (D'Angelo et al. 2005; Esser et al. 2001; Esser and D'Angelo 2003; de Vreese and Elenbaas 2008). Concerns about the effects of such reportage on public cynicism about politics (Cappella and Jamieson 1997; Valentino et al. 2001; de Vreese 2004) have been usefully balanced by other research (McNair 2000; D'Angelo and Lombard 2008) that illustrates how media reportage of political strategy or process can provide citizens with important information about both political behaviour and communication and media involvement in political processes.

The 'game' of political communication can also be understood alternatively as a competition, a contested arena governed by rules and conventions that structure and regularize behaviour and legitimize subsequent results of the process. The game may not be pretty at times, and it may be frustrating to view and actually cause alienation and disengagement, but we may also consider why the process occurs the way it does. If interviews, debates and press conferences are' understood as struggles over the meaning of important public issues and over who has the right to exercise considerable political power, then perhaps we should expect the communicative encounters to be combative and highly disciplined. This is not to excuse obfuscation or bad journalism, but it is to ask us to consider whether it is realistic, and even desirable, in effect, to take the 'politics' out of political communication. Specific instances of language use and performance can prompt us to demand better quality political communication from those who profess to represent us politically, or those who speak journalistically on our behalf, but it is argued here that such demands need to be couched within an understanding of both the dialogical character of language (Bakhtin 1981, 1986; Crossley and Roberts 2004) and the agonistic character of democratic politics (Mouffe 1993, 2000). Both these accounts of language and politics highlight that interviews, debates and press conferences are fundamentally contestable encounters. Political communication, then, can perhaps be cast legitimately as a 'game', albeit a serious one. It follows that, given our own stake in its process, we should understand the rules of the game.

We start our understanding of political games in this chapter with a discussion of the relationship between the institutions of journalism and politics. We will note that, while journalism – and the media more generally – has become central to politics, the two institutional sites still exert particular influence over the behaviour of their respective practitioners. The contrasting interests of these institutional domains inform much of the discursive struggles that we will examine later in this book. The next section of the chapter will provide a brief overview of the way that power is encoded in questions and answers, and we will also consider the different kinds of interaction that occur across political interviews, leaders' debates and press conferences. We will examine the various roles of the public in such interactions and discuss in more detail our understandings of the dialogic basis of language and the agonistic basis of democratic politics. It will be explained that we can use these theoretical approaches to argue that the function of interrogative forms of political communication should be cast less in terms of producing truth, consensus and mutual understanding and more in terms of keeping the political open. We will argue that the production of truth is not the primary goal of political communication; rather, it is persuasion, the cultivation of trust, and the mobilization of public opinion. Finally, we will outline the methodological approaches that inform our analysis of interrogative exchanges between journalists and politicians.

Political and Journalistic Fields

The contemporary political landscape may be in a state of flux, but the rules, conventions and values of journalistic and political institutions still govern the practices, texts and performances of political communication. We can understand the ways in which these institutional domains shape the behaviour of politicians and journalists through reference to Bourdieu's concept of 'field' or 'fields of action'. Fields, such as the media, the legal and the corporate fields, as well as other social domains such as the family, are institutional sites that are governed by their own internal dynamics, but they also relate to one another in complex ways in the constitution of societies. The *institutional* status of fields refers not so much to their formal, organizational identity as to the way they facilitate 'relatively durable set[s] of social relations which *endow*...individuals with power, status and resources of various kinds' (Thompson 1991, p. 8; original emphasis).

Fields circumscribe what is 'thinkable', 'doable' and 'sayable' within particular domains, and this effect is realized by factors such as the conditions of entry to a field, the productive requirements of the field and its competitive dynamics, as well as by the available vocabulary and discursive register. Bourdieu stresses the relative autonomy of fields in such a way that differentiates his theory from Marxist analysis, which would account for a field's power more directly from its relationship to the economic mode of production (Thompson 1991, p. 29). That said, fields are always sites of struggle for the power, prestige and authority that derive from the specific domains, which are rendered by Bourdieu as forms of capital or profit. As such, Bourdieu sometimes uses related terms, such as 'market' and 'game', as synonyms for field, and these terms highlight the transactional and competitive basis of the domains.

Bourdieu's theory highlights the centrality of communication and forms of symbolic power in the exercise of cultural practices. Symbolic power is the power 'of constituting the given through utterances, of making people see and believe, of confirming or transforming the vision of the world and, thereby, action on the world and thus the world itself' (Bourdieu 1991, p. 170). Symbolic power is intimately connected to the exercise of other forms of power, such as political power and economic power, and in order to exercise symbolic power people must have access to resources involving the 'means of information and communication' (Thompson 1995, p. 16), which include particular skills, competences and knowledge.

The political and journalistic fields are each constituted by a complex structure and set of conventions that give definition to the particular domains of practice. Politicians undergo a specialized form of training – a 'sort of *initiation*, with its ordeals and its rites of passage' (Bourdieu 1991, p. 176; original emphasis) – that includes the acquisition of relevant bodies of knowledge (party history and current organization, institutional operations, economic data, political theory, etc.) as well as the cultivation of certain modes of deportment and ways of speaking (to fellow politicians, media professionals, members of the public, etc.). Bourdieu limits the political field to electoral politics and institutionalized political power, and he notes how the development of the field has been facilitated by the increased professionalization of politics, encapsulated in bureaucratic party structures and the influence of political consultants (Thompson 1991, pp. 25–6). The political field has a significant degree of autonomy – institutional and party structures dictate roles, discourses, and norms of behaviour – but equally the political field is defined – more so than other fields, such as business, science and higher education – by a greater public 'porousness' and engagement with other related fields, such as the media or journalistic field. Bourdieu (1991; see also Thompson 1991, pp. 27–8) notes that the discourses produced by politicians are influenced by two kinds of constraint that work in an antagonistic relation. Firstly, the political field is partly determined by an internal, relational logic whereby the expression of individual political discourse is always necessarily defined through the positions and values of political opponents. Secondly, success and authority in the political field are also determined by the ability of politicians to appeal to groups and individuals outside the political field. Political success, then, emanates from the negotiation of the antagonistic relation between these two broad constraints.

The operations of the political field are very much influenced by its entanglements with the journalistic field. Like the political field, the journalistic field is central to the structures and play of power because it is inextricably connected to, and interacts with, a number of other fields and also public opinion. Bourdieu's work on the journalistic or media field has attracted considerable attention and is subject to varying evaluations (Benson 1999; Benson and Neveu 2005; Darras 2005; Davis and Seymour 2010; Hesmondhalgh 2006; Schudson 2005; Webb et al. 2002). It remains difficult to assess, for example, the degree to which the journalistic field impacts on the processes of the political field, and to what extent the political field equally imposes its influence on the journalistic field (Darras 2005; Schudson 2005; Webb et al. 2002). In accord with field theory,

Bourdieu acknowledges the internal logics and dynamics of journalism – it can be claimed, for example, that the journalistic field has a degree of autonomy through professional codes of ethics that enshrine commitments to freedom of speech, the public's right to know, and accurate and unbiased reporting (Webb et al. 2002, p. 183). It is claimed, however, that the journalistic field has 'very low autonomy', and there is a focus on the increasing influence of the journalistic field over other fields due to its growing commercialization (Bourdieu 2005, p. 41). The journalistic field is said to be a 'very heteronomous field, which is structurally very strongly subordinated to market pressures, [and this] in turn applies pressure to all other fields' (Bourdieu 1998, p. 54).

In his book *On Television*, which was written for a more general audience and designed to provoke public debate, Bourdieu outlines a number of quite conventional criticisms of journalistic performance and argues that the public vision of politics is deleteriously influenced by media reportage. Journalistic reportage is said to produce a 'depoliticization' of, or 'disenchantment with', politics (1998, p. 6). This occurs because, increasingly, television dictates the news agenda (ibid., p. 50) and its journalistic framework highlights news that is dramatic visually and controversial at the expense of analysis (ibid., pp. 19, 51). Journalism's ongoing need for novelty and the competitive requirement for 'scoops' generates a kind of 'structural amnesia' (ibid., p. 7) that prevents sustained debate, and the production demands of journalism, particularly the increased speed of news production, mean that ideas are always evaluated within existing conceptual frameworks (ibid., p. 29). While these criticisms have some merit, Bourdieu's critique of journalistic performance is nonetheless also overdrawn and insufficiently sensitive to the complexities of media representation, the contributions of popular media to political process, and the particular functions and requirements of the journalistic field. While we can question Bourdieu's criticisms of journalism, the concept of field is used here because it focuses on the significance of internally generated practices and modes of sensemaking while also highlighting the particular interactions that occur between specific social domains; it also highlights the production and circulation of different kinds of capital without succumbing to economic reductionism.

These descriptions of both the political and the journalistic field need to be supplemented with a more detailed understanding of the ways in which the successful practice of contemporary politics is dependent upon various kinds of expertise and skills associated with the journalistic field. In their account of 'media capital', Davis and

Seymour (2010) refer to the kinds of resources and authority accrued by politicians through contacts with journalists, knowledge about media practice and values, and performance skills in various journalistic and media genres. Media capital is necessary in the acquisition and maintenance of the various forms of cultural, social and symbolic capital that, in turn, are integral components of successful action in the political field. Media capital, then, does not refer simply to credit gained from direct media performance but, rather, to a regime of knowledge, skills and esteem that is gained and exercised through a range of public and private encounters and associations with journalists and media contexts, and which is linked to different types of audiences or publics. Media capital can be generated within the contexts of the political field (internal media capital) – relations with political colleagues, opponents and other political actors, including journalists – or it can be generated outside the political field (media meta-capital), through interaction with journalists, and directed to the populace. A further means of distinguishing it is to categorize the media capital of an individual politician in terms of their institutionalized position (institutionalized media capital) and their individual personality (individualized media capital). Another way of gaining symbolic capital through the media is via 'mediated performance capital': 'Performances can contribute to the accumulation of each of the four forms of media capital identified and potentially sets up a dynamic exchange between forms generated within and external to the political field' (Davis and Seymour 2010, p. 744). As Davis and Seymour (ibid., p. 743) state, media capital can simply be generated quantitatively, through numbers of media appearances and the size of media outlets and on the basis of the kinds of audiences that bestow symbolic capital. It is also generated, as they note, more discursively in the ongoing media performances of political leaders, and this is the object of scrutiny for us here.

In our analyses in the succeeding chapters of this book we are seeking to show the relationship between the performances and discursive struggles in the texts of the interrogative encounters and the requirements of the respective political and journalistic fields. For Bourdieu, it is the structural basis of fields that facilitates and exerts power: the ability of individual politicians to impose their vision as the objective reality in communicative exchanges is realized primarily through the resources they are able to harness as a result of their institutional subject positions within a given field. Bourdieu is therefore dismissive of the kind of 'discourse analysis' that seeks to elucidate the significance of communicative interaction without prioritizing the pre-existing structuring of those subject roles and discourses. Despite this,

Bourdieu's more sociologically informed theory has been enhanced by a range of studies that consider how these structural parameters and processes can be engaged in the examination of the production and performance of political discourse (Boussofara-Omar 2006; Chouliaraki and Fairclough 1999; Reisigl 2008; Wodak 2011). This body of specific work has done much to bridge micro-analysis of political language and macro-processes and structures. Such work emphasizes that fields are not static structures and are subject to change. Struggles occur over the hierarchy and boundaries of fields, as well as over the capital that derives from access to the discursive and other resources of fields – that is, struggles over the 'capacity to constitute the given, and…to do so in a legitimate style which gives credibility to a vision of the world' (Chouliaraki and Fairclough 1999, p. 104). Bourdieu's theory, however, cannot account for *how* such struggles occur; it lacks 'the specific "grammar" of symbolic control' (ibid., p. 107). This, then, is our object of scrutiny here: how the political game is played out through communicative interactions in mediated political interrogative exchanges. We will seek to show how the socio-cultural practices and social relations of the political and journalistic fields are encoded in, and reproduced through, language use.

Journalistic and Political Interaction

We now consider the nature of the specific communicative interactions that occur between politicians and journalists. The power of the exchanges between individuals in political interviews, debates and press conferences derives largely from the *face-to-face* confrontation of the exchanges. We are reminded of the bare, interpersonal drama of leaders' debates and media interviews when we watch a presidential candidate stumble in response to a question from the debate moderator or when we see a prime minister angrily point her finger at her interrogator across the table. These interpersonal exchanges, however, are also *institutional* exchanges: the participants speak as representatives of the political and journalistic fields, and, as such, the exchanges differ from everyday conversation. The institutional exchanges of political interviews, leaders' debates and press conferences structure power differentials between the participants, with differing expectations about access to information and rates of participation in the exchange. Interviews, debates and conferences are also more goal-oriented than everyday conversation (Drew and Heritage 1992, p. 49; Craig 2010a, p. 79). These kinds of interactions are 'front-stage' interactions (Goffman 1959; Thompson 1995) where individuals are disciplined by professional standards of discourse and performance, although the motor of communicative exchanges in political talk formats is often the disjuncture between this front region and perceived political 'realities' that lurk in the back stage of political practice. These exchanges are, of course, also *mediated* events that facilitate a type of interaction between the participants of the interpersonal exchange and the general, viewing or listening public. The significance of these dramatic interpersonal exchanges stems from their *public* status and are profoundly influenced by their orientation towards the audience of the programme. As such, there is a 'double articulation' to broadcast talk (Scannell 1991, p. 1). As I have noted previously (Craig 2010a), the *dissemination* of interviews, debates and press conferences is not just the transmission of an already completed exchange but, rather, a constitutive feature of the communicative act.

There is a fundamental *interrogative* relationship between journalists and politicians that is manifested most directly in the questions and answers that occur in interviews, debates and press conferences. A question, however polite, is an implicit command to answer. However open a question might be, it offers information and frames an issue in a particular way, and this framing of questions structures the power relations between interviewer and interviewee. The posing of a so-called 'wh-question' (where, what, when, why) is usually an open question where the interviewer is acknowledging a deficit of understanding and the question seeks to elicit knowledge or information from the interviewee. The interviewer can sharpen the challenge to an interviewee by asking a polar question, where the scope of the reply is theoretically limited to yes or no. Questions can be asked with a negative or positive orientation, making it difficult to provide an answer that opposes that orientation, and often journalistic 'questions' are in fact grammatically structured as statements where there is an even more direct challenge. In this sense, while interviews are often presented as equal exchanges where the participants have the freedom to have their say, the reality is that such communicative exchanges are highly structured. That said, such exchanges are also defined by their dialogic status, where the meanings and values of the issues are necessarily problematic. An interviewee has to confront a set agenda of questions and accede to the journalist's authority, but they also engage in a struggle over meaning as they negotiate the framing of questions in order to advance their understandings and interests.

The nature of the interaction between journalist and politician varies considerably across different types of mediated political

interrogative exchanges. The particular dynamics of political interviews, leaders' debates, press conferences, current affairs forum television and political celebrity interviews will be discussed in more detail
in later chapters, but here the variations that occur in journalistic and
political subjectivity and performance across these genres are initially
contrasted, so we can be aware that successful contemporary political
communication practice requires individuals to exercise flexibility
across a range of media genres as they communicate to a range of constituencies. Most political interviews are dyadic encounters, and this
highlights the intensity of the interaction, although interviews can
sometimes occur with two political opponents or involve a panel.
Alternatively, the interaction in leaders' debates focuses more on the
participating politicians. Leaders' debates also assume a variety of
formats and often feature some journalistic participants in addition to
the host of the event, who might nonetheless be the main questioner of
the candidates. Politicians may have to engage not only with their
opponent and journalists but also with a live studio audience. The
drama of the interactions that occurs in such debates is determined
largely by their common context of election campaigns, while political
interviews and press conferences are a more regular feature of the
political media landscape. Press conferences can take a variety of
formats but often feature a large number of journalists where the politician is usually able to exercise greater control over the length of the
interaction and which journalists pose questions.

Broadcast media interviews, leaders' debates and press conferences
are brought together here in this study because they are prominent
instances of politicians and other public figures directly encountering
questions from journalists and where that interrogative encounter
forms the basis of a media programme or text. It is in these extended
encounters that the interactions between the journalistic and political
fields are most prominently exhibited and where subjectivity and
performance are integral to communicative and political success.
Interviews are, of course, the basis of much print, broadcast and
online reportage, and selections from those interviews, in the form
of quotations and reported information, are subsequently reworked
in journalistic texts. The broadcast media encounters that are analysed here occur across a spectrum of institutional spaces and television programmes – from the White House to Hollywood studios, and
from flagship, political talk shows on British and Australian public
broadcasters to daytime US variety chat shows. The diversity of these
programmes is also informed by the subjectivities of the presenters/
interviewers, who embody mixes of 'journalistic' and 'show business'
personas.

These kinds of distinctions across media interview-based programmes emphasize the variability in the negotiations between the
political and journalistic fields that is sometimes lost in sweeping
denunciations of the quality of political reportage. Interactions
between politicians and journalists are profoundly influenced by the
communicative contexts of the programme genre: our analysis in
chapter 6, for example, shows that the appeal of current affairs forum
television derives partly from more open exchanges, where politicians
have greater freedom to deviate from the strictures of the political
field, and where they are open to scrutiny not just from the programme host but also from other panel participants and the studio
audience. Insights into issues of political authenticity and journalistic
credibility, which trouble so many evaluations of contemporary political communication, can be derived from close scrutiny of the language use and performances of different kinds of interviews, debates
and press conferences. Relations between the political and journalistic fields are informed by antagonism or conflict, and this informs the
usually combative nature of political interviews, leaders' debates and
press conferences, prompting charges about the unduly negative focus
of political journalism that, in turn, generates public cynicism and
political disengagement (Cappella and Jamieson 1997). Such observations, however, can be supplemented with an awareness of the sometimes informal, entertaining and mutually beneficial exchanges
between journalists and politicians in different media contexts and
the 'leakage' of politics across the different kinds of media genres
that establish a range of power relations between politicians, journalists and respective audiences.

The Public in Political Talk Formats

A focus on the interpersonal interaction between politicians and
journalists in interviews, debates and press conferences can also distract us from comprehending how such exchanges are profoundly
determined by their orientation to the viewing public. These are not
just exchanges that occur in public, as we have already noted, and
they are not communicated to a passive, pre-existing public; they are
more substantively the means by which public formation occurs.
While the analyses in the following chapters will dissect the nature
of the exchanges in genres of interviews, debates and press conferences to show the power relations between the political and the
journalistic fields, they will also demonstrate both how such interactions are shaped by and, in turn, shape the broader political and

cultural environment and how their public dissemination and reception inform the structure and meanings of the interactions.

The public is a complex entity that is manifested in various ways throughout the following case studies. The public is both an object, 'voiced' into existence through the discourse of the participants in the interrogative exchanges, and a subject, when members of the public speak for themselves and question their political representatives (Craig 2004). The mediated basis of modern public life was outlined in the previous chapter, and this helps us understand the extent to which the public is a figure of representation, its identity and values subject to discursive struggle. The public, as witness and participant, is vital in the interactive exchanges that will be investigated here; the legitimacy of the exchanges is generated through their public status. As Coleman and Ross (2010, p. 22) remind us, public space, understood as 'a social configuration comprising practiced and experienced relationships of interaction', is defined by characteristics of accessibility, universality and visibility. The analysed programmes are informed by the need to provide access for the public to their political representatives. This access should be a generalized access, providing 'room for all voices, regardless of their status, background, or mode of expression' (ibid., p. 26). Some of the communicative genres, such as current affairs forum television and the leaders' debates, do this explicitly, while others, such as the political interviews and the press conferences, feature only elite voices, and they variously realize the principle that the concerns of a diversity of people are raised. The programmes importantly offer public visibility, providing the performing politicians with a stage but also opening them to general scrutiny.

Publics are further characterized by their possession and exercise of rationality in perceived contrast to other types of public formations, such as crowds. Publics ideally carry with them an explicit political or civic identity and a sense of agency with an active role in self-formation (Craig 2004, pp. 60–1). Public reason is crucial in the performances by participants and in the subsequent reportage and reception of the mediated political interrogative exchanges. As we will see in the subsequent analyses, there is a range of different types of public performance, but the publics are primarily disciplined entities where the manner and limits of participation are controlled by programme producers. While publics are traditionally characterized by the use of reason, the following analyses will demonstrate how effective public participation needs to be more broadly conceptualized and is also enabled through performance and by the exercise of emotion and satire. Of course, mediated publics are often simultaneously audiences, where membership is more 'individualized' and processes of commercialization and commodification are highlighted. Studio observers of *The View*, for example (see chapter 7), represent the more traditional audience, denied the opportunity to participate other than to applaud and cheer, whereas the audiences in the leaders' debates and the current affairs forum television programmes are more strongly marked as public actors. As will be observed in the analysis of *Q&A*, the public has a collective identity and also facilitates individual expressions of difference, both of which are crucial to its legitimacy as a public.

Our focus is on programmes and exchanges that constitute the conventional, mass-mediated public sphere, but of course such an entity is now complicated by the input of social media and the Internet. Now more than ever the public is a fragmented entity, and specifically with our analyses we can witness different kinds of public participation within the one programme. In chapter 6, for example, there is a differentiation between the disciplined questions of the studio audience and the more diverse public expressions of opinion that occur through the Twitter feed on *Q&A*. Facilitated by forms of social media, publics increasingly have more involvement in the production and meanings of mediated political interrogative exchanges. This increased agency, or 'produser' status (Bruns 2008), enriches the meaning potential of programmes and complicates the traditional division between production and reception. In chapter 4, it will be noted how the Twitter feed throughout the debate informs the subsequent 'expert' political commentary that once had a pre-eminent role in directing public opinion.

Interviews, debates and press conferences, then, are profoundly porous events that take place in the turbulent flow of public discourse (Craig 2010a, p. 85). The discussion in the encounters we will examine attempts to shape and fix the meanings of issues and events and, as such, refers to past comments and opinions, and projects expected and desired commitments and outcomes. That is, the discussion is always part of an ongoing public conversation and is moulded by, and informs, the temporality of public discourse. Our analyses, then, will sometimes include examination of the news media reportage of the interrogative encounters as well as the social media discussion. Was the news media reportage of the press conference, for example, in accord with the politician's framing of the event or relationship?

Contestability in Language and Politics

The political games that we see in the language use and performances of both politicians and journalists in interviews, debates and press conferences attest to the fundamental contestability of language and politics. It is axiomatic that there is a contest of ideas in these kinds of interrogative encounters, but our negative perceptions about the clashes and evasions can divert us from a comprehensive appreciation of both the dialogic nature of language and the agonistic basis of democratic politics. This appreciation provides a perspective on the power struggles that occur between politicians and journalists, and it has significant ramifications for how we regard the truthfulness of political discourse and the trustworthiness of those involved. Ultimately, this appreciation informs our understanding of the actual purposes of media-based interrogative encounters as means to ensure ongoing challenges to political order and the marshalling of public opinion.

It is hard for us to appreciate that the words we use are not fully our own. The dialogic character of language emphasizes that its use is always historically and culturally embedded and that every time we speak we are drawing on, and engaging with, pre-existing meanings. The so-called Bakhtin Circle of theorists, who were working in Russia in the early part of the twentieth century, outlined this understanding of language. For Bakhtin (1981, pp. 293–4):

> The word in language is always half someone else's.... All words have the 'taste' of a profession, a genre, a tendency, a party, a particular work, a particular person, a generation, an age group, the day and hour. Each word tastes of the context and contexts in which it has lived its socially charged life; all words and forms are populated by intentions.

This dialogic understanding of language has ontological consequences: our utterances are not the sole product of our individual consciousness, independent of others. Instead, as Maybin (2001, p. 69) summarizes: 'The dialogic quality of communication means that there is always at least one other respondent voice implicit in any utterance, and an implied dialogue with that voice shapes the form and meaning of the utterance.' For the Bakhtin Circle of scholars, the utterance is the basic unit of analysis, and all texts – not just verbal interaction – are informed by a dialogic orientation. Our utterances are, in turn, structured by speech genres that govern rules of interaction and ways of acting and inform our evaluations of communicative encounters. Genres refer to the 'use of language associated with and constituting part of some particular social practice' (Fairclough 1995b, p. 56). Speech genres span all communicative situations, from institutional interactions – such as political interviews – to everyday encounters where we greet a neighbour or play a game with a child.

Our implication in the dialogic orientation of speech genres does not deny individuals a sense of agency – an ability to use words to produce meanings and bring about action. Certainly words and discourses can have relatively fixed meanings that permit mutual understanding and facilitate ideological dominance, but the very openness of language also enables contestation. Bakhtin (1981) distinguished between centripetal forces that standardize, limit and produce the authoritative discourses associated with political centralization and centrifugal forces that allow for diversification and contestation by groups and individuals. As such, language use always involves a struggle over meaning and embodies the conflict between different individuals and social groups. In one sense, an argument about the fundamental contestability of language may seem obvious when considering encounters such as interviews, debates and press conferences. However authoritative a political figure, the very structure of interrogative encounters highlights not only opposing points of view but also the selections and emphases that an individual speaker uses in order to convince others. An emphasis on the contestability of language does not, however, preclude the possibility of agreement or the exercise of rationality, only that such formulations are always provisional and grounded in the particular contexts of the dialogue that is taking place.

The approach here, then, emphasizes the *rhetoric* that is exercised in political interviews, leaders' debates and press conferences. Rhetoric can be defined simply as 'the art of persuading others' (Charteris-Black 2005, p. 8). As Fairclough (2000, p. 96) has noted, rhetorical style is 'not an invariable way of using language; it is rather a mixture of different ways of using language, a distinctive repertoire.' As we have already remarked, the deployed rhetorical styles of politicians and journalists are dependent upon a range of factors, such as the institutional roles of the participants, their individual personality and identity, and the particular speech genres in which they are operating. Rhetoric extends beyond language use to consider bodily performance, including the use of sound, gestures and expressions. Unlike more structuralist approaches to language, the Bakhtin Circle, and the social semiotics tradition more generally, directs our attention to the specificities of language use and behaviour, and this understanding informs the selection of case studies in later chapters.

The understanding of the contestable character of language use, and the emphasis on the social uses of language, mirrors the agonistic character of modern democratic politics. To say that modern democracies are 'agonistic' is to stress the openness and perpetual struggle that informs political activity. Again, it is hard for us to appreciate, given the concrete manifestations of institutional power which exist in modern democracies, that democracy is 'instituted and sustained by the dissolution of the markers of certainty' (Lefort 1988, p. 19). As Claude Lefort (1988; 1986, pp. 303–4) noted, the execution of the sovereign king in the French Revolution meant that suddenly there were no more ultimate guarantors of truth, authority was diffused throughout society, and sovereignty was relocated in the indeterminate figure of 'the people'. This radical change meant that society itself became problematic, and debate on the future direction of society was facilitated by an explosion in journalism. In France there were only about half a dozen political newspapers at the start of 1789, but by the end of the year more than 130 newspapers had been formed; it is believed that 184 journals were launched the next year and 335 in 1790 (Hartley 1996, p. 82). Journalism, then, was the vital instrument that enabled both the prolific expression of ideas and an emerging collective political consciousness (Hartley 1996).

The democratic revolution introduced a tension between two fundamental political features that is central to our understanding of the agonistic basis of modern democratic politics: expressions of both liberty and equality. The inauguration of modern democracy enabled people to exercise individual freedoms and expressions of difference, but it also fostered the power of equality through recognition of popular sovereignty. Put simply, this tension is embodied in different political theoretical traditions: liberalism extols the rights of individuals over any idea of the common good, whereas communitarianism argues that democracy and citizenship are concerned more centrally with the relations we have with others and with community formation.

Building on her earlier work with Ernesto Laclau (Laclau and Mouffe 1985), Chantal Mouffe (1993, 2000) further develops ideas about the fundamental indeterminacy in modern democracies and the tension between expressions of liberty and equality in her formulation of an 'agonistic pluralism', which accounts for the conditions by which a radical democratic politics can arise. Mouffe argues that the pluralism of modern democratic societies, and the absence of any substantive common good, means that the political task is the construction of alliances, the formation of a 'we' in the face of political opposition. For Mouffe, the indeterminacy of democracy means that there is nothing potentially that cannot be politicized and that 'the political' is not restricted to particular institutions or levels of society. Specifically, she distinguishes between 'the political', which refers to 'the dimension of antagonism that is inherent in human relations, antagonism that can take many forms and emerge in different types of social relations', and 'politics', which is the 'ensemble of practices, discourses and institutions which seek to establish a certain order and organize human coexistence in conditions that are always potentially conflictual because they are affected by the dimension of "the political"' (Mouffe 2000, p. 101). The antagonistic process of political community formation occurs because of the relational basis of identity: every identity is affirmed through relations of difference. Any attempt to establish an ultimate consensus and the formation of an established political unity must, then, involve a suppression of difference. As such, Mouffe is fundamentally critical of theories of deliberative democracy where there is a focus on the processes and procedures by which public reason is exercised in order to resolve social problems, and where social unity is seen as the goal of the democratic process. She proclaims that it is impossible to have both 'perfect liberty and perfect equality' (ibid., p. 10) and, as such, we can conclude that 'pluralist democratic politics consists in pragmatic, precarious and necessarily unstable forms of negotiating its constitutive paradox' (ibid., p. 11). Once we accept 'the impossibility of a world without antagonism' (Mouffe 1993, p. 4), the task is to build a pluralistic democratic order that permits such political contestation. Here, Mouffe invokes the idea of the *'respublica'*, which refers to the ' "grammar" of political conduct' (ibid., p. 65), or the norms and rules of political conduct that are adhered to by different political projects and enterprises within a political community. Her understanding of the *respublica* extends beyond its singular and rational conception as the 'rules of the game' in liberal theory in her insistence that it is itself always a site of struggle: 'the *respublica* is the product of a given hegemony, the expression of power relations, and…it can be challenged. Politics is to a great extent about the rules of the *respublica* and its many possible interpretations; it is about the constitution of the political community' (ibid., p. 69; original emphasis).

The indeterminacy of democracy is manifested in its temporality, and we see this operating in journalistic interrogations of politicians. The claiming, exercise and maintenance of political power in democracies is premised upon the ability to persuade others to grant power on the basis of future promises which are subject to ongoing scrutiny with regard to a future adjudication of political performance. That is, democracy unfolds through 'a play between anticipatory authorization and retrospective accountability' (Barnett 2003, p. 28). Journalism is, of course, the major societal mechanism that provides that scrutiny, but it is this democratic temporality that informs so much of the discursive struggle between journalists and politicians in inter-views, debates and press conferences. Such agonistic interaction between journalists and politicians is based upon attempts to fix both the terms of future accountability and subsequent judgements about performance, whether it is a promise to reduce a budget deficit or to fix a broken hospital system. Political media discourse is littered with declarations about ongoing commitments to past promises, acknowl-edgements and explanations about current difficulties, and attempts to delineate the anticipated forward projection of events, actions and outcomes. Of course, ultimately, a public judgement is made at an election, but the public decision that is made at that time also con-tinues the next cycle of 'anticipatory authorization'.

The contestable character of media interviews, debates and press conferences is also manifested in expressions of modality. In social semiotics, modality refers to the truth-value of a proposition and the speaker's orientation towards the subject (Simpson 1993, p. 47), and it is part of a broader linguistic framework regarding the language of evaluation (Martin and White 2005). For our purposes, we can simply note the frequency with which the discursive struggle between politicians and journalists revolves around queries and judgements about the veracity of information and statements. Political discourse is peppered with definitive statements, articulations of probability and possibility, and various kinds of hedging and evasion. Of course, a categorical assertion ('The prime minister *is* brilliant...', 'The country *was* wrong...') carries the highest possible truth claim, but varying degrees of modality can be expressed with regard to truth and obligation (Richardson 2007, p. 60). Truth modality varies across a spectrum from a categorical assertion to lesser degrees of truthfulness ('The debates *will/can/could* go ahead...', 'I *know/believe/understand/suspect* the minister will be in trouble...'). Obligation modality 'refers to future events and, specifically, the degree to which the speaker/writer believes that a certain course of action or certain decisions *ought* or *should* be taken' (Richardson 2007, p. 60; original emphasis). Of course, the motor of journalistic inquiry is the attempt to determine the truth, but, as we will see in the following analyses, the status and 'degrees' of truthfulness are subject to constant interpretation and struggle. We should also note that across the different types of interrogative exchanges there are varying implicit expectations about truthfulness: political interviews are more 'agonistic' and are often prefaced upon a scepticism that a singular truth will derive from the interaction, while political celeb-rity interviews tend to be informed more by a belief that the interview subject will be more forthcoming about the truthfulness of the discussed subjects.

This preceding discussion about the contestability of language and the agonistic basis of politics highlights that *trust*, rather than truth, is the primary goal in mediated political interrogative exchanges. Political speech is successful not so much because it demonstrates a singular truth but because it persuades others that the person speaking has the authority and ability to successfully implement that which they are promising (Bourdieu 1991, pp. 190–1). As Bourdieu (ibid., p. 192) has noted, political capital stems from the political field itself, but political capital is also granted 'in and through representation, in and through trust, belief and obedience'. The notion of trust is central to modernity: Giddens (1990; see also Washbourne 2010, pp. 46–9) has observed how complex abstract systems engender a form of trust, so that, when we turn on a light or get cash out of an automatic teller, we take it for granted that most of the time there will be an appropriate and desired outcome. This passive form of trust has declined as forms of expertise in social fields – medical, scientific, political – have been subject to greater scrutiny and challenge, and increasingly a more active form of trust is required that employs more direct forms of communication in order to justify its authority. In politics, the generational trust in the political system and the political class has eroded, and this has meant that individual political leaders must more actively seek the trust of the electorate. This, in turn, influences the character of political rhetoric: individual leaders must seek trust not only on the basis of their expertise and the clarity of their logic but also on their ability to identify with the interests and concerns of voters. The dimensions of political trustworthiness (or lack thereof) can be encapsulated in reliability, competency and media engagement (Brants 2013, pp. 16–18). Politicians are judged according to their ability to be honest, faithful to their stated intentions, and responsive to the public. They must also demonstrate they have the skills and character to mobilize people and solve problems. They are also judged trustworthy if their media engagements are not based on self-promotion and strategic electoral advantage.

The contestable nature of language use and democratic politics, and the primacy of trust over truth, has major ramifications for how we understand the task of journalists in their questioning of politicians. The interrogative basis of political interviews, leaders' debates and press conferences is, of course, driven by a desire to clarify positions on issues, policies and strategies – to 'pin down' politicians on understandings and commitments – so that the public are informed and politicians can be subject to accountability. Ultimately, these interrogations seek the truth, but this is no simple matter, and the nature of the truth that underlines and informs these encounters can vary in different circumstances. Sometimes, for example, the implied truth is posited as more 'open-ended' and the journalist will proffer counter-arguments and propositions as a means of testing the viability of a politician's argument. The journalist may voice the concerns of political opponents or may simply play the 'devil's advocate'. At other times, the underlying truth is offered as a more concrete reality that the interviewee denies, and this often produces a more antagonistic encounter. An embattled political leader may, for example, doggedly claim her position is secure despite obvious manoeuvrings against her, or she may insist that the government's economic policies will lead to a lower budget deficit despite economic data and opinion that suggest otherwise. In both of these cases, and however skilled the journalist may be in forensic questioning, the interview is not characterized by a resolution and an agreement about the truth. Instead, what such scenarios suggest is that mediated interrogative encounters highlight and probe differences and map the terrain of opinion on a particular issue. In doing so, they establish the grounds upon which we can decide whether to trust the politician. It follows, then, from what we have determined about the contestable nature of language and the indeterminacy of democracy that the primary task of journalists is to keep the political open. While politicians will seek to fix the meaning of issues in order to further their self-interest (however well intentioned or socially desirable), the indeterminacy of democracy requires that the general interest be always subject to contestation, and this perpetual provocation of public discourse occurs through journalism. This argument is a counter to public cynicism that is informed by the belief that politicians never tell the truth, and it is not an advocacy for the kind of interviewing style that is motivated by a sentiment that wishes a 'plague on both your houses'. Instead, it is an argument that sees the political games in interviews, debates and press conferences as the necessary and legitimate play and critique of power.

Methodology

The discussion so far has already highlighted that this study draws upon a range of theoretical approaches, given we are examining the language and performances of journalists and politicians as well as the broader public and institutional contexts within which interrogative encounters occur. The specific analyses in the later chapters are informed by a critical reading approach that seeks to emphasize the power struggles that occur through the language use and performances of both journalists and politicians in interviews, debates and press conferences. This approach offers an interpretation of the meanings of utterances, interactive relations, and communicative and political strategies that is informed by the theoretical framework that we have outlined in this chapter and the preceding chapter. We will be providing a close reading of specific instances of language use, drawing attention, for example, to the types of question asked, the lexical choices of interviewees and interviewers, the different registers that are used by participants, and the various argumentative strategies across the range of interrogative exchanges.

We are not applying a single linguistic methodological procedure here, but there are some specific bodies of research that have been influential in our approaches to the study of media language use. The work of Steven Clayman, John Heritage and others (Banning and Billingsley 2007; Clayman and Heritage 2002b; Clayman et al. 2006, 2010, 2012), which examines forms of aggressive questioning by the White House press corps of US presidents, gives us insight into not only the general historical decline in deferential journalism but also the specific discursive strategies that journalists employ in their questioning of presidents. The dimensions of aggressive questioning which have been identified can be summarized as

- adversarialness, which is 'the extent to which questions pursue an agenda in opposition to the president or his administration';
- accountability, which is 'the extent to which questions explicitly ask the president to justify his policies or actions';
- assertiveness, which is 'the extent to which questions invite a particular answer and are in that sense opinionated rather than neutral';
- initiative, which is 'the extent to which questions are enterprising rather than passive in their aims'; and
- directness, which is 'the extent to which questions are blunt rather than cautious in raising issues' (Clayman et al. 2010, p. 233).

These dimensions are coded according to the formal aspects of question design used by the journalists and cover matters such as the statements that preface questions, the type of question asked, and whether there are follow-up questions.

We also draw on research that has examined the argumentative strategies deployed in media interviews, debates and press conferences. There is a range of types of justifications and discursive strategies that are used in the arguments proffered in mediated political discourse, from the identification of external factors that explain why actions have not occurred through to commitments about future actions. These argumentative strategies are termed 'topoi' and refer to 'the obligatory premises of an argument, whether explicit or implicit' (Wodak 2011, p. 42). Topoi draw our attention to the fact that media interviews, debates and press conferences do not feature rational arguments so much as the mobilization of different types of common-sense reasoning, captured in phrases such as 'It costs too much', 'This action is consistent with what happened previously', or 'Most people believe this to be the case'. Wodak (ibid., p. 44) provides a list of common topoi, such as the topos of numbers ('if sufficient numerical/statistical evidence is given, a specific action should be performed'); the topos of reality (which 'tautologically infers that[,] as reality is as it is[,] a particular action should be performed'); the topos of history ('because history teaches that specific actions have specific consequences, one should perform or omit a specific action in a specific situation'); the topos of authority ('if one refers to somebody in a position of authority, then the action is legitimate'); the topos of threat ('if specific dangers or threats are identified, one should do something about them'); and the topos of urgency ('decisions or actions need to be drawn/found/done very quickly because of an external, important and unchangeable event beyond one's own reach and responsibility'). In addition to this range of research, this particular study identifies the way that an action/verbal binary is deployed in media interviews, debates and press conferences. Journalists can challenge political efficacy by highlighting that promises and discussion have not materialized in action, and politicians can invoke the action/verbal binary to challenge political opponents and journalists and also to underline their own political power. Such a binary partakes in the popular opposition of language and speech to power, where 'weak' language/speech is opposed to the 'reality' of deeds, even though of course action is also taken in and through speech and writing (Austin 1975; Chilton and Schaffner 2002; Searle 1969).

This study is informed more broadly by both the principles and techniques of critical discourse analysis. Critical discourse analysis is a wide-ranging and pluralistic approach to the study of language and social practices (Chouliaraki and Fairclough 1999; Fairclough 1995b; Wodak 2011) and is importantly both a theory and a method (Chouliaraki and Fairclough 1999, pp. 16–17). Put simply, critical discourse analysis combines both linguistic and social understandings of discourse. Linguistic approaches to discourse focus on specific uses of language and the rules of interaction in particular contexts. Structural approaches to discourse (Foucault 1972) concentrate more on the social domains of statements and interactive exchanges within which, and through which, meanings are produced, including hierarchies of knowledge and the establishment of power relations. Critical discourse analysis maintains that these understandings of discourse exist in a dialectical relationship: 'In critical discourse analysis, language-as-discourse is *both* a form of action...through which people can change the world *and* a form of action which is socially and histori-cally situated and in a dialectical relationship with other aspects of the social' (Jørgensen and Phillips 2002, p. 62; original emphasis). Critical discourse analysis maintains that all language use consists of three integrated aspects: it is a text; it is a discursive practice that involves the production and consumption of texts; and it is a social practice (Fairclough 1992). It is also informed by a particular political and pedagogical purpose: it acknowledges both that its research projects are themselves interventions in knowledge production and the social uses of knowledge and that it has the goal of revealing the sense-making processes involved in the formation and inequalities of social relations and structures. This final point is important for us to consider here: the goal of this book is to promote greater literacy about contemporary political communication and to help foster an approach to the power struggles that occur between journalists and politicians that will lead not to more cynicism but to greater public engagement.

Conclusion

This chapter has outlined what may be considered an unconventional take on the dynamics between politicians and journalists across inter-rogative exchanges that occur through the media. Invoking the idea of a 'political game', we have forwarded the argument that we can see such tussles between journalists and politicians as legitimate and necessary struggles over the meanings of public issues and policies. In so doing we can acknowledge our frustrations as politicians seek to evade questions or as journalists focus unduly on differences between political colleagues with a political party, but we also need to recognize that such discursive strategies and struggles occur because power is at stake. This argument about how we should evaluate the interactions between politicians and journalists derives from an understanding about the fundamentally contestable nature of lan-guage and the indeterminacy of democracy. We discussed how the discourses of politicians and journalists are structured by their institutional roles and their placements within particular 'fields' and how such power struggles are encoded in language use. We also considered the interpersonal and mediated bases of these interrogative exchanges, the power relations that are coded in questions and answers, and the different ways those exchanges function in political interviews, leaders' debates and press conferences. And we discussed the various ways in which the public is invoked and participates in such exchanges. Finally, we outlined the methodological basis that will inform our case study analyses in the remainder of the book.

3

Political Interviews

Introduction

In the rest of the book we will demonstrate how our earlier discussion of political games and televisual performance are played out in particular communicative encounters between politicians and journalists. In this chapter we examine political interviews – the most frequent and high-profile forms of interrogative media encounters with politicians. Even though political leaders generally now engage in more careful management of their appearances, political interviews remain a staple of journalistic output compared to other encounters, such as leaders' debates, which are more singular events. We are focusing on extended interviews with political leaders from mainstream parties on leading broadcast current affairs programmes or 'political talk shows', such as *Insiders* and *7.30* in Australia, *Newsnight* and *The Andrew Marr Show* in the UK, and *Meet the Press* and *This Week with George Stephanopoulos* in the US. These are important 'flagship' programmes and their featured interviews often set the news agenda for the following day. Of course, political interviews can be conducted with a variety of political actors, and it is perhaps unfortunate that these kinds of programmes often do not involve a broader range of political actors. Nonetheless, the leaders featured in these chapters are important and powerful figures in representative democracies, and it is crucial that they undergo the kind of scrutiny that is afforded by political interviews.

Political interviews may involve a number of participants, but they are primarily dyadic encounters between a journalist and a politician involving discussion of contestable matters relating to the public good. While there are a variety of genres of news media interviews, the accountability interview with a public figure (Montgomery 2008) is the object of our analysis here. Such interviews inquire into so-called hard news information relating to issues and policy, though they also probe into political strategy and the effects such matters will have on changing political fortunes. As was discussed in chapter 2, political interviews are institutional exchanges, and there are clearly demarcated roles for both interviewers and interviewees that designate the implicit rules of the interaction and the power relations that inform such interaction. The interviewer, for example, must provide the interviewee with the opportunity to respond to questions, but equally they have the right to interject and challenge an answer that is deemed unsatisfactory. Although an interviewee has the freedom to frame their answers as they wish, they must to some degree accede initially to the question, and it is difficult for them to issue a fundamental challenge to the authority of the interviewer. The dyadic nature of political interviews and the active negotiation of these 'rules' over important and contestable issues are the reasons why the 'political game' is such a prominent feature of such exchanges.

Broadcast interviews are a well-established feature of the political communication landscape, but they are also evolving within the contexts of the contemporary television and media industry. As we will see, such interviews have historically developed from a deferential mode of inquiry into a more adversarial form of questioning; however, within the contexts of an increasingly hybrid media system (Chadwick 2013) there continue to be emerging features of interviewing across the kinds of genres we will be examining in this book and within the accountability political interviews that we are examining in this chapter. A programme such as *The O'Reilly Factor* on the Fox network in the US, for example, can be defined as something of a 'hybrid political interview' (Hutchby 2011), given that it shares features of the more conventional adversarial interview but also allows the often dramatically emotional expressions of the host's opinions. More conventional accountability political interviews also increasingly feature 'meta-discursive' work, where there is a more reflexive reference to the dynamics of the interaction itself ('I'm not saying you are...', 'If you would just let me finish...'), suggesting that the conventional turn allocation sequences are under increasing strain in the encounters (Montgomery 2011). Equally, as will be illustrated in the following case studies, modern political interviews are increasingly characterized by 'micro-arguments' (ibid.), where there is a sustained sequence of assertion and counter-assertion between interviewers and interviewees over a single topic that involves the journalist explicitly invoking a judgement on the politician's answers. Such emerging forms and features point to the growing prominence of the role, input and personality of the journalistic persona in accord with the more performative televisual requirements of reportage that was noted in the opening chapter.

Broadcast interviews are vitally important and high-profile acts of political communication, and politicians must be able to manage the rigours of these interrogative encounters successfully. In 2013, the UK prime minister, David Cameron, initiated a reshuffle that involved cabinet minister Chloe Smith, who had indicated she wished to step down from her duties. It was widely reported that Smith's demotion was partly associated with a disastrous interview that she conducted with Jeremy Paxman on *Newsnight*. As the following analyses will show, political interviews are dramatic and performative encounters requiring both politicians and journalists to be able to exert their opinion powerfully while also embodying a professionalism that skilfully negotiates the generic parameters of the interview format. The longer length of political interviews means that interview-based current affairs and political talk shows are often scheduled later in the evening or on a Sunday morning, but equally their extended duration is an increasingly valuable feature in a news environment that is compressed into headlines, sound bites and Twitter feeds.

In this chapter we will firstly establish the historical contexts of the political interview. The interview may seem like an obvious and natural way to gain information, but the interrogative character of journalism generally, along with the accompanying critical scrutiny of public figures and public life, is a modern phenomenon and arose out of particular historical circumstances. The chapter will then investigate the complex communicative structure of political interviews, where they are both intense interpersonal encounters and, simultaneously, media events in which a 'distant' viewing public plays a crucial role in the unfolding exchange between the two participants. We will critically evaluate political interviews against the ideals of dialogue while noting their important function of maintaining the contestability of the political. It will also be discussed how the dissemination of political interviews is an integral feature of the structure and meanings of such encounters. Finally, this understanding of political interviews will be supported through two case studies: David Cameron's appearances on *The Andrew Marr Show* and the interviews of the former Australian prime minister Kevin Rudd on *Insiders* and the *7.30 Report*. As noted in the preface, these instances have been selected because they illuminate the behaviours of the respective individual high-profile leaders, and we should caution against making representative claims about the genre of political interviews on the basis of a limited number of case studies. Nonetheless, the analyses do show the discursive struggle that occurs between journalists and politicians and their respective attempts to align themselves with the general public.

History of Political Interviews

While the term 'interview' entered the English language in 1514, the news interview became a regular feature of journalism in the United States only in the last quarter of the nineteenth century (Clayman and Heritage 2002a, p. 26). Indeed, what we would recognize as modern reporting did not feature in the US press until the 1820s. Before that time, newspapers were a mix of essays and opinion articles, letters and announcements (Schudson 1994, p. 565). Early reporters may have sought information from authoritative figures and other newsworthy individuals and relayed the substance of public statements, but they did not formally engage in a question and answer exchange and they did not print quotations from their informal inquiries. The earliest newspaper interview is said to be between President Martin Van Buren and James Gordon Bennett of the *New York Herald* in 1839, and it includes novelistic commentary from Bennett about the setting of the interview and his thoughts about the exchange (Bell and van Leeuwen 1994, p. 29). The novelty of the early interviews meant they were regarded 'as an independent genre of journalism separate from reporting and regarded as a news event in itself, a journalistic coup' (Schudson 1994, p. 574). Over time the interview was incorporated into everyday news-gathering techniques and became viewed as a more formal, on the record exchange with the use of direct quotations, although Schudson (ibid., p. 575) notes that, as late as 1914, a leading newspaper such as the *Baltimore Sun* could go for days without featuring a direct quotation on its front page.

Journalistic interviews were seen initially as an invasion of privacy, and their interrogative character was at odds with the deferential demeanour of journalists towards political and social elites. The interpersonal nature of interviews meant they were judged not to carry the import of public announcements and formal speeches. They were also seen as inauthentic forms of communication that allowed journalists to make the news rather than to report it. They did, however, also enhance the prestige of journalists and facilitate greater autonomy from the control of editors. As Schudson (1994, p. 583) has noted: 'The rise of the interview coincides with the rise of newspaper reporters as relatively autonomous workers who self-consciously achieve an occupational identity.'

The interview was suited to broadcasting, and it became a feature of programming once early radio producers realized that the medium required something more than the simple reading of the written word. Interviews facilitated the conversational and more informal discourse that was necessary for radio to flourish. Successful radio programmes in the United States subsequently moved to the new medium of television. Edward R. Murrow's radio programme *Hear it Now* became *See it Now* on CBS television in 1951, and NBC's *Meet the Press* moved to television from radio in 1947 (Clayman and Heritage 2002a, p. 28). The late 1950s and early 1960s saw a decline in deference to political elites, and questioning in television interviews became more vigorous and combative. The timeliness and relevance of political interviews in Britain had been hampered by the fourteen-day rule, which prevented public discussion of matters that were to be considered by Parliament in the coming fortnight, but this was dropped in 1957. Equally, the introduction of commercial broadcasting in 1955 introduced innovations in news reportage and production and a more aggressive orientation towards politicians than the respectful and benign approach of BBC interviewers. In particular, the interviews of Robin Day adopted an adversarial approach that had not previously been seen in that country. Day's interview of Harold Macmillan when he quizzed the prime minister about the possible sacking of the foreign secretary is often invoked as a key interview of the time, and it marked the beginning of the modern relations between journalists and politicians that characterize political interviews to this day.

In more recent decades interviews have, of course, become a staple of political communication, and we expect to see our political leaders regularly offering themselves to rigorous scrutiny in these encounters. In this sense, such interviews are part of a more generalized, more forthright and aggressive political journalism. In the United States, programmes such as ABC's *Nightline*, hosted by Ted Koppel for many years, embodied the adversarial style of interviewing, although PBS's *NewsHour* (originally *The MacNeil/Lehrer Report*) has stood out as one place where more extended and less aggressive interviews have occurred. In the UK, a tradition of adversarial interviewing has been established by journalists such as Jeremy Paxman on the BBC's *Newsnight*, John Humphrys on the BBC radio programme *Today*, and Andrew Neil on *The Daily Politics*. In Australia, the modern adversarial interviewing style was initially adopted by the ABC pro-gramme *This Day Tonight*, which started in 1967, and the national public broadcaster continues to host a number of interview-based shows such as *7.30* and *Insiders*. Following the early success of *This Day Tonight*, commercial television networks adopted successful and popular interview-based programming in subsequent decades, with shows such as *A Current Affair* and *Sunday*, although there has been a decline in such programming on commercial networks in more recent years.

Dialogue and Dissemination

The frustration that is sometimes experienced when watching politi-cal interviews derives partly from the perceived distance of such encounters from a true dialogue, where there is a considered appraisal of different points of view and some kind of consensus or conclusion is reached. The interviewee often seems to be defending an entrenched position, while the interviewer is attempting to catch them out by exposing the deficiencies of their argument, and in the end we finish where we started. We noted in chapter 2 the dialogic basis of lan-guage and the agonistic basis of politics and argued that the ongoing contestability of political discussion is a necessary and legitimate feature of democratic societies. How, then, should we consider the nature of the interaction that occurs in political interviews? Should we judge them negatively when they fail to realize the ideals of dia-logue, or do we need a different way of evaluating them?

While we have a colloquial understanding of dialogue as a con-versational exchange between two or more people, the ideals of dialogue reveal a much richer form of interaction and also posit more onerous responsibilities on the participants. As Cissna and Anderson (1994, p. 10) have noted: 'Dialogue implies more than a simple back-and-forthness of messages in interaction; it points to a particular process and quality of communication in which the participants "meet", which allows for changing and being changed.' More specifi-cally, dialogues have the following features: they have an extended duration; they are a reciprocal group activity; their participants seek common ground and are open to new ways of thinking; they have respect and goodwill; and they appreciate the value of the dialogue regardless of the result. This understanding of dialogue is some way from the cut and thrust of political interviews – a point that has been highlighted by those who study dialogues: 'Dialogue studies have often treated the mass media as an iconic Other, the very embodiment of the impersonal relations that undermine mutuality' (Pauly 2004, p. 243). Broadcast political interviews are more accurately understood as forms of institutional dialogue which are more explicitly goal oriented, and there are different roles for participants based on unequal access to information and expectations about rates of participation (Drew and Heritage 1992). Job interviews and doctors' consultations are other examples of such forms of interviews. Political interviews, however, are also different from other forms of institutional dialogue because there is not the same kind of asymmetrical power relationship between interviewer and interviewee or such a shared, centripetal focus to the discussion. In many forms of institutional dialogue the questioner explicitly exercises their power and authority over the interviewee in seeking information, as in a teacher questioning a student, or there is common agreement about the goal of the dialogue, as in the case of an open group discussion among company employees about ways to ensure future profitability. Political interviews do, of course, feature differential power relations between interviewer and interviewee, but the institutional dialogue of political interviews is characterized by each of the participants possessing institutional authority in a context of relatively open debate. In another context, for example, a lawyer may question a policeman in a trial, but the freedom of the questioned person to extrapolate in the formulation of a response is limited and they are less able to challenge the authority of the questioner. Political interviews in this sense are unique because, while they are rule-governed encounters, they are also comparatively open exchanges over highly contestable matters between individuals, both of whom possess considerable institutional authority.

The dialogues of political interviews are informed primarily by a power struggle over the meaning of the topics under discussion. As was noted in chapter 2, language always involves the use of power: the question form itself, for example, establishes power relations between discussion participants. In political interviews participants may not be open to alternative arguments or to change, as in ideal dialogues, but there must be a negotiation of the terms of alternative positions and a defence of established positions. Given that considerable power is at stake in the interpretation of issues and debates, it should be expected that participants would be disciplined and controlled in their use of language. As such, while in political interviews we may indeed end up where we started, we have nonetheless witnessed the testing of arguments, enabling us to better evaluate the basis of a politician's position. Perhaps, then, the goal in political interviews should not be to eradicate power but to make it more explicit and to evaluate its use in different communicative encounters. Following the discussion in chapter 2, the purpose of political interviews is subsequently less the discovery of truth and more the delineation and interrogation of different points of view.

There are different strategies that interviewers may employ to provoke an interrogation of the interviewee's position. Sometimes, for example, politicians face a particular challenge – it may be from a political opponent or an issue that requires resolution – but it is not in the interviewee's political interest to publicly acknowledge the challenge. The task for the interviewer is to raise the implicit political reality and to have the politician acknowledge the dilemma and explain how they will manage the matter. The conflict generated in such interviews also derives partly from different framing of politics: the journalist is keen to explore the political ramifications of the discussed dilemmas, while the politician is keen either not to acknowledge the dilemma or to limit the discussion of the challenge to the 'front stage' of politics. This kind of negotiation occurs in political interviews because politicians must always speak in the public interest and not acknowledge the self-interest that motivates their actions and discourse.

Political interviews are more than their interpersonal dynamics; they are media events. They are not only disseminated to a viewing public but their public orientation informs the structure and content of the exchange. This is obviously signalled at the beginning of interviews, where there may be a direct address to the viewers. In this way the ensuing interview is marked as a public conversation. Similarly, politicians do not usually object personally to the interviewer when they are quizzed in an aggressive manner because they understand that the interviewer is asking implicitly on behalf of the public. The relative lack of reciprocity in political interviews and the unequal contributions of the participants to the discussion also derive from recognition that the primary recipient of the politician's answer is the public. It follows that there is much more to the public dissemination of political interviews than a simple acknowledgement of the political and cultural contexts of the exchange. In this sense they have a porous nature where they inform, and are informed by, broader political and public forces. For all the animated exchanges between interviewer and interviewee, the dialogue is differentiated from everyday conversations because the subject of the interaction is not primarily the relationship between the participants but, rather, public issues. Political interviews, then, are moments in a stream of public discourse where there is an attempt to fix or negotiate a plurality of other circulating viewpoints and to establish the primacy of particular narratives that explain previous comments or events and anticipate future commitments and outcomes.

Case Studies

We now turn to an analysis of particular examples of contemporary political interviews featuring the UK prime minister David Cameron and the former Australian prime minister Kevin Rudd. The case studies are designed to demonstrate how the power struggles between journalists and politicians are manifested in language use, how politics is framed and how the political field is managed by the politicians, and how the interviews are vehicles for the performance of the habitus of the politicians and journalists.

David Cameron on *The Andrew Marr Show*

The Andrew Marr Show is one of the BBC's leading television current affairs programmes, together with *Newsnight* and the current affairs forum show, *Question Time* (see chapter 6). Broadcast on Sunday mornings, it revolves around interviews with leading politicians but usually includes an interview with other public figures, such as actors or singers who are promoting recent work. In addition it features two or three guests, often journalists and lower-profile politicians, who dissect the Sunday newspapers with Marr. The analysis here is of three interviews Marr conducted with David Cameron over six months. The first interview was on 21 July 2013 in the garden of 10 Downing Street when Marr was still recovering from a stroke he suffered earlier that year. The second interview was conducted on 29 September 2013 at the time of the Conservative Party conference, and the final interview occurred on 5 January 2014.

Before an examination of the language use can occur, it is necessary to sketch the specific dynamics of the political and journalistic fields that are manifested in the analysed interviews, along with the habituses featured in the exchanges. It follows from field theory that the meanings of the interviews derive significantly from the particular institutional placement and political temporality of the interactions within particular journalistic and political fields. The status of *The Andrew Marr Show* (and the *7.30 Report* and *Insiders* in the following case study) as a flagship, serious current affairs programme on the national public broadcaster provides it with an authority that stems from codified ideas of public service broadcasting and manifested in independent and highly professionalized journalistic practice. The host's journalistic authority is reflected in the fact he lends his name to the programme. Marr was previously a political editor of *The Economist*, editor of *The Independent* newspaper, and political editor of BBC News. The status of the programme in the current affairs hierarchy facilitates a rigorous, more combative orientation towards political interviewees, and the meanings of particular instances of language use, including more colloquial expressions, are also generated partly through their placement in such authoritative journalistic contexts. As Darras (2005, p. 163) reminds us, there is an isomorphic relation between a national broadcaster and the types of people and issues that are featured on such shows, although it is the authority of the political field rather than the authority of particular programmes or journalistic judgements that yield media appearances (ibid., pp. 170–1).

David Cameron came to the position of prime minister following the successful negotiation of a coalition agreement with the Liberal Democrats after the 2010 election did not yield a party with a sufficient majority to govern alone. Cameron's claiming of the position of prime minister capped a remarkable political ascension that was partly facilitated by a background in, and knowledge of, media, as well as an aptitude in media and public performances. Cameron initially captured the position of opposition leader in 2005 after entering parliament only in 2001. His surprise elevation to the position of leader of the Conservative Party was due in no small way to his strong performance at the party conference, where all the leadership candidates delivered speeches. In addition, Cameron drew on the social capital he had accrued through his work in various offices of leading Conservative politicians and the internal media capital he had accrued over time through his dealings with political journalists in the course of that work, as well as through his time as head of communications and director of corporate affairs with the television company Carlton Communications (Davis and Seymour 2010).

Cameron's habitus is a successful amalgamation of the media capital that derives from knowledge of, and skills associated with, contemporary journalism and the cultural and social capital associated with an elite British education and upbringing. Cameron's mother is the daughter of a baronet, and Cameron was educated at Eton and studied philosophy, politics and economics at Oxford. While at Oxford, he was a member of the aristocratic Bullingdon Club (as were both Boris Johnson and George Osborne) although he has expressed embarrassment over his involvement in the club (Sparrow 2009). In his public performances, then, Cameron draws on his experience in the media industry to demonstrate the kind of media proficiency that is increasingly required of contemporary national leaders. His political persona also involves an active negotiation of the elite background that helped him ascend to the leadership of the Conservative Party and the projection of the character of a family man who is able to identify with the concerns of 'ordinary' voters. It is no accident, in this sense, that Cameron has actively courted appearances across a range of 'non-political' media outlets where he has highlighted his everyday, family life (Booth 2013; Mason 2013; Wintour 2013).

The three interviews will be analysed here to reveal the discursive struggle that occurs between Marr and Cameron and the prime minister's production of his particular political habitus. Throughout we witness struggles between the interviewer and interviewee over the process of answering questions, including disagreements over the meaning of contestable terms and the assignation of degrees of modality to events and claims. We also see a different framing of politics in the way both Marr and Cameron discuss issues. Marr emphasizes the possible pragmatic outcomes of issues in contexts of political conflict, while the prime minister emphasizes the role of himself and the political process in negotiating between different interests over time and managing the relationship between the political field and other fields. Cameron also spends considerable time in the interviews outlining a particular political subjectivity, where he prioritizes the responsible exercise of power and offers an appropriate balance between the political and the personal, including the presentation of himself as an affective subject.

A central feature of the Downing Street garden interview is Marr's struggle to have the prime minister disclose whether he had 'talked' to political consultant Lynton Crosby about the government's decision to delay the introduction of plain paper packaging for cigarettes. The discussion continued the media agenda of the week, and Marr alludes to this in his opening move in the exchange. In addition, he flags a challenge in his ironic use of 'favourite' and his open invitation, but grammatical command, to discuss the political consultant: 'Okay, well let's turn to another of your favourite newspaper stories. Tell us about Lynton Crosby' (*The Andrew Marr Show* 2013a, p. 6). The issue had mushroomed over the week because Cameron had insisted on declaring that Crosby (who has links to the tobacco industry) had not 'intervened', but he had refused to deny he had 'talked' to him about it, and this obfuscation continued in the interview:

> *Marr*: You have told me absolutely everything except the question that I was asking, which is have you talked to Lynton Crosby about this?
>
> *Cameron*: I think I have answered the question. He has not intervened...
>
> *Marr*: (*over*)   You haven't actually, Prime Minister.
>
> *Cameron*: ...in any single way.
>
> *Marr*: But you won't tell me whether you've talked to him about it.
>
> *Cameron*: Well I think, as I've said, he hasn't intervened in any single way. I think you'll find that is an answer.
>
> *Marr*: Yes, but it's not quite an answer to the question I asked.
>
> *Cameron*: Well, it's the answer you're getting (*laughs*). (*The Andrew Marr Show* 2013a, pp. 7–8)

This exchange is an example of a micro-argument, and it exemplifies several features of political interviews, language use, and relations between the journalistic and political fields. Firstly, the interview is a valuable opportunity to draw upon, and also extend investigation into, the existing media agenda. The prime minister's prevarication over the issue in previous days is rendered explicit by the interview's extended question and answer exchange. Marr demonstrates the dimension of aggressive questioning of assertiveness given his 'questions' are opinionated and invite a particular answer, and the sustained probing of the topic also makes it clear that the prime minister will remain steadfast in his political strategy. Secondly, the issue revolves around the significance of the variation in meaning between 'intervened' and 'talked'. Cameron risks the loss of political capital if he admits that he had discussed the issue with Crosby but attempts to defuse the matter by maintaining that no improper influence was exerted in the course of the making of the decision. What may seem to be a trivial distinction to some becomes politically significant because the terms have different effects, with regard both to the turn-taking process of the interview and to the boundary maintenance between the journalistic and political fields. To say that Crosby had not 'lobbied' Cameron or 'intervened' in the decision is to close down further discussion, whereas to admit 'talking' to Crosby, while still denying influence, prompts further questions and inquiry into the back-stage operations of the political field. Cameron calculates that the loss of face by appearing deceptive in not acknowledging he and Crosby had talked about plain paper packaging of cigarettes is less than the potential political damage that could occur if the issue was further investigated. As we see, the exchange ends with a standoff between interviewer and interviewee, where Cameron dictates the nature of the 'answer' he will provide even though Marr indicates its unsatisfactory status. The challenges both interviewer and interviewee offer to each other is, nonetheless, softened by Marr's qualification ('not quite an answer') and the prime minister's laugh.

The three interviews reveal that contestation often flows from the different ways in which journalists and politicians frame politics. Journalists will often focus on conflict between participants, investigate the machinations of the political field, and adjudicate or speculate on the practical outcomes. Alternatively, politicians must negotiate whether they will position themselves in conflict with other participants: sometimes they will seek either to position themselves as beyond the conflict or to defuse the conflict they might have with others, both within and outside the political field, through emphasizing their conflict management skills and processes of negotiation. The Number 10 garden interview, for example, opens with an extended discussion about actions that are needed to restrict search engine results on child pornography images. The interview narrative is prompted by the interviewer's claims that the major Internet companies are intransigent and that the government has not been successful in forcing them to change, as the following sequence of Marr's interventions throughout the exchange illustrates:

So you haven't persuaded the Googles and the Yahoos yet to do what you want?

...

Okay, so if I'm running an internet company search engine based in California and I simply say to you, 'Terribly sorry, I'm not interested, I'm not going to cooperate', what is the stick? What can you do? Apart from asking Google to pay their taxes, I suppose, what more can you do?

...

Because you see this is a power thing. It's the power of the global internet companies versus the power of national governments, and so far the companies have had it mostly their own way. (*The Andrew Marr Show* 2013a, pp. 3–4).

In response, Cameron emphasizes the complexity of the process and notes the actions the Internet companies have already implemented while also warning that he will implement legislation if negotiations with the companies are not fruitful:

> Well we're on the case. This is going to be a big campaign. This speech is the start of something; it's not the end of it. There are some specific steps we can take right now: give the Internet Watch Foundation resources and ability to take down images; work with the companies to take down images that have been identified; make sure the police run a really tough campaign to find these images and find the people putting them up. But the final piece of the jigsaw, which is even more responsible behaviour by the companies – and, as I say, they're not doing nothing, but I want them to do more – we need to do more work on that. (*The Andrew Marr Show* 2013a, p. 3)

In contrast to Marr's framing of the issue, Cameron presents government as an enabling mechanism, managing relations between various institutional actors, while reserving its ultimate political authority if the actors from the corporate field are not responsive to the need for change. The prime minister, then, seeks to promote a different kind of political agency through the *responsible* exercise of power: he demonstrates that his status enables him to act if required, but he downplays conflict and defers the exercise of power, emphasizing instead the virtues of negotiation and process.

The discourse of politicians is also defined against the values and positions of political opponents, and there is much in the three interviews that probes the respective standings of the government and the opposition over policy, such as economic management and energy prices, in the context of the scheduled 2015 national election. Marr highlights the conflict between the Conservatives and Labour, and the prime minister must argue for the actions and plans of the government and criticize the opposition, but Cameron also at times seeks to emphasize his authority as leader of the government by portraying himself above the immediate concerns of the news cycle and the strategic manoeuvrings that constitute the political game. In a discussion in the 5 January interview on the government's economic performance, Marr undercuts Cameron's discourse with a peppering of references to the government's standing in the polls:

> *Cameron*: We're one of the fastest growing countries now in the Western World, but we can't be complacent, the job isn't even half way done. This is a vital time...
>
> *Marr*: (*both together*) And Labour are nine points ahead.

Cameron: Also, this is a vital time in our country's history and the opposition are basically committed to undoing our good work. They want to borrow more, spend more, tax more, I mean for them…

Marr: (*over*) And yet the public are in favour of that apparently if you look at the polls.

Cameron: Well we've got, you know, sixteen months till the next election. This year for me is a year about governing, it's about delivering. It's about putting in place the elements of that long-term plan. I'm content that the public will judge me and the government I run and the party I run in 2015, but the public need to know that the opposition are committed to undoing all that good work, it will be like handing back the keys to the people who crashed the car in the first place. They've learnt nothing about the absolute mess they made of the economy when they were in power.

Marr: I have heard these messages before and yet they are nine points ahead. What is the Cameron problem here? (*The Andrew Marr Show* 2014, pp. 6–7)

The prime minister continues to outline the 'difficult decisions' the government has made in policy areas of welfare, education, small business and pensions, before declaring: 'I think perhaps politicians, media, all of us, we spend too much time on the sort of daily strategy political battle – who's up and who's down. I'm not really interested in that' (ibid., p. 7).

This exchange, then, reveals the prime minister shifting the focus of his discourse in response to the interviewer's questions, moving from a political attack on his opponents to a seemingly contradictory declaration that he is not interested in such contestation because he is preoccupied with the difficult task of governing. After the second intervention from Marr, Cameron is forced to implicitly acknowledge that his criticism of the opposition is blunted by current polling, and he responds by shifting the temporality of the political contest to the next election. He then further backtracks by seeking to reframe his engagement in the political field as not primarily concerned with the conflict with his political opponents. We can now note how the narrative of this exchange is driven not so much by the logical interrogation of statements as by the struggle of the interviewee to rework the framing of political relationships in a way that preserves his own political authority.

The third major theme of the interviews with the prime minister that we will discuss here is the production of Cameron's political habitus, which is substantially constituted through his self-promotion as an *affective* subject. Of course, political interviews are sites where the professional identity of the participants is foregrounded and per-formed, and there is ostensibly rational discussion about important public issues. Political interviews, however, cannot be exclusively characterized in this way, particularly given the emphasis on the personality and character of leaders in contemporary politics, the culture of political celebrity, and the fundamental importance of cultivating a rhetorical bond with the electorate. Across the three interviews Cameron's personal life, and his identity as a parent and husband, is both invoked by the interviewer and noted in the inter-viewee's answers. Across the interviews Cameron variously 'worries desperately' about the availability of pornography on the Internet, notes his children 'absolutely adore' holidaying in Cornwall, and declares he is 'incredibly proud' of the NHS, that he has 'huge sym-pathy' for victims of flooding, and that he is 'passionate' about the institution of marriage. We see his shifting invocation of himself as both a politician and a parent, and the alignment between himself and the nation, in the discussion about Internet pornography. He starts by declaring: 'I'm concerned as a politician and as a parent about this issue' before ending the discussion with the following exchange:

> *Cameron*: ... And I think it might take a bit of an argument to get it, but it's an argument on behalf of Britain's parents and children I'm prepared to have.
>
> *Marr*: I know you're making a speech on Monday about access to pornography for children. I'm talking about legal pornography, but nonetheless pornography that children in millions and millions of homes in Britain can get and are watching.
>
> *Cameron*: Well we need to do more on this as well. And I speak as a parent...
>
> *Marr*: (*over*) Is that possible? [i.e., to do more]
>
> *Cameron*: I've got a nine year old...
>
> *Marr*: Yeah.
>
> *Cameron*: ... a seven year old and a soon-to-be three year old. I worry desperately about this and I know parents do because you know when we're offline, you know there are rules about what films you can see in a cinema, what age you have to be to buy alcohol or cigarettes or what have you. (*The Andrew Marr Show* 2013a, p. 5)

Here Cameron invokes different forms of self-nomination as he nego-tiates both identification with other parents and at the same time a differentiation from those parents that provides the basis of his political authority. He speaks as a parent, noting the ages of his own children, but in the very next sentence he separates himself from 'parents', and earlier he states he is willing to have an argument with global corporations '*on behalf* of Britain's parents and children' (emphasis added). This shifting self-nomination is not the product of deception or confusion but the necessary discursive work a political leader must deploy in the production of a successful political habitus. In the interview discussion on this subject, the prime minister must demonstrate comprehensive knowledge of the legality and politics of the issue as well as a professional ability to act and to manage relations between institutional actors, but he must also express an *emotional investment* in the issue and embody an appropriate subject of affect.

In this exchange Cameron outlines his willingness and ability to speak on behalf of Britain's parents about the protection of their children, and throughout the three interviews he attempts to interpellate a national public that is unified through its sharing of the same kinds of emotions and values he expresses. In some ways the nation is unified in Cameron's discourse through its differentiation from others. The prime minister, for example, extols the universal service of the NHS as a source of 'pride' for the nation but argues against 'medical benefit tourism': '...our NHS is a national treasure. We can all be incredibly proud of it and it's right that we all pay in to it and everyone here has access to it for free but people who come to our country, who don't have the right to use it, should be charged for it and we're putting that in place' (*The Andrew Marr Show* 2014, p. 2). Equally, Cameron declares that the public is defined through the common desire to be able to express its opinion on the issue of UK membership of the European Union: '...what most people in this country want, is actually a real choice' (ibid., p. 5). The nation, then, is defined through the ongoing negotiations of the unity/difference binary. This is the fundamental basis upon which the meanings and identity of nations are established. In his discourse on the British public, the prime minister variously promotes the freedoms of individuals, the values, allegiances and identifications that unite 'us', and the shifting relations with other places and peoples against which the British public is delineated.

Cameron also speaks of the British public as *economic subjects*, and he negotiates principles of 'fairness' and types of government intervention across different economic issues. Across the three interviews, the British public is constituted as a unified moral and economic entity. The divisions that exist across subjects of public debate are attributed to conflicts within the political or parliamentary sphere, and the political agency of the public is only rarely acknowledged, such as Cameron's declaration in the 21 July interview that '…the British people are, I always think, a tough but fair taskmaster' (*The Andrew Marr Show* 2013a, p. 17). In the 29 September interview, a discussion on the housing market and the government's introduction of a help-to-buy scheme ends with these comments by the prime minister:

> This is not something totally new in our country. Most of our life times Andrew, it's been possible for people to go out and buy a flat with a 10% deposit and if we don't do this, then it will only be people with rich parents who can help them with the deposit, who can get on the housing ladder. That's not fair, it's not right, it's not the sort of country I want to live in and that's why it's important we bring this forward. (*The Andrew Marr Show* 2013b, p. 6)

Marr subsequently shifts the discussion to another economic issue, invoking the principle of fairness that Cameron had just mentioned:

> *Marr*: So we've been talking about fairness, in effect. Both of the other parties are now in favour of a mansion tax on properties above two million pounds. What's your view and can you be clear about what you would do in government…
>
> *Cameron*: I don't think it is a good idea. I want to live in a country where people work hard, they save, they put money in to their home and I think it's right that people pay council tax, it's right people pay stamp duty and we put that up. It's right people pay a decent top rate of tax and it's 45p in the pound in this country. But to go after some-one's house every year with a wealth tax, I don't think that is a sensible thing to do. (Ibid.)

The economic *divisions* within the British nation are highlighted in the help-to-buy scheme and mansion tax discussions, where 'fairness' is framed differently at opposite ends of the wealth spectrum in accord with the conservative economic philosophy of the prime minister. Cameron is prepared to intervene in the housing market to help those who are struggling to buy their first home, but he does not think it is 'a good idea' or a 'sensible thing to do' to intervene at the upper end of the housing market. He must implicitly address the perceived lack of fairness in not imposing a mansion tax, and he does so by outlining the other taxes that people pay. As such, across both ends of the wealth spectrum, Cameron wants a nation of citizens who work hard, save, and put their money into property. Of course,

Cameron is required to address both housing issues because Marr has adroitly set them together in the sequencing of the discussion, and he also seeks to highlight divisions within the political field by noting that both Labour and the Liberal Democrats support the mansion tax.

Kevin Rudd on *Insiders* and *7.30 Report*

Our second case study of political interviews features the former Australian prime minister Kevin Rudd, who experienced a turbulent political time as the national leader. He was elected in 2007 on the wave of strong popular support, but poor political management subsequently led to a leadership challenge by his deputy, Julia Gillard, and Rudd lost the leadership of the party in 2010, only to return as prime minister for a brief time in 2013 before losing the national election later that year. The analysis here is based on interviews in the months preceding his political downfall on two of the Australian Broadcasting Corporation's (ABC) leading current affairs programmes. The first interview, by Barrie Cassidy on the *Insiders* programme, occurred on 28 February 2010, and the second, by Kerry O'Brien, was on the *7.30 Report* (since retitled as 7.30) on 12 May 2010. Rudd's downfall that year stemmed from a number of political crises in the preceding months, including the deferral of an emissions trading scheme following the failure of the Copenhagen climate change talks, the disastrous implementation of a home insulation scheme, difficulties implementing changes to the hospital system, and the proposed introduction of a mining tax.

As was noted at the outset of the previous case study, we can focus initially on the authority of the participants within the hierarchies of their respective fields. The authority of the programmes analysed here also derives significantly from their individual hosts. O'Brien and Cassidy occupy remarkably similar habituses: both have high-profile status as veteran ABC journalists; both were previously press secretaries to former Australian Labor prime ministers (O'Brien for Gough Whitlam and Cassidy for Bob Hawke); both had conventional journalistic career trajectories, working as cadet journalists and in print journalism as well as television; and they are of a similar age (O'Brien is five years older) and were born in country towns. Both, then, are established Australian journalistic and political insiders, and their authority in the journalistic field and their journalistic subjectivity facilitates a shared framing of politics and understanding of political and media relations. It is the correspondence between O'Brien and

Cassidy's 'symbolic weight' (Darras 2005, p. 161) within the journalistic field and the prime minister's status in the political field that facilitates their communicative exchanges. More particularly, even though they have Labor backgrounds, O'Brien and Cassidy both have a history of antagonism with Rudd: for a period of time Rudd did not appear on *Insiders*, a point raised publicly by Cassidy; and O'Brien had previously contrasted Rudd's dealings with the media unfavourably with those of former prime minister John Howard (Craig 2010b, p. 44).

The habitus of Kevin Rudd, its constitutive features and its placement within the political and journalistic fields, forms a central site of struggle in both the *Insiders* and *7.30 Report* interviews. Rudd's language use and political character as prime minister was always the subject of intense media and public fascination. On the one hand, Rudd, a former diplomat and Mandarin speaker, was criticized for his convoluted language and verbose dissection of policy detail. On the other hand, he cultivated something of a nerdish political character and often employed Australian slang in a bid to appear more human and more accessible to the electorate. The significance of Rudd's habitus and the way it informed his leadership style assumes particular importance given his placement in the political field of the Australian Labor Party. Rudd, of course, had great power as party leader and prime minister, and he had a background in the Labor Party, having worked for the former Queensland premier Wayne Goss. Unlike previous Australian Labor prime ministers, however, Rudd had something of an 'independent' status in the party. His authority, then, was relatively presidential and his ascension to the post was significantly realized through the force of his habitus and his media meta-capital. While this was initially sufficient to compensate for his deficiencies of internal media capital (Davis and Seymour 2010, p. 742), this imbalance also gave his leadership a greater fragility, as we saw profoundly in his subsequent loss of the prime ministership.

The effectiveness of Rudd's leadership is presented as profoundly determined by his communicative style: how, and to whom, he speaks, as well as the values that are expressed through his speech. His style, and his personal management of it, is addressed in the *7.30 Report* interview when O'Brien raises the issue of 'brand' Rudd: '...you've spent the best part of two years building up your political capital. How have you managed to damage brand Rudd so comprehensively in such a short time this year?' (*7.30 Report* 2010). The prime minister attempts to deflect the personal angle of the question, responding 'the Government's going through a tough time at present', but O'Brien persists with his initial framing: '...I said brand Rudd, you said the

Government. I'm talking about Kevin Rudd, I'm talking about your image, your credibility, your brand' (ibid.). After Rudd again deflects the question, saying such a question is not for him but for political commentators, O'Brien sharpens the interrogation with a statement that includes a negative orientation: '...you can't possibly suggest that this does not exercise your mind at all, that you are so focused, you're so focused on Government that you're not concerned about whether you're losing support going into the next election?' (ibid.). It is only then that Rudd directly answers the question: 'Kerry, look I'm human like anyone else and of course, you'd, um, um, be inhuman if you weren't affected by developments from time to time, that's just the truth of it' (ibid.). Rudd quickly moves on from such a confession, locating his and the government's difficulties with the broader contexts of the political field, particularly with regard to the Carbon Pollution Reduction Scheme:

> What's the reality that I had to confront there? Well two realities. One is that the Liberal Party backflipped and voted our legislation down, having negotiated an agreement with Mr Turnbull to get it through. That is the reality we had to confront and the second reality is this, that when we got to Copenhagen it didn't produce the sort of progress and the global agenda that we all had hoped...(Ibid.)

This exchange is another micro-argument, and it represents a struggle over the relative authorities of an individual habitus and the political field – O'Brien wants to locate political agency with the individual while Rudd seeks to downplay his agency given the contexts of the political field. The invocation of Rudd's leadership as a 'brand' highlights the manufacture and commodification of political leadership. Implicit in the use of the term is an acknowledgement of the political project involving the institutional construction and management of a political self, but equally 'brand Rudd' is attributed with legitimacy through reference to the 'political capital' that had been accrued by the prime minister through his personal popularity. Here, then, Rudd is criticized not for a lack of authenticity but because he has lost his feel for the 'political game'. While the interviewer seeks to elicit the views of Rudd the individual, the prime minister tries to refuse this interpellation and instead promotes his public persona as leader of the government. In this sense, there is a discursive struggle over the privileging of Rudd's institutionalized media capital as leader of the government and his individualized media capital (Davis and Seymour 2010, p. 743). Rudd engages in this strategy because he understands successful political discourse requires that his own political stratagems and interests are not publicly highlighted. The exchange here is motivated by a previously noted (Craig 2008) disjuncture in the framing of politics between journalists and politicians, where the former are often interested in the meta-narratives of politics and, as such, scrutinize the intentions behind, and the effects of, political actions, while the latter attempt to limit their disclosures to descriptions and accounts of their public political performances. In essence, there arises a paradoxical situation where individual leadership style is integral to political success and subject to close scrutiny but leaders must not be seen to promote their self-interest.

The prime minister employs an action/verbal binary to undermine the authority of the journalistic field and portray his own political efficacy through practical engagements and actions, but the primary goal of Rudd's deployment of the action/verbal binary is to establish his pre-eminent association with the Australian public, particularly given that so much of his political authority derived from his media meta-capital. The authority of the journalistic field stems from its powers of mediation: it has direct access to political and community leaders, such as the prime minister, and conveys the comments and opinions of those figures to the public. Journalistic authority stems largely from its honest broker role, representing the interests of the public, but journalists such as O'Brien are also physically disassociated from the public. His engagement with the public operates more at a discursive level, assessing public opinion polls and the circulation of news media discourse about public opinion. Rudd exploits this disassociation and exerts his authority through his direct, personal engagements with members of the Australian public. It follows that we can not only note Chouliaraki and Fairclough's critique of Bourdieu's insufficient acknowledgment of the importance of mediation, and maintain the importance of news media interviews as 'significant political events in their own right' (1999, p. 103), but that we also need to highlight how the nature of mediation *itself*, and the political and social relations that are established through such mediation, can be the site of struggle between different fields. Davis and Seymour (2010, p. 742) are right to stress the need for political actors to cultivate productive relations with journalists, given that they connect the political field and wider citizenry, but we also need to note how often there is discursive conflict in media contexts *between* the political and journalistic fields as they vie for identification with the public.

This struggle between the respective authorities of the political and the journalistic fields for identification with the public continues in the *7.30 Report* interview when the prime minister comments on his extensive touring of hospitals around the country. O'Brien's status in the journalistic field derives from his *national* profile, but Rudd seeks to undermine O'Brien's authority by highlighting not only his media-centred isolation from the public but also his ignorance of *regional* media and its more direct communication with particular constituencies. In an extraordinary exchange, the prime minister invokes the layered constitution of the journalistic field and *overturns* the established hierarchy of that field for his political advantage:

> *Rudd*: Ah, Kerry, ah if, um, you'd come down the Queensland coast with me and the New South Wales coast to practically all the major centres, um, in those, ah, regions with their local hospitals and sat with the local doctors and nurses and allied health professionals and the patients and spoken to each of their local media perhaps not read by you in the studio where you are this evening, let me tell you...
>
> *O'Brien*: I do occasionally step outside it but go on...
>
> *Rudd*: No, I'm making a serious point to you. Do you read the *Mackay Mercury*? Do you read the *Bundaberg News Mail*? Do you read the *Maryborough Chronicle*? I mean these are papers which are reporting what's happening on the ground in their communities. (*7.30 Report* 2010)

This example also further illustrates Rudd's idiosyncratic use of language in his engagement with interviewers. In particular, he often deploys rhetorical questions, either as a direct means to challenge the interviewer, as we see in the example just cited ('Do you read...'), or as a means of framing the context of his answer, as we saw earlier: 'What's the reality that I had to confront there?' In addition, he often commences his answers with phrases that implicate the interviewer: 'You know something, Kerry...', 'Can I just say, Barrie...'. This strategy, while seeming to accede to the interviewer's authority, actually establishes Rudd's control over his interrogators in a way that doesn't draw attention to the exercise of power.

The *Insiders* and *7.30 Report* interviews also focus extensively on the *management* of the political field, and this more pragmatic orientation is highlighted over the values or philosophies informing policy action. Management can be differentiated into *internal* relations within the political field and *external* relations between the political field and other fields. While Rudd's political authority is granted by his position in the political field, he must, nonetheless, be seen to exercise this authority and enhance it through the successful navigation of political exigencies. An example of such a navigation of the internal relations of the political field occurs in the opening segment of the *Insiders* interview, where Cassidy quizzes the prime minister about the demotion in the past week of environment minister Peter Garrett, who had overseen the home insulation scheme. In the exchange, Rudd charts a delicate path between exerting his authority through his act of demoting Garrett and downplaying the political damage that ensued from such action:

> *O'Brien*: Now that you have stripped Peter Garrett of his responsibilities for energy efficiency, does that make him a second-class Minister?
>
> *Rudd*: What it means is that when it comes to the key task of environmental protection, which is the core responsibility of the Department of the Environment, that's where he now focuses his energies.
>
> ...
>
> *O'Brien*: But if he was a first-class Minister as you insisted all week, you wouldn't have had to do that.
>
> *Rudd*: Well, look, let's just call a spade a spade, Barrie. There's been real problems with the implementation of this program, there've been real problems with compliance and the Minister has had those responsibilities removed from him. That's just a fact. As far as other responsibilities are concerned, which is those of environment protection, which are important for the nation, where Peter has been active for a long period of time, taking tough and hard decisions on Traveston Dam, on the pulp mill in Tasmania and other significant projects, in Western Australia and elsewhere... these are areas where his impartiality has never been questioned, his diligence has never been questioned and his effectiveness has never been questioned. (*Insiders* 2010)

In this exchange there is a tension between Rudd's attempt to exert his authority in direct, plain speech and his desire to play down both his involvement in the decision and the damage to the reputation of the government and its ministers. He tries to invoke a 'no-nonsense' response both to the questions and to his actions with comments such as 'let's just call a spade a spade, Barrie' and 'That's just a fact'. Of course, Rudd is required to utter the cliché about spades because he had previously attempted to evade the question, and when he does answer the question directly his expression nonetheless deletes his agency in the process: 'the Minister has had those responsibilities removed from him.' Similarly, the more formal nominalization of 'the Minister' is contrasted with the subsequent section of Rudd's answer, where the minister is identified informally by his first name, his decisions in other areas of environmental policy are outlined in detail, and a tricolon is employed to emphasize the minister's competency.

Rudd's management of relations of authority with external fields of action is also a prominent feature of both interviews. The *7.30 Report* interview, for example, opens with O'Brien relaying critical comments by the CEO of the mining company Rio Tinto about the government's proposed resources tax and its impact on future resource development. Rudd's authority is dependent upon his ability to establish good relations between the political field and the business field, particularly the powerful resources sector that provides much of the nation's wealth:

> *O'Brien*: ...Can you afford to ignore that warning?
>
> *Rudd*: Ah, Kerry, I think it's entirely predictable that large mining companies will complain about what the Government has put forward....It reminds me, very much, of the debate which was kicked off back in the mid '80s when we bought in the petroleum resource rent tax....So it's fairly predictable that we're gonna have complaints. We think the right thing to do is to, um, obviously consult with the industry, we've said we're open to do that on questions of detail of implementation, of transition, but I've got to say Australians need to have a fairer share of these profits being earned from a resource which the Australian people own...(*7.30 Report* 2010)

In his reply Rudd downplays the charges by the mining industry through reference to historical precedents. That is, he deflects the political threat by again engaging in the discursive strategy of modulating, where he 'regulate[s] the perception of external environmental threats...[and] institutional imperatives to act' (Wodak et al. 2011, p. 605), although this time he invokes the topos of history to justify his conclusion. Rudd also seeks a balance between exerting his authority (declaring that the tax will be implemented and maintaining his consistency on the issue) and presenting himself as reasonable and open to negotiation. In this sense, the example highlights the discursive tension in political leadership between building consensus through acts of consultation and alternatively exercising political authority through actions. Once again, however, as we have seen in previous examples, Rudd's primary purpose is to align his political leadership with the interests of the Australian people.

Conclusion

This chapter has examined political interviews – those interrogative exchanges between politicians and journalists where the exercise of political games is perhaps most clearly observed. It has been seen that an ability to master the conventions of interview performances is essential for a successful career in contemporary politics. We considered the history of political interviews, noting that the rise of the interview as a genre of reportage coincided with a growing journalistic autonomy and distinct professional identity. The communicative form of political interviews was discussed by contrasting the ideals of dialogue with the institutional type of dialogue that occurs in broadcast journalistic interviews. We discussed the way that power struggles occur between politicians and journalists in interviews and also how the interviews need to be understood not only as interpersonal communicative encounters but also as media events that are disseminated to the viewing public. This discussion, and the theoretical framework that was established in the opening two chapters, was then applied to our case studies: David Cameron's appearances on *The Andrew Marr Show* and the interviews of Kevin Rudd on *Insiders* and *The 7.30 Report*. These analyses initially examined the status of interviewers and interviewees in the journalistic and political fields respectively but then proceeded to demonstrate how the power and authority of both protagonists were manifested in the exchanges. Across the case studies, we revealed and analysed the kinds of discursive struggles that occur between the participants, most notably the differences in the way they frame politics. The case studies also revealed how the interviews were often contests between the journalistic and political fields for an authority that derived from identification with, and the capacity to speak for, the public. They highlighted how politicians must effectively negotiate a range of relationships beyond the immediate challenge from the journalistic field: within the political field they must successfully account for external relations with political opponents and internal relations with colleagues, and they must enact governance through their management of other fields, most notably the field of business. In addition, the case studies focused on the importance of the habitus of both political leaders: how their backgrounds and communicative style are mobilized in mediated performances, where the expression of affect is crucial in conveying a sense of authenticity and personal engagement with the concerns of voters.

4

Leaders' Debates

Introduction

Unlike political interviews that occur on a regular weekly basis, leaders' debates are more exceptional events that feature primarily during election campaigns. While leaders' debates have been introduced in the United Kingdom only recently, they have been a regular feature of election campaigns in many other countries for several decades. It has been noted that 'Participating in political debates has become as common for candidates as kissing babies, eating "rubber" chicken dinners, raising money, and launching attack ads' (Carlin et al. 2009, p. 9). Leaders' debates are often high-pressure and widely watched television programmes because they are judged to be significant indicators as to who will soon be the next political leader. As such, they can provide exciting television: it has been claimed that leaders' debates provide 'human drama at its rawest' (Schroeder 2000, p. 201). The drama stems from the very 'debate' between candidates: the direct clash of ideas and personalities rarely occurs at any other time in modern political communication. Some have noted the 'conversational violence' in television debates that restricts the conversational rights and integrity of a participant and unduly influences the direction of the conversation (Luginbühl 2007). Others have taken a very different view, likening leaders' debates to television game shows with excited contestants, a 'prepped' audience, a celebrity emcee, and the ultimate prize of national leadership (Drucker and Hunold 1987).

These comments suggest that both positive and negative evaluations can be made about televised leaders' debates. Their positive
features include their attraction of large audiences and their educational impact. Research has shown that the content of discussion in
such debates is overwhelmingly focused on issues (Birdsell et al.,
2002, p. 207). They are focal points in an election campaign, and
many, otherwise disengaged citizens will watch the programmes to
assess the candidates. There is a large body of research on the effects
of leaders' debates on the public and their voting patterns which has
struggled to offer definitive conclusions, but there is evidence
that debates enhance viewer learning about candidates and their
issues, that previous non-voters are more likely to vote after viewing
them, that non-aligned viewers are most strongly influenced by them,
and that their effects 'co-mingle' with other campaign information
(An and Pfau 2004; Birdsell et al. 2002; Coleman 2000; Pfau 2002;
Senior 2008). In addition, as Coleman (2000, pp. 10–11) has noted,
televised debates help both to equalize the access of candidates to
mass media and to provide equal political opportunity. They bring
together on the same stage current leaders and lesser-known candidates with varying degrees of pre-existing public support whose
respective performances are clearly contrasted. This is important in
an environment where the increasingly exorbitant costs of campaigns
can hinder the prospects of poorer candidates and parties. Debates
also force candidates to speak to the positions of their opponents and
require television broadcasters to consider how the medium can best
serve the public in providing important political information (ibid.).
Pfau (2002, p. 251) maintains that political communication scholars
'believe that debates are superior to other communication forms in
that they offer an opportunity for candidates to advocate the relative
superiority of their positions via a communication venue that facilitates clash, depth, and unfiltered access.'

Leaders' debates, nonetheless, have also been subject to a range of
criticisms. Televising them is said to give undue emphasis to the image
and performances of the participants at the expense of the content
(Kraus 2011; Lang 1987; Roper 1998). Much has been made of high-
profile instances where radio listeners of debates have judged the
encounters very differently from television viewers – the most famous
example being the 1960 US presidential debates, where an unshaven,
perspiring Nixon was perceived by radio listeners to be the 'winner'
of the debate but the younger, more telegenic Kennedy was more
convincing for viewers. Leaders' debates also contribute to the trend
of giving almost exclusive focus to party leaders during election campaigns at the expense of broader involvement by political parties and

other political actors, including the public. The 'presidentialization' (Mughan 2000; Poguntke and Webb 2005) of politics has been charged with overemphasizing the individual character and style of campaigning leaders, diminishing the focus on the policies that differentiate parties. Leaders' debates have also been criticized because they are not debates in the best sense of the term, where there is a shared and thorough interrogation of respective viewpoints, but, rather, are comprised primarily of a series of independent and relatively short answers to a large range of questions.

In this chapter we will firstly examine the structures and formats of leaders' debates. Like political interviews, they are instances of interpersonal communication but also complex mediated events. Their organization and format differ across different countries, are partly dependent upon the nature of the political system, and are often subject to political wrangling. The range of formats will be examined, from formal presidential debates to informal town hall meetings where members of the public are the primary questioners. We will discuss how the nature of interactions between participants varies according to the structure of the debates, and we will scrutinize the roles and influence of moderators in managing that interaction. And we will highlight how the more active role of the public and the use of online technology have in some instances recently brought innovations into the dynamics of the events. The impact of debates in the context of election campaigns will also be considered. There is now an extensive history of leaders' debates in election campaigns in countries such as the United States, Canada, Australia and New Zealand, and the particular national contexts have influenced both how they function and their effects. We will consider these effects with regard to issues such as the promotion of underdog participants and the impact on voting patterns. The case studies in the chapter will analyse the historic leaders' debates in the UK 2010 election campaign and the US presidential debates between Barack Obama and Mitt Romney. The analyses of these particular debates reveal that the performances of the politicians depend less on direct journalistic interrogation and more on interaction with other participants and the studio audience. Again, we should caution against claiming a more general, representative status for these particular debates. They have been chosen nonetheless because of their high-profile status and their relatively recent occurrence. Furthermore, the UK debates were the first of their kind and had a large impact on the election campaign, while the US debates illustrate the evolution of the genre in the context of the growing power of social media.

Formats and Structures of Leaders' Debates

The previous chapter noted how the public dissemination of political interviews informs and complicates the apparent simplicity of the interaction between interviewer and interviewee. Leaders' debates are even more layered communicative encounters because they include at least two participants, there is variation in format that affects the interpersonal dynamics, and because the studio audience can sometimes play an active role. Leaders' debates, then, are comprised of multiple communicative relations where participants have varying access to voice, performance and representation; different powers to influence the narrative; and diverse forms of political agency and effect.

Leaders' debates span a range of possible formats. The most common involve a sole moderator, a moderator and panel of journalists, or, in so-called town hall debates, candidates moving around more freely on a stage and answering questions from the assembled members of the public. They can involve a range of participants, from the two main party leaders to panels featuring a range of contributors from across the political spectrum. It can be argued that the more presidential style of debate, featuring two main party leaders, is less appropriate in multi-party systems or where a parliament is elected by proportional representation, where a range of minor parties have some influence in processes of governance. This, in turn, raises the issue of how the format is determined and who chooses the participants. In some countries there are informal and often protracted negotiations between political parties and broadcasters, but in the United States the debates have been organized since 1986 by the Commission on Presidential Debates. There has been a single moderator in the US since 1992, but debates in other countries still sometimes feature an additional panel of journalists. A panel of this type ensures that one individual does not exert too much influence over the debate and that there is a representative spread of journalists across print and broadcast media and perceived political orientations. Equally, and ironically, more questioners can mean that politicians are subject to less scrutiny.

The interaction between politicians is, of course, the main point of leaders' debates. We want to see not only the side-by-side presentation of policy details and political values but also the questions, rebuttals and challenges between the candidates. This interaction animates debates and provides their main drama, and it is often where the strengths and weaknesses of political performance are most evident. The interpersonal dynamics between politicians, however, is very much dependent upon the format. Debates have different rules and design which influence performance: whether there are opening statements and follow-up questions or rebuttals; whether there are time limits, and how strictly they are enforced; and whether candidates are seated, stand, or can walk about the set. As already noted, the discussion is sometimes dominated by candidates' responses to questions from the moderator. There is often a freer form of interaction in town hall meetings, and occasionally politicians may energize a debate by overriding the rules in order to converse – as occurred between Kevin Rudd and Tony Abbott over health policy before the Australian 2010 election campaign.

The genre of the leaders' debate requires particular performative skills, and different politicians have been known to perform best in particular formats. Bill Clinton, for example, was well noted for his engaging performances in town hall debates. Debates compel politicians not only to present their own ideas skilfully but also quickly to evaluate and critique, in an effective rhetorical manner, the discourse of others. Helen Clark, the former prime minister of New Zealand, was noted for her sharp debating skills (Craig 2007). Successful political discourse in leaders' debates, however, cannot be solely combative. Politicians must also present themselves as reasonable individuals who are able to express positive political visions and mobilize consensus and unity. Equally, performative skill requires a productive synthesis of substance and style. Leaders' debates have been criticized for prioritizing style at the expense of the substance of verbal discourse: while it is true that, as televisual events, they give prominence to the visuality of the candidates and their performances, we should not overlook the fact that it is often through the reportage of style and performance that the substance of the content of debates is conveyed. Successful communication does not derive necessarily from the demonstration of political truths but from the presentation of a habitus that fuses political authority with performative style: politicians must convey their knowledge and expertise as well as an appealing and engaging personality. Part of the performative authority of a politician derives from the way they exploit the setting of the debate and interact with the audience. In one prominent example from the 2010 Australian election, the then opposition leader, Tony Abbott, decided to move from the stage at a so-called People's Forum debate down to the level of the audience. As he later explained: 'If you're up on a stage behind a lectern you're almost by definition lecturing to people. But the whole point of these events is not to lecture to people, it's to engage with them' (cited in Younane Brookes 2011, p. 65).

Debates also offer a stage for the journalists who act either as moderators or as panel members. Moderators introduce the debate, when they have the opportunity to outline the significance of the encounter. They perform the important function of imposing discipline on the participants and seek to ensure the fairness of the process, allowing equal opportunity to speak and ensuring that interruptions to answers do not occur, or are at least kept to a minimum. Some individuals distinguish between their role as moderator and as journalist. Jim Lehrer, who has moderated US presidential debates since 1988, has said: 'When I do the debates I very consciously take off my journalism hat and serve in the role of the moderator. I keep the time, I enforce the rules' (cited in Minow and LaMay 2008, p. 178). Lehrer rightly suggests that the role of the moderator, unlike the more active interrogative role of an interviewer, is to facilitate the discourse and interaction between the politicians, but nonetheless the dividing line between the roles of moderator and journalist is not easily maintained. Moderators have great power because they ask questions. Sometimes the selection of questions is solely the work of the moderator and not shared with others, and sometimes there is consultation over the formulation of questions. In addition, moderators cannot help but actively contribute to the evaluation of the debate through their decisions to discipline participants and to ask follow-up questions. Moderators are usually high-profile and influential journalists, and they sometimes exercise an interventionist and critical approach to their role. Such an approach, however, is usually disparaged. The debate hosts in the New Zealand 2002 election campaign, for example, were subject to much public criticism for their self-promotion and lack of respect for the party leaders, leading to more restrained and courteous performances by moderators in the 2005 election campaign.

The audience at leaders' debates is posited as an active participant or at least an acknowledged presence. While all forms of interrogative political communication are premised upon the existence of an audience, the context of an election campaign highlights the need for public involvement and judgement in leaders' debates. As already suggested, the role of audience members varies across different formats: they are relegated in some debates to a mute presence in the shadows of the studio lights, in others their questions and opinions are 'voiced' through the moderator, while in town hall meetings they have the opportunity personally to quiz the leader of the country on national television. More recently, televised debates have included questions posted on YouTube. Some studio audiences consist of party supporters while others are exclusively 'non-committed' voters.

Beyond the studio audience there is, of course, the viewing or listening audience, and sometimes the views of a selected audience (often non-committed voters) are represented on screen through the debate in the form of a so-called 'worm'. While this offers 'public' feedback as the discussion unfolds, the public also finds expression in opinion polls that are conducted immediately after the debate. The inclusion of questions from members of the public can add variability and unpredictability: while some are often formally posed, mimicking the style of a journalist or moderator, and deal with conventional topics, others are 'softer' or less sophisticated than the questions of the media professionals; yet others can raise unexpected issues, and their personal framing can suddenly shift the tone of a debate. In the 2010 Australian election, a question in one of the town hall meetings about same-sex marriage rights unexpectedly elevated the issue to prominence in the campaign.

Leaders' Debates in Election Campaigns

We gain a better understanding of leaders' debates when we examine the broader context of election campaigns, where debates are now considered as conventional, focal points (An and Pfau 2004; Carlin et al. 2009) – an essential part of the 'democratization process' (Coleman 2000, p. 7). They are also popular events, although the percentage of the overall electorate who watch them has fallen in the United States since their introduction. Well over 80 per cent of the television audience watched the US presidential debates in 1976, and more than 58 million people watched the first of the debates between Barack Obama and Mitt Romney in the 2012 presidential campaign (Obama–Romney debate 2012). There has been considerable research conducted on the evolving character and effects of election campaigns (Chau 2007; Farrell and Schmitt-Beck 2002; Norris 2000; Sanders 2009), which are obviously critical periods in democracies. They are characterized by a blizzard of different forms of political communication, such as news stories, advertising, tweets, opinion polls and public events. We should not forget that election campaigns are also cultural events – 'distinct but nonetheless in continuity with the flow of everyday life of the local population' (Chau 2007, p. xii). Contemporary 'postmodern' campaigns (Norris 2000) are now highly professionalized and managed events, but they also remain at times unpredictable affairs, and a gaffe on the campaign trail or an unanticipated news event can suddenly change the focus of a campaign. It can be argued that campaigns are now more important because of increased volatility in the electorate, with less established class identities aligned to major parties, but equally it can be argued that pre-existing political allegiances and levels of economic prosperity dictate electoral success more than do campaigns.

Leaders' debates have a long and distinguished background from before the introduction of mass, audio-visual media. Contemporary debates are always overshadowed by the mythology that has grown up around the seven senatorial debates between Abraham Lincoln and Stephen Douglas in 1858, when candidates spoke for an hour on the future of slavery, followed by a rebuttal of an hour and a half and then a summary speech of half an hour (Coleman 2000, p. 4). The first radio debate in the United States occurred in 1948 between the two leading Republican Party candidates, Harold Stassen and Thomas Dewey, and the first televised debate took place eight years later between Democratic Party primary candidates Adlai Stevenson and Estes Kefauver (ibid., p. 6). The famous first US presidential debates between John F. Kennedy and Richard Nixon propelled the format into the political consciousness of the nation, although there was a hiatus in debates until 1976, when Jimmy Carter and Gerald Ford shared the same stage. The town hall format was introduced in the presidential debates in 1992. While US presidential debates attract global attention, many other countries have been conducting political debates for decades: Sweden has broadcast debates since the late 1950s, Canada had its first televised debate in 1962, and West Germany has held debates regularly before elections since 1969 (ibid.). In New Zealand the first televised leaders' debate took place in 1969, but Australians had to wait until 1984, when the prime minister Bob Hawke and Andrew Peacock went head to head. While there is a general similarity in the range of formats that are employed across different countries, we should be cognizant that the way debates unfold is influenced not only by the particular political system but also by the 'speech culture of the nation' (Isotalus and Aarnio 2006, p. x). Isotalus and Aarnio (2006), for example, note how the main function of discussion in Finnish culture is to maintain harmony, and this informs conduct in their leaders' debates.

Leaders' debates are televisual events and also increasingly Internet events, most notably through the inclusion of video questions posted on YouTube – a practice that has now occurred across a number of leaders' debates, including those before the London mayoral election, the Spanish presidential election, Greek and New Zealand elections, as well as for US presidential elections and debates between Democratic and Republican candidates. They not only feature individual video questions, but their online transmission enables a variety of means of public engagement, such as the posting of comments and hyperlinks on the comment sections of websites, the tracking of links of particular video clips, instant searching on terms mentioned, and participating in live blogs and online discussion boards (Kirk and Schill 2011). In this sense, leaders' debates are part of the broader trend where the Internet and social media are transforming both how candidates campaign and how the public interact with candidates and one another. To what extent the inclusion of online questions qualitatively changes the dynamic of debates and ushers in substantively greater public engagement remains an open issue (Craig 2009; Kirk and Schill 2011; May 2008; Tryon 2007). Questions are screened and selected by producers, and those from members of the public often cover conventional topics, although their very articulation, sometimes involving colloquial language and often being filmed in living rooms and bedrooms, helps to ground politics in the everyday concerns of citizens (Craig 2009). Equally, there are suggestions that such innovations are helping to reach a broader audience: the CNN YouTube debate in the US presidential election campaign in 2008 amassed the largest audience in cable news programming for those in the 18- to 34-year-old range (May 2008).

The number and timing of debates, as focal points of election campaigns, becomes a crucial issue for candidates and campaign teams. In Australia, some campaigns have featured only one debate in the early stage of the election campaign, largely because the incumbent prime minister was not a strong debater. In contrast, the 2005 New Zealand election featured five television debates, including one between the finance spokespersons for the parties, and a number of radio debates. Televised debates are significant markers in the narratives of election campaigns, charting the changing fortunes of candidates: they are often presented as either the first 'battle' or the 'last chance' for a candidate to convince voters. After the 2010 UK election, the prime minister David Cameron complained that the three debates had assumed too much influence over the election campaign, and this was one reason why the same kind of format was not replicated in the 2015 election campaign. Leaders' debates cover main policy areas that are central to the election, but it is a convention that new policies are not announced during debates. In this sense, while political debates have a high informational value, they function primarily as moments in the campaign where there are explicit contrasts and evaluations of already available policy detail.

Leaders' debates can be seen to give an advantage to an opposition leader, given they are afforded equal status with incumbents on a shared stage, and consequently sometimes prime ministers can decide not to take part in debates during a campaign, particularly if they hold a strong lead in public opinion polls. The Australian prime minister Bob Hawke decided not to have debates in the election campaign after their introduction in 1984. A decision not to participate, however, must factor in criticisms that the leader is avoiding public scrutiny. Anecdotally, leaders' debates do often provide an 'underdog effect', where opposition candidates, and particularly those who are perceived to be poor debaters, are judged to have performed well. Mitt Romney received positive media coverage following the first of the debates in the 2012 US presidential campaign, John Key surprised the public with strong performances in the debates with Helen Clark in New Zealand in 2008, and the Australian prime minister John Howard was regularly judged to have been out-debated by a range of opposition leaders. Often, however, the underdog effect does not translate into electoral success, as attested by the Romney and Howard examples, and it underlines the fact that leaders' debates are but one feature of complex, multifaceted election campaigns.

Our perceptions of leaders' debates are strongly influenced by the reportage of the encounters. Debates are often immediately followed by 'recap' programmes where the highlights and lowlights are dissected and political commentators offer their own evaluations. Journalists and commentators inevitably focus on who 'won' and who 'lost'. The very structure of debates and the competitive nature of elections influence the adoption of such an evaluative framework, but they can also reduce debates to 'zero-sum' games that can sideline the substantial amount of information conveyed. This journalistic framework in the reportage of debates is in accord with the more general criticism that journalists reduce elections to a 'horse race'. Opinion polls, often commissioned by news media outlets, also seek instant public assessments of who won a debate, and this, in turn, reinforces a particular kind of journalistic reportage. In addition, post-debate reportage can reshape public opinion. One famous example of this phenomenon was following the 1976 presidential debate between Carter and Ford, when polls that judged Ford the winner were dramatically reversed a day later after news media reportage and commentary focused on his gaffe that Eastern Europe was not under Soviet domination (Birdsell et al. 2002, p. 211). Such an example emphasizes that the meanings and effects of leaders' debates cannot be contained within the event itself. News media reportage and poll findings influence perceptions about debates, but more broadly the debates influence longer-term 'relational' judgements about the persona of candidates, and their effects inform and 'co-mingle' with other electoral communicative forms and content

(Pfau 2002). This extends beyond news reportage to other influential forms of media, including social media and television political satire programmes.

UK 2010 Leaders' Debates

The United Kingdom 2010 election was historic because it was the first time that leaders' debates had featured in an election campaign in that country. The debates became the major feature of the campaign and dominated media coverage. The impetus for televised leaders' debates during the campaign came from Sky News in 2009, with the subsequent agreement of ITV and the BBC. Not surprisingly, the then opposition leader, David Cameron, quickly announced his support for the debates, particularly given his ability as a televisual communicator and Prime Minister Gordon Brown's perceived lack of appeal as a media performer. Brown also agreed to appear, not least perhaps because the Labour Party was trailing in the opinion polls, and significantly both leaders agreed to the proposal that the Liberal Democrats should also have a presence on the debate podium. Three debates were held over three weeks of the election campaign. The first was hosted by ITV on 15 April, the second was hosted by Sky on 22 April, and the final one was screened on the BBC a week later. The debates had individual areas of policy focus: domestic, foreign and economic affairs. The format was the same across all three, with brief opening and closing statements, questions from a studio audience, and short answers, with subsequent opportunities for the leaders to engage in direct dialogue with each other. The televising of the leaders' debates attracted a mass audience. The ITV debate was viewed by 9.68 million people; only *Britain's Got Talent* was watched by more people on the channel that week. Viewing figures dropped for the second debate on Sky News, but the final debate on the BBC attracted 7.43 million viewers (Wring and Ward 2010, p. 803).

The prominent feature of the debates was the acclaim Liberal Democrat leader Nick Clegg received for his performances, particularly in the opening debate. Clegg had previously had a low national profile, but his frequent invocations of a 'new' politics, in contrast to the two major parties, and his personable engagement with studio audience members, contributed to his positive reception. A poll after the first debate found 61 per cent of respondents believed Clegg had won, in contrast to 21 per cent for Cameron and 17 per cent for Brown (Wring and Ward 2010, p. 805). The popular news media responded in different ways to Clegg's sudden elevation in the nation's consciousness: the positive reportage dubbed the phenomenon 'Clegg-mania', while several right-wing newspapers engaged in a range of attacks on the Liberal Democrat leader (ibid., p. 807). While it has been argued that the debates did influence voters' thoughts and decisions during the campaign, it has also been noted that the election result for the parties was relatively in accord with opinion polls prior to the first debate (Pattie and Johnston 2011). Our focus here is to show how Clegg's language and performance skills contributed to his favourable reception in contrast to his opponents. We will argue that Clegg successfully mobilized a habitus of affect and that this was integral to his success. The analysis will also investigate the interactions between Brown, Cameron and Clegg and the way that expressions of both consensus and conflict were integral to the debates.

The three debates form a striking example of the kind of political discourse and mode of engagement that yields successful political communication in leaders' debates. This is evident when we contrast the strategies of Nick Clegg with those of the then prime minister, Gordon Brown. The Labour leader's inability to convey a media-friendly persona was widely noted: even Brown himself acknowledged this in the second debate, contrasting his 'substance' with the ability to perform in the encounters: 'If it's all about style and PR, count me out. If it's about the big decisions, if it's about judgment, . . . delivering a better future for this country, I'm your man' (Sky debate 2010). In the debates Brown adopted the strategy of *debating his opponents*, whereas Clegg primarily *talked with* the studio audience and the public. Brown constantly challenged both Clegg and Cameron on details from their party manifestos, noting when they had not answered his question, and often demonstrating his displeasure with them by shaking his head and smiling in a grimly ironic manner. The prime minister demonstrated good command of policy detail and also sometimes offered an effective critique of the comments of others, but the negative framing of his discourse and performance was not conducive to engaging with the public.

Clegg, more so than his opponents, engaged with questioners, almost always referring to them by name and sometimes seeking to identify them amid the studio audience. He also made a point of explicitly responding to the questions: 'I think discipline is important, of course. I think creativity, which I think is the point you're saying, Joel – I'm not allowed to ask you questions, that's against the rules, but just nod if – good! I think creativity is important in the classroom' (ITV debate 2010). Clegg not only referred to the questioners but also sometimes deferred to their expertise and aligned himself with their concerns. In the latter part of the final debate, a question from a teacher prompted the following responses from Clegg:

> Of course Gordon Brown's right to say there's a link, Michael. You know this better than we do. You know there's a link between poverty at home and underperformance in the classroom.
>
> ...
>
> Why not focus the money on where it's really needed, and also use the money that we can save elsewhere, as I explained to Michael, to invest in those individual children who need that individual care. It could be Saturday morning classes, evening classes, one-to-one-tuition, the smaller class sizes, all the things that I know as a parent and Michael no doubt knows as a teacher makes the most dramatic difference to a child's education. (BBC debate 2010)

This alignment between the Liberal Democrat leader and the audience was reinforced visually through a cutaway of the teacher nodding his head. While one might think that debates would prioritize the use of the first-person pronoun – with declarations that '*I* have the right policies' – successful contemporary political discourse is also increasingly attuned to the importance of highlighting the political agency of the public through second-person mode of address. President Obama, for example, in his post-election speech after winning a second term of office, declared: 'Whether I earned your vote or not, I have listened to you, I have learned from you. And you have made me a better President' ('Obama' 2012). This production of political authority by politicians through the discursive delegation of it to others also occurred in Clegg's comments. In the second debate, for example, he noted:

> Firstly, Mary, you need to be given the power to sack any politician who's proved to be corrupt. It's something I advocated in the past, it's something I put forward in Westminster. Both David Cameron and Gordon Brown's party didn't support that. They now say, which is good, say they do welcome that. You're the boss, you're the boss. (Sky debate 2010)

Clegg's success in the debates derived not only from what he said to the audience members but also *how* he made his comments. While all the candidates were obviously conscious of the performative demands of the debate format, Clegg, more so than the others, displayed empathy for the audience members through the tone of his voice and the emphasis in the delivery of his comments.

Particularly when he was speaking about an injustice or unfairness, the Liberal Democrat leader would give an adjectival emphasis together with a slowed delivery to convey his feelings, as the following excerpts show:

> Millions of ordinary people are simply struggling to pay the fuel bills, to pay the petrol prices, to pay the weekly shopping bills. What I'm...I'm totally with you on this Adina. I think it's *just wrong...*
>
> ...
>
> I've now had enough people in tears in my constituency office where I'm an MP in Sheffield, because they've been given money one moment, they've spent that money on the children, on the heating bills, and then suddenly they get a letter, out of the blue, from the Government, saying you've got to pay the money back. That is *so unfair...*(BBC debate 2010; emphasis added)

These examples reveal how Clegg was able to convey himself as an *affective subject* who is able to forge an emotional connection with the electorate. As we saw in the previous chapter in our analysis of David Cameron's performances on *The Andrew Marr Show*, this skill is a general feature of contemporary political discourse, but it is particularly powerful here because the politician is able to engage directly with members of the public (unlike in a political interview) and also because it stands in contrast to the ostensible purpose of the event, which is to debate his or her political opponents. As we will see, the ability to manage conflict and consensus in interactions with other debaters is still, of course, a fundamental feature of debates, but the analysis here demonstrates that engagements with the audience are also crucial to success in such encounters.

In this sense, members of the audience were crucial to the discourse and interpersonal dynamics of the debates, even though they were required to be silent throughout the event, with no applause or interjections, and those individuals who were fortunate enough to quiz the leaders were not allowed follow-up questions. The debates, nonetheless, only featured questions from the public, with the moderators limited to the occasional restatement of questions and observations that candidates could answer the question more specifically. The active role of the public in posing questions to political leaders not only influences the discourse of politicians and their interactions with each other on stage but also offers a relatively rare moment when the public's agency is on show and they can potentially influence the democratic process. The UK debate audience, however, was a disciplined public, given the selection process of the questioners and their restricted ability to engage in dialogue. The questions covered conventional political topics and were posed to all candidates in a polite and generalized manner. In this way, the audience was more restricted than some others, such as those in the town hall debates in Australia, where a greater number of questioners sometimes posed idiosyncratic questions, and those in current affairs forum television programmes (see chapter 6).

The presence of audiences also influenced the debates' content because they prompted accounts about the everyday experiences of people whom the politicians had encountered on the campaign trail. More so than in conventional political interviews, the leaders peppered their answers with stories of their engagements with members of the public in a way that underlined the argument of the debater and grounded their authority in knowledge about the exigencies of everyday life and their knowledge of local problems, as the following excerpts demonstrate:

Cameron: …I went to Crosby the other day and I was talking to a woman there who had been burgled by someone who had just left prison. He stole everything in her house. As he left, he set fire to the sofa and her son died from the fumes. That burglar, that murderer, could be out of prison in just four-and-a-half years. The system doesn't work, but that sort of sentence is, I think, just completely unacceptable in terms of what the public expect for proper punishment.

…

Clegg: …This government spent £12 billion on a computer testimony in the NHS which doesn't work, yet I was in Burnley the other day. I think Jacqueline was saying you come from Burnley. As you know, they've closed the A&E department there. I think you now have to travel 25 miles to Blackburn. (ITV debate 2010)

The prevalence with which all three political leaders used such stories suggests it was a deliberate political strategy, although post-debate research by IpsosMORI (2010, p. 4) indicates it was an unsuccessful strategy.

The debates were also characterized by expressions of difference and conflict, as each leader sought to distinguish himself from his political opponents. Such debate is, of course, the driving narrative force of these encounters, and there were several lively exchanges between the leaders that presented a clear contrast between the parties over a range of policy issues. The presence of three participants provided for a broader and more complex range of disagreements and agreements, in contrast to those debates that set only one candidate against another. Gordon Brown, for example, strongly criticized his opponents throughout the debates – likening them at one stage to his own 'two young boys squabbling at bath time' (Sky debate 2010) – but equally he was aware of potential future coalition arrangements and, as such, frequently noted that he agreed with Clegg.

Each of the candidates was seeking political advantage through the exploitation and management of conflict. This occurred through a number of different strategies: sometimes one would note absences or deficiencies in the policies of the others, sometimes one would acknowledge the detail of his opponents but argue the policy needed to be further developed, and sometimes one would exploit conflict between the two other candidates to appear reasonable. In the first debate, an extended exchange about healthcare involved a string of comments that noted the deficiencies and absences of the policy of other parties:

> *Brown*: ...The main point to recognize is this: David will not give you the guarantee that you'll see a cancer specialist in two weeks, or the guarantee that you'll have a GP in the evenings and weekends.
>
> ...
>
> *Cameron*: ...The government has had 13 years to fix these problems, and it hasn't done. Gordon Brown talks about cancer, but what he's not telling you is that there are people in our country...who had to sell their home to get the cancer drugs.
>
> ...
>
> *Clegg*: This is a phoney debate....David Cameron, you simply cannot seriously suggest that we should believe that you can cut the deficit immediately as you want, then have a whole blizzard of tax breaks...and provide huge lashings of extra money to the public services. (ITV debate 2010)

While public discussion about leaders' debates often focuses on the negativity of such exchanges, politicians must nonetheless be able to demonstrate effective debating skills and engage in combative discussion in a professional manner to display their expertise and authority. The expression of conflict does not, however, have to be directly combative. In the debates, leaders sometimes sought to appear reasonable through agreement, while also differentiating themselves by noting that the policies of others were insufficient. In the first debate, for example, Cameron noted that proposed border control measures did not go far enough: 'As well as border controls that Gordon talks about, and I support strong border controls, I think we need to go one step further and have a proper border police force so we can combine at our borders, customs, immigration, security and police' (ITV debate 2010). At other times, debate participants were able to capitalize on conflict between the other two in order to forge positions of consensus. In the first debate, for example, Cameron observed, after an exchange between Clegg and Brown over political reform: 'Well, it's rather difficult, because Gordon says Nick agrees with Gordon and Nick says that Nick doesn't agree with Gordon. Let me try and find something we're all agreed on that we could change' (ITV debate 2010).

While each of the three leaders interrogated the positions of both of their opponents to seek political advantage, Clegg was again successful because he was able to differentiate himself and the Liberal Democrats from the 'old' major parties and, somewhat paradoxically, align himself with the electorate by portraying himself as 'outside' or 'beyond' politics:

> I think this is partly what's been going wrong for so long. We have both major parties running government over the last 20 years talking tough about immigration and delivering complete chaos in the way in which it's run. I'm like anybody else. I just want a fair, workable immigration system...
>
> ...
>
> I'm not sure if you're like me, but the more they attack each other, the more they sound exactly the same. Look, Joel's question – let's go back to the question. (ITV debate 2010)

In the implementation of such a strategy, the Liberal Democrat leader promoted himself as a practical problem-solver and someone who had the capacity to act rather than just talk about a political dilemma. In the final debate, for example, he criticized the leaders of both major parties in their management of immigration:

> Maybe I should explain, rather than having David Cameron and Gordon Brown, very much in the style of old politics, making misleading claims. I think there is a problem. It's a problem I didn't create, you didn't create, they created it.... You can pretend as much as you like, David Cameron and Gordon Brown, that somehow you can deport people when you don't even know where they are. I'm coming up with a proposal. It might be controversial, but it's dealing with the way the world is. Get real. (BBC debate 2010)

Equally, Clegg employed the same kind of action/verbal binary that we saw in the analysis of Kevin Rudd in the previous chapter in order to portray his opponents as inconsistent and ineffectual. While the actions of politics are implemented through discourse, this portrayal reinforces popular perceptions of a *disconnection* between discourse and action in politics:

> I have to say to both David Cameron and Gordon Brown, what bothers me is that I hear the words, they sound great. But, you know, it's not just what you say, it's what you do. Why is it that when I put forward, Liberal Democrats put forward, a law which would have given all of you and everyone watching now the right to sack their MP if their MP is corrupt, the Labour MPs voted against it, the Conservative MPs didn't even bother to vote. (ITV debate 2010)

The UK leaders' debates demonstrated that political leaders had to show expertise and authority through their ability to critique forcefully the positions of others but, ultimately, that the encounters were not primarily about the process of debate with political opponents or with the debate moderator. Instead, the primary interrogative process was between the politicians and the audience, and Nick Clegg was perceived to have been the strongest performer because he most effectively identified with the public. The Liberal Democrat leader achieved this identification through accounts of everyday engagements with the public, through personal engagement and validation of the concerns of questioners, through his performance as an affective subject, through aligning himself with the public as 'outside' the machinations of the major political parties, and through the use of an action/verbal binary. As has often been witnessed in the history of leaders' debates, Clegg benefited from an 'underdog' and 'outsider' status. Equally, as we have seen subsequently, he has experienced a reversal of that status: his public appeal diminished after his engagement in the political field as deputy prime minister, and he was judged to have performed poorly in 2014 in debates with the new political 'outsider', Nigel Farage. At the 2015 election the Liberal Democrats suffered serious losses and Clegg resigned as leader of the party.

US 2012 Presidential Debates

The two years between the innovation of leaders' debates in the 2010 United Kingdom election and the 2012 US presidential election witnessed an explosive growth in social media usage that now has significant ramifications for the public reception of, and engagement with, such debates. The prominence of the televised debates in the UK campaign saw the election dubbed a 'TV election', even though some studies (Ampofo et al. 2011; Chadwick 2011) have noted the influence of social media during that campaign. Nonetheless, by contrast, much coverage of the Obama–Romney debates focused on the rise of social media, and specifically Twitter, with headlines such as 'Twitter Won the Presidential Debate' (Bennett 2012) and 'How Twitter is Winning the 2012 US Election' (Mills 2012). While it is true that leaders' debates are still television events, they are also now much more than this in the age of the Internet and social media.

The 2012 US presidential debates featured two prominent issues that will provide the core of our discussion here. Firstly, as noted, they were characterized as the Twitter debates, and we will move beyond the interaction between the candidates to explore the roles of social media in the public discourse about the debates, which includes media reportage and commentary and public opinion polls. Secondly, a major talking point was the perceived poor performance of President Obama in the opening debate and the surprisingly strong performance of the Republican candidate Mitt Romney. We will examine the language and performances of both candidates and use the analysis to highlight the generic requirements of modern television debate discourse and performance.

Twitter and the Obama–Romney Debates

The first debate between President Obama and the former Massachusetts governor Mitt Romney attracted even more public interest than normal for a US presidential debate: it was then the most tweeted event in US political history (Morgan 2012), generating 10.3 million tweets during the 90 minutes of the encounter – about twice as many as in all of the debates during the previous presidential campaign in 2008 (Peterson 2012). Public interest was also reflected in the television viewing figures: more than 58 million Americans watched the debate, either on cable or on one of the four leading broadcast networks, up from the 52 million people who watched the corresponding first debate between Obama and John McCain in 2008 (Obama–Romney debate 2012). The debates were also live streamed on YouTube and Xbox Live. In addition, there was commentary and analysis by YouTube Election Hub partners such as the *New York Times*, the *Wall Street Journal*, Al Jazeera English, and BuzzFeed.

The most tweeted moments from the debate related to interactions between the candidates and the moderator, Public Broadcasting Service's (PBS) Jim Lehrer, about the lengths of speaking times – in particular when Lehrer quipped, 'Let's not', in response to Romney's request to add another comment to his answer. Another exchange that attracted high levels of tweets was Obama's mischievous remark to Lehrer that 'I had five seconds before you interrupted me', and a lot of Twitter flow was generated by Romney's comment during his proposed budget cuts, when he invoked Big Bird, the popular character from the famous children's programme *Sesame Street* (Ngak 2012): 'I'm sorry, Jim. I'm going to stop the subsidy to PBS. I'm going to stop other things. I like PBS. I love Big Bird. I actually like you too. But I'm not going to – I'm not going to keep on spending money on things to borrow money from China to pay for it' (US debate 2012).

This activity on Twitter suggests it is the *drama* of the debate, the interactions between candidates and moderators, that provoke public interest, but there was also evidence that there was a more substantive engagement with the issues raised. Discussion about Medicare and vouchers was another prominently tweeted topic, and Google announced that the four most searched terms during the debate were Simpson–Bowles (the bipartisan commission on fiscal reform), Dodd–Frank (the financial reform law), who was winning the debate, and Big Bird ('Social media weighs in' 2012).

Twitter and other forms of social media are radically transforming the ability of individuals to participate in ongoing public debate. Twitter, the micro-blogging site where messages are limited to 140 characters, provides a more open service than other social media, such as Facebook. There are different ways to structure the content of tweets: direct tweets to individual accounts; re-tweets, where messages are shared and distributed through a user's network; and hashtags, which facilitate easy categorization and sharing of content. The reception of televised leaders' debates is enriched through the process of live-tweeting, enabling mass social conversations to occur as the event unfolds. Lehrer's retort of 'Let's not' to Romney resulted in 158,690 tweets in a single minute. Early research has suggested that the process of two-screen 'social watching' (McKinney et al. 2014), where people watch a televised political programme while interacting with others online, facilitates greater engagement with the content (Houston et al. 2013) and that the 'amount of tweeting during a debate was positively related to learning more from the debate' (ibid., p. 558). The ability of Twitter to foster involvement in the debates was noted by media commentators:

> We're seeing a shift in not only media, but in major historical moments like political campaigns. What Twitter does is add a new dimension of participation, allowing people from all over the world to share their thoughts and feelings in real-time about something that's really

important. In this case, it's the next President of the United States. (Olanoff 2012)

An inquiry into social media usage reveals the highly differentiated public consumption of leaders' debates and the increasingly complicated and reflexive nature of public opinion production. In 2012, only 13 per cent of Americans used Twitter, and most tweeters were from among the younger generation, who were more likely to favour the Democratic Party. In addition, Twitter reactions were often at odds with general public opinion (Mitchell and Hitlin 2013), and there is evidence that users display greater reflexivity about public opinion and a critical engagement with public opinion polls (Ampofo et al. 2011). While Twitter users were predominantly of a younger demographic, the overall television viewership of the first Obama–Romney debate was very much skewed to an older age group: nearly half were over 55 (Murse 2012). The audience, then, of the 2012 presidential debates was highly differentiated, with different demographics more heavily represented across traditional mass media and newer online and social media.

The promise of a social media service such as Twitter is that it allows greater public involvement in public debate and, subsequently, that there is a more equalized and democratic public discourse. The evidence from the 2012 presidential debates suggests Twitter usage did provide the public with greater agency, but equally that a hierarchy of voices persists within social media that replicates broader social inequalities. Twitter responses provided individuals with the opportunity to support, critique and supplement candidate information in a way that enriched public debate. One prominent example came from the astrophysicist and science communicator Neil deGrasse Tyson, who challenged Romney's attack on PBS by tweeting 'Cutting PBS support (0.012% of budget) to help balance the Federal budget is like deleting text files to make room on your 500Gig hard drive' (Ngak 2012). His comment was re-tweeted 50,294 times. The Twitter commentary on the debates was directed and influenced by celebrity interventions. Liberal comedian Bill Maher's tweet during the first debate, 'I can't believe I'm saying this, but Obama looks like he *does* need a teleprompter' (original emphasis), confirmed public perceptions about the president's performance in the debate, as one posting on a debate article noted:

> I 'watched' the debate for the first time 100% on Twitter. Within 10 minutes I knew Obama was losing it. Half way through I knew he was toast. How? When Bill Maher tweeted out 'I can't believe I'm saying

> this...but Obama looks like he DOES need a teleprompter.' So, while
> I did 'listen' to friends on twitter, media personalities have massive
> influence on what is then retweeted and amplified by the general
> public. Media personalities still matter. (Cited in Olanoff 2012)

This response is in line with research that examined Twitter usage
during one of the 2012 Republican primary debates, which found
that media and political elites seem to exert greater influence on
public conversations than ordinary tweeters and that alternative
citizen frames, which challenge conventional media understandings
of the debates, are not forthcoming (Hawthorne et al. 2013, p. 558).
Equally, the networked basis of Twitter facilitates broad and comprehensive social connections, but tweets on political subjects, like most
other forms of political discourse, are highly partisan. Himelboim,
McCreery and Smith (2013, p. 154) found from their study that
'Twitter users are unlikely to be exposed to cross-ideological content
from the clusters of users they followed, as these were usually politically homogeneous.'

The use of Twitter has had an impact on the role of conventional
post-debate commentary. Public evaluations of leaders' debates are
significantly shaped by the post-debate commentary of influential
journalists and political commentators, but the more immediate and
voluminous Twitter flow during the debates has undercut that particular influence. As Ampofo, Anstead and O'Loughlin (2011) have
noted, the *commentariat* of 24-hour rolling television news has given
way to the *viewertariat*, who are those 'viewers who use online publishing platforms and social tools to interpret, publicly comment on,
and debate a television broadcast while they are watching it' (Anstead
and O'Loughlin 2011, p. 441). This viewertariat does not replace
commentators but, rather, complicates and enhances media commentary: post-debate television commentary now is informed by the
exchanges that have already occurred online.

The use of Twitter has also meant that the speed of interaction
between politicians, journalists and the public has increased. Political
staffers engage in instantaneous 'spin' to try to counter trending
online criticisms of their candidate's performance, and more generally
there is the growing necessity to quickly exploit positive opportunities
and defuse controversy. It has been noted that the 24-hour news cycle
is now the 21-minute news cycle due to the influence of Twitter
following an incident at a rally on the 2012 presidential election
campaign trail, where Romney joked, in response to the 'birther'
conspiracy advocates who had questioned whether Obama was an
American, that no one had asked to see his birth certificate. His

comment was tweeted three minutes later and appeared on the website of Politico after four minutes; video of the comment could be viewed on Buzzfeed after five minutes, and the Romney team had a clarifying statement 21 minutes after the initial comment (Mills 2012). As such, the media contexts of leaders' debates, and politics more generally, are informed not so much by news cycles as by 'political information cycles', which are 'assemblages in which the personnel, practices, genres and temporalities of supposedly "new" online media are increasingly integrated with those of supposedly "old" broadcast and press media' (Chadwick 2011, p. 25). The tight control of the news cycle that was previously imposed by politicians and political staffers is harder to sustain in a social media environment.

Obama's First Debate Performance

The major talking point from the first of the presidential debates in Denver between Obama and Romney was the unexpected strong performance from the Republican candidate and the lacklustre showing by the president. Obama's political success has been partly built upon his oratory skills and his debating acumen, but Romney was judged to have been the 'winner' of the debate in most social and mass media coverage. Pro-Obama writer Andrew Sullivan from the *Daily Beast* tweeted during the debate: 'Man, Obama is boring and abstract. He's putting us to sleep. I get his points but he is entirely wonky tonight. And he is on the defensive' (Woolf 2012). Such perceptions, together with the observations we have made about the UK 2010 leaders' debates, underline the contemporary performance requirements for political debates. If Gordon Brown's problem was that he thought the primary communicative task was to debate his opponents, Obama's problem was that he did not strike the right balance between detail and direct 'cut-through' discourse. The pithy, usually colloquial language of social media and the sound bites of much television commentary are stark counterpoints to the debate discourse, but cumulatively it could be argued that this kind of media discourse environment is exerting greater pressure on candidates to employ language that is accessible and to perform in a personable manner.

This, in turn, raises questions about the balance between 'substance' and 'style' in leaders' debates and the role of reason in such encounters. Establishing a binary between 'substance' and 'style' in evaluations misunderstands the necessary fusion between the two features that exists in debate discourse (Craig 2007). Successful participants must negotiate the generic and performative contexts of television debates while also exhibiting a political proficiency that convinces voters. The first Obama–Romney encounter was significant because Obama did not make any major gaffe or error, unlike previous high-profile examples of debate losses such as when Al Gore sighed dramatically in the 2000 debate, or when George H. W. Bush glanced at his watch during a debate in 1992 (Bai 2012). In addition, as Robert C. Rowland notes, Obama constructed strong arguments during the debate. His analysis shows that 'Obama made 42 effective points, against 30 for Romney,.... Obama cited evidence on 69 occasions, against 51 citations for Romney...[and] Obama effectively responded to a Romney charge 46 times, against 25 effective responses by Romney' (2013, p. 534). The president's problem, however, was that he 'did not effectively present these arguments' (ibid., p. 535) and that he 'did not accurately analyze the interest and knowledge level of the national audience' (ibid., p. 539). In contrast to Romney's approach of presenting concise points, often without supporting evidence, Obama often 'tried to explain the underlying rationale behind his positions' (ibid., p. 538). We see this in two examples from the debate. In his opening answer on his plan for the economy, Romney noted:

> My plan has five basic parts. One, get us energy independent. North American energy independent. That creates about four million jobs. Number two, open up more trade, particularly in Latin America; crack down on China if and when they cheat. Number three, make sure our people have the skills they need to succeed and the best schools in the world. We're far away from that now. Number four, get us to a balanced budget. Number five, champion small business. (US debate 2012)

In contrast, Obama countered Romney's approach to Medicare with an extended answer that included a direct address to the audience, as well as political context detail, reference to supporting research, and a concession to his political opponents:

> For – for – so if you're – if you – you're 54 or 55, you might want to listen, because this – this will affect you. The idea, which was originally presented by Congressman Ryan, your running mate, is that we would give a voucher to seniors, and they could go out in the private marketplace and buy their own health insurance. The problem is that because the voucher wouldn't necessarily keep up with health care inflation, it was estimated that this would cost the average senior about $6,000 a year. Now, in fairness, what Governor Romney has now said

is he'll maintain traditional Medicare alongside it. But there's still a problem, because what happens is those insurance companies are pretty clever at figuring out who are the younger and healthier seniors....So I don't think vouchers are the right way to go. And this is not my own – only my opinion. AARP thinks that the – the savings that we obtained from Medicare bolster the system, lengthen the Medicare trust fund by 8 years. (US debate 2012)

We noted at the beginning of this chapter that leaders' debates offer comparatively extended and unfiltered opportunities for politicians to explain and to be quizzed on their policies and for the public to assess candidates side by side. That said, the first Obama–Romney encounter and its public reception raised questions about the educative potential of such debates. Commentators noted that part of Romney's success derived from the moderating of previous policy positions outlined during the Republican presidential primaries and his very selective citing of studies to support his policies, and Rowland argues that his success in the debates stemmed partly from a lack of this contextual political knowledge by viewers (2013, p. 534). Equally, the criticisms of Obama's performance, where '90-second answers on complex topics' were considered 'long-winded and wonky' (ibid., p. 543), show little media and public tolerance for any kind of complexity. These judgements about the debate, and the examples from Romney and Obama's answers, suggest less propensity to engage with the relatively extended narratives of answers and also a declining role for reason in leaders' debates.

Conclusion

We have noted in this chapter the exceptional status of leaders' debates, given that they occur in the heated contexts of election campaigns. Their communicative complexity has also been identified, given they involve, across a range of possible debate formats, direct interactions between politicians, politicians and debate moderators and panels of journalists, as well as frequent direct input from audience members and members of the general public. As the analysis of the 2012 US presidential debates revealed, this communicative complexity is compounded by social media usage that allows individuals to contribute to a public discussion as the event unfolds. The analysis of the role of Twitter in the debates highlighted a number of features: the differentiated nature of the viewing public between an online and televisual audience, the hierarchy of voices on Twitter that influence the stream of online debate, and the impact Twitter has on conventional post-debate television commentary. Importantly, we can note that the plurality of voices in the social media responses to the debate highlights the increasingly dialogic and agonistic nature of mediated public discourse. With the use of Twitter, debates, and other forms of political media events such as press conferences, are *more open texts*, with the possibility of journalistic and public checking, critiquing and challenging within the event as it unfolds.

The chapter also allowed further consideration of the importance of political performance in mediated interrogative encounters. The analysis of the historic leaders' debates in the 2010 UK election highlighted how Liberal Democrat leader Nick Clegg's language use and performative skills established a connection with both the studio audience and the general public. This 'connection' was facilitated primarily by a habitus of affect, where Clegg demonstrated his personal, emotional empathy for others. As such, the analysis highlighted the irony that success in the leaders' debates derived less from the 'debate' with political opponents and more from the constructive engagement with the audience. That said, it also revealed that success depended crucially on the management of expressions of conflict and consensus and an appropriate balance between identification with the audience and the exhibition of authority. It has been argued that political communication in leaders' debates requires the fusion of style and substance and that such events provide the opportunity for extended interaction; however, the chapter ended on a cautionary note in its observation that President Obama was perceived to have failed in the first debate because of the developed nature of his answers, where he provided context, balance and supporting evidence. This particular example attests to the restricted parameters of contemporary political discourse and the limited role for the exercise of reason, and it is, in turn, a cause for concern about the ability of such high-profile media events to contribute to an informed electorate.

5

Press Conferences

Introduction

Press conferences are high-profile encounters between political leaders and journalists. In the turbulent flow of everyday political life there are numerous occasions when politicians engage with journalists. In corridors after meetings, in airport lounges, or on the steps of parliament there are relatively spontaneous and informal gatherings where groups of journalists can try to quiz politicians. Press conferences are distinguished here from such moments by the advance notice provided about the occasion, their more formal status, and their more extended duration. US presidential press conferences have been defined as public events 'where reporters either permanently or temporarily accredited to cover the president ask questions on a variety of subjects without any control by the president and his staff on what is asked' (Kumar 2003, p. 226). It is also noted that presidents and their staff cannot restrict who attends a press conference and that they are on-the-record events whose transcripts cannot be altered (ibid.).

Press conferences may be held as routine events, but they are usually called because of a particular newsworthy announcement involving the release of new policy, a political crisis, a national disaster, the end of a summit or meeting, or an update during an election campaign. The press conferences of national political leaders are newsworthy events in themselves, given the elite nature of the personnel involved, but it is this heightened specificity of an announcement that lends press conferences their drama and sometimes triggers adversarial moments between journalists and politicians. Press conferences are contrasted with the regular news briefings that are chaired by representatives of the political leader. In the United States the White House press secretary will meet with journalists and provide details of the president's schedule for the day and whom the president has seen, and they also speak for the administration on current newsworthy issues. In the United Kingdom, the official spokesperson at Number 10 Downing Street will usually brief journalists twice daily on the prime minister's schedule and events, though without providing political comment. These briefings are increasingly becoming less important, given that much of the information is made available earlier and outside the briefings.

Unlike political interviews, politicians instigate press conferences and this allows them to choose the timing and the length of the event. They are also able to try to exert some control over the framing of the event with a customary opening statement before fielding questions. As such, press conferences provide politicians with an opportunity to take the lead on an issue, to try to shape news coverage, and to reach a large and broad audience to explain the reasons for their actions. When the Australian prime minister Julia Gillard was subject in 2012 to allegations about her past actions as a lawyer, she called a press conference that did not finish until journalists had exhausted their lists of questions, enabling Gillard to defuse the issue ('Gillard in marathon press conference' 2012; Keane 2012). While press conferences are open encounters, politicians are able to select the questioners, limit follow-up questions and, to some degree, avoid those journalists who might adopt a more critical perspective.

Alternatively, press conferences can be risky affairs for politicians. It has been noted that politicians are unlikely 'to be able to control the trajectory of the discussion and more likely to be boxed into answering a question on an issue they may prefer not to discuss' (Rottinghaus 2009, pp. 301–2). The cumulative force of an audience of journalists can place greater pressure on politicians. In this sense, press conferences are communal media events rather than individual interviews, which are determined more by the particular personalities of interviewers and are more likely to be branded and promoted by a particular news outlet. Like a political interview, a press conference may be broadcast live, but it may also act as a site where information is gained for subsequent reportage. Press conferences are mainly structured through direct interpersonal encounters between politicians and journalists, although online technology has allowed more people to participate (Jacobs 2011).

Political press conferences are held in all Western democracies, but they serve somewhat different functions in different political systems. In the United States the president is more likely to hold press conferences because he or she has 'no constitutional forum for public communication' (Seymour-Ure 2003, p. 202). In contrast, at least historically, prime ministers in the United Kingdom were subject to processes of cabinet government and by the belief that the parliament, the House of Commons, was the appropriate forum for both announcements and political scrutiny. The increasingly presidential nature of political leadership, as well as the rise of television broadcasting, meant that press conferences have become a more prevalent form of public communication (ibid., pp. 197–202).

The frequency of press conferences has become an issue in some countries, as political leaders have sought other means to communicate with the public or simply sought to avoid media scrutiny because their government is unpopular or is fighting off a crisis. UK prime minister David Cameron has been criticized for his lack of press conferences (Eaton 2013), and the then Australian immigration minister Scott Morrison was subject to media criticism when he cancelled weekly press briefings that prevented journalists from questioning him on the controversial issue of asylum seekers (Farrell 2014). Equally, the importance of press conferences may be devalued if they are held too frequently (Seymour-Ure 2003, p. 175).

Our object of scrutiny here is political press conferences, but press conferences are, of course, more generalized communicative encounters that are deployed by a range of institutional and newsworthy individuals, from the police through to rock stars. However, we will use the term '*press* conference' even though such events are obviously attended by different types of journalists. While the terms 'media conference' and 'news conference' are also sometimes used in contemporary journalism, the seemingly more antiquated use of 'press conference' persists in everyday journalistic and political discourse. In this chapter we will first discuss the history of press conferences, providing the context of the contemporary trends of frequency and performance. The different types of press conference will then be outlined, differentiating between solo domestic conferences and two-party conferences that involve pairs of national leaders. We will provide a summary of the nature of the performances and the language use of both politicians and journalists across these types of press conferences. The contrasting formats will be elucidated through an analysis of conferences that feature US President Barack Obama. Analyses will be offered of Obama's White House press conference in August 2013, when he commented on US and Russian relations, and of the joint bilateral press conferences and briefings held by Obama with Russian President Medvedev during his term of office. These will highlight the varying degrees of politician and journalist interaction, the different forms of political discourse employed, the negotiations of conflict across the press conferences, and the body language and disciplined performances in the exchanges. The analyses will also consider news media reportage of the press conferences.

History of Press Conferences

The modern press conference is an invention of the twentieth century. While reporters in the nineteenth century occasionally went to the White House to question presidents, there was not even a regular White House beat until the 1890s (Kumar 2005, p. 174). Although President Theodore Roosevelt cultivated relations with the press, it was President Woodrow Wilson who, in 1913, gave the first formal press conference where journalists could ask whatever they liked and all accredited reporters were able to attend (Smith 1990, p. 26). Wilson implemented press conferences for pragmatic reasons: rather than conducting interviews with individual reporters, the format enabled him to answer all questions at the one time (Kumar 2005, p. 175). Many journalists preferred the more informal and selective meetings with Roosevelt, where more newsworthy information was usually disclosed (ibid., p. 176) but Wilson's open encounters paved the way for the more adversarial relationship between journalists and politicians in modern press conferences (Smith 1990, p. 26).

During subsequent decades press conferences struggled through changes and varying degrees of commitment by presidents: Warren Harding required reporters to submit questions in writing before meeting him, and Herbert Hoover's relationship with the press deteriorated after he favoured some reporters over others and took no follow-up questions (Smith 1990, p. 31). Many of Hoover's press conferences involved him declaring he had no news, and no questions were posed (Kumar 2003, p. 223). Indeed, one conference in 1933 started with the president remarking: 'Well, I have one question today, and I am not quite in a position to make an adequate reply to it, so this is a famine day. I am sorry to say. I have nothing on my mind, and apparently you have nothing on yours very much. I am sorry I haven't anything' (Kumar 2005, p. 176). In the years following Franklin Roosevelt's administration, press conferences became more formalized: they gradually developed into on-the-record events and were broadcast electronically (Kumar 2003, p. 224). It was President Kennedy who exploited fully the *televisual* potential of press conferences. Kennedy implemented live televised conferences and, building on his skills as a media performer, is said to have 'created *the press conference as public spectacle*' (Seymour-Ure 2003, p. 179; original emphasis). The live broadcasting of press conferences was a high-risk strategy but, as Smith (1990, p. 41; original emphasis) notes: 'If a president can perform *successfully* under these adverse conditions, spontaneously answering contentious and quarrelsome questions in a format where no editing is possible, then he can lead the country.'

In more recent decades there have been some general trends in US presidential press conferences, including fewer domestic solo conferences, more joint conferences with other national leaders, and the increased use of other forms of engagement with journalists. As Kumar (2005, pp. 187–8) has noted, in the decades since 1981,

> presidents took four actions that altered their relations with the press: reduced their number of traditional presidential press conferences; reshaped this forum into a diplomatic tool by bringing foreign leaders onto the White House stage; increased the number of one-on-one and group interviews they did with domestic and foreign reporters; and developed short question-and-answer sessions as vehicles for answering reporters' queries on a fairly regular basis.

In the United Kingdom, prime ministers had given press conferences in earlier decades, but it was not until Tony Blair's tenure that Britain had regular, wide-ranging, open and on-the-record press conferences, although even these did not occur until three years into his premiership (Seymour-Ure 2003). Private, off-the-record briefings of journalists were given during Ramsay MacDonald's time, and before the Second World War Neville Chamberlain also regularly and privately briefed journalists. During the 1960s and into the early 1970s, Harold Wilson and Edward Heath saw the lobby a few times per year and conducted airport and in-flight meetings with journalists. Blair's more presidential style of leadership and his proficiency as a media performer partly accounted for his adoption of the presidential style of press conference, but such meetings also provided him with an opportunity to attempt to influence the news agenda and speak directly to the public. For Blair's first press conference the lobby were asked to select 45 journalists, international correspondents were allotted 30 seats, and 15 political commentators were also invited (ibid., p. 172).

These historical notes reveal a history of changing relations between politicians and journalists. During the nineteenth and into the early twentieth century political leaders sought contact with editors and proprietors rather than reporters, and, despite President Wilson's innovation, press conferences for several decades were often subject to strict political control, with prior submission of questions and an off-the-record status. The rise of television elevated press conferences to public events and allowed politicians to speak more directly to the people, bypassing to some extent the need for access through journalistic selection and interpretation. Presidential press conferences 'can be effective tools to generate news coverage', and 'many of the president's own words penetrate news coverage' (Eshbaugh-Soha 2013, p. 560), particularly when they are solo domestic conferences held in Washington. The broadcasting of press conferences, however, also provided journalists with a public profile, particularly when they became known for their interrogations of the president. More aggressive questioning has been the trend since the late 1960s (Clayman et al. 2010), and this partly explains why domestic solo conferences are now held less frequently and why other means of engaging with journalists and the public are incorporated into political communication strategies.

Types of Press Conference

The two main types of press conference held by political leaders are those encounters where an individual leader faces journalists, usually to discuss domestic political issues, and those occasions where a pair of national leaders host a joint press conference after a meeting or series of talks and report on their discussion. Press conferences conventionally start with an opening address that attempts to frame the issues that have prompted the event, and then there is a question and answer session.

The ability of a politician to control the agenda of questions through their opening remarks is limited: a study of Eisenhower and Reagan news conferences found that the content of more than 80 per cent of journalists' questions differed from that of the opening remarks (Clayman and Heritage 2002b). As stated in the introduction, the politician can ironically benefit from the presence of a large number of reporters because they are able to choose from the bidding journalists, and the ability of journalists to ask follow-up questions is limited. Journalists often seek to counter this limitation by asking complex questions or building in another question when they are selected. As Clayman and Heritage (2002b, p. 758) have noted, a follow-up question demonstrates journalistic initiative, given it violates the convention of one turn per journalist, and it often represents a challenge to the politician, indicating that the previous answer was inadequate or in some way incomplete, although other research (Eriksson 2011) indicates that follow-up questions are not necessarily indicators of adversarialness and may depend partly upon whether the press conference is broadcast. Smith (1990, p. 107) notes that follow-up questions can take the form of clarifications, elaborations or consistency questions. While a politician may seek to avoid particular journalists who may be more critical and negative in their questions, it is often the case that journalists will pursue a line of questioning concerning a newsworthy issue which the politician is avoiding or about which they have inadequate knowledge.

Press conferences are usually considered as adversarial encounters between journalists and politicians, and, as discussed in chapter 2, the different forms of aggressiveness in question design have been mapped by Clayman and Heritage and others. Their schema of questions includes initiative, where the question is enterprising rather than passive; directness, where the question is expressed bluntly; assertiveness, where the question presupposes a particular answer; adversarialness, where the question is overtly critical of the politician; and accountability, where the question demands the politician justify their statements or actions (Clayman et al. 2010). There is no doubt that press conferences are often adversarial encounters, but equally it has been suggested that they are often characterized by an exchange model of communication where there is greater cooperativeness than aggressiveness (Eriksson and Östman 2013). According to Eriksson and Östman's (2013) study, journalists seek information in press conferences and are more adversarial in the subsequent construction of news stories, when the words of political leaders are critiqued and other sources are used to provide different perspectives.

This discussion about the interpersonal dynamics in press conferences also needs to be alert to the differences between domestic solo press conferences and two-party press conferences involving national leaders: the former is usually characterized by a greater number of questions and more aggressive probing by journalists, and the latter commonly feature more diplomatic language and more restrained questions (Banning and Billingsley 2007). The joint international conference is not the usual form of encounter we consider when discussing press conferences. While joint conferences were occasionally held in earlier decades (Kumar 2003, p. 233), they are now more widespread: 'Joint press conferences went from being nonexistent in the Reagan administration to representing 41.5 per cent of the press conferences of President George H. W. Bush, [and] 67.9 per cent of those held by President Clinton' (ibid., p. 235). This shift represents an attempt by politicians to exert greater control over journalists in their press conference interactions.

Joint press conferences are rendered more complicated by the presence of, and interactions between, two political leaders, as well as the dual national political contexts that impact on the encounter. In addition to the immediate audience of journalists, the leaders are consciously addressing their respective national audience and the audiences of other global political leaders. These differences can be quite pronounced when the participants come from nations where there are divergent traditions of press freedom and political opposition. Joint press conferences are also 'meta-communicative' encounters: they are reports of another communicative encounter (diplomatic talks) that otherwise remains private. The joint conference is a carefully stage-managed event where there has been detailed consultation and planning between leaders and their staff about what will be discussed from their meeting and how the details will be conveyed.

Joint press conferences are intended to portray a positive, diplomatic front and, as such, can be rather staid and formulaic events. In this way they provide a stark contrast to a leaders' debate, where differences are highlighted and interrogated and the discourse can be overtly negative. Political differences in joint press conferences are nonetheless negotiated in the conference discourse and expressed in a subtle and sub-textual manner. Joint press conferences thus represent a 'complex interplay of opposites: so far as the two main participants (politicians) are concerned, we see positivism versus conflict of interests; deep ideological divisions versus constructive, cooperative face; controlling specific and transparent contributions from other participants, especially the press, on the one hand, and diplomatic, vague, evasive, often non-communicative statements from the politicians' (Bhatia 2006, pp. 195–200). Journalists are well aware of the subtle inflections of meaning that are expressed in joint press conferences and are able to decode such discourse in their reportage (ibid., p. 194).

The contrast between solo and joint press conferences underlines the importance of performance. While most modern politicians are well coached for specific encounters, the solo press conference is arguably the interrogative site where politicians must most visibly 'think on their feet' as they field often probing questions from a variety of those present. The interactions with journalists may be less animated in joint press conferences, but nonetheless such events require an even greater degree of disciplined bodily performance from politicians, given they are even more highly ritualistic encounters and expressions of power and difference are conveyed in a finely drawn and less straightforward manner.

Case Studies

We will now illustrate these issues about the interactions, language and performances with an analysis of press conferences that feature US President Barack Obama. We will firstly examine a solo press conference that the president held in the East Room of the White House in August 2013. The wide-ranging agenda featured discussion about reforms to governmental surveillance processes following the revelations of Edward Snowden and the deteriorating relations with Russia following that country's decision to offer Snowden asylum. The conference also included questions on US drone strikes in Yemen, the choice of the next Federal Reserve chairperson, the implementation of healthcare law, and the anniversary of the attack on the US embassy in Benghazi. The joint press conference to be scrutinized features President Obama and Russian President Dmitry Medvedev in June 2010, and this press conference was also held in the East Room of the White House. The questions from US and Russian journalists covered topics such as the US withdrawal of troops from Afghanistan, Russia's entry to the World Trade Organization, Chinese currency levels, and the deteriorating situation in Kyrgyzstan. Both these conferences, then, feature discussion about US–Russian relations, and this provides us with a point of contrast between the differing formats and styles of the two encounters, but equally we must note that they occurred at different times and were dealing with different issues. In addition to their common treatment of US–Russian relations, the two press conferences have been selected because they feature the sitting US president at the time of writing, and we can contrast Obama's different performances across the two encounters. These case studies were not special or unusually dramatic press conferences, but nonetheless even in such 'routine' events there is value in dissecting the language use and performances to understand the power relations that are at play in such interactions.

President Obama's Solo Press Conference

A presidential press conference carries connotations of elite political authority and accountability as the leader of the nation faces up to leading political correspondents from major national news organizations. Before a word is spoken, the press conference of President Obama conveys meaning. The formal staging of the event exhibits a semiotic richness, as the president stands in the East Room, with its portraits of previous political leaders, before a lectern with the presidential seal, in front of ornate, golden drapes and the US and presidential flags. In contrast to other political interrogative encounters – interviews and debates are usually held in the comparatively neutral spaces of television studios – the president is speaking in the press conference from the domain of the political field, from the site of his political authority, and this physical location of the White House influences the interpersonal dynamics between him and the journalists.

The occasional status of a presidential press conference also lends a newsworthy appeal. Modern politicians, including Obama himself, have been criticized rightly for holding fewer open press conferences, and scheduled events do not always yield lively exchanges and the disclosure of dramatic information. In addition, press conferences compete with a blizzard of appearances across a variety of media genres and platforms. Nonetheless, and partly because of the ubiquity of contemporary mediated political performance, presidential press conferences retain a distinctive status: their formal setting and scale, with a room full of journalists, mean that presidential press conferences are very much *media events*, where there is both a symbolic and a real display of political accountability, where politicians open themselves to scrutiny, and where journalists are seen in their collective task of interrogating the policies and discourse of elected representatives.

The timing and content of presidential press conferences nonetheless must also be understood within the broader context of particular political strategies and media performances. President Obama's conference in August 2013 followed a month of other, very different media performances where he was seeking to highlight Republican intransigence in Congress, in contrast to his self-proclaimed more practical approach to problem solutions and his own willingness to negotiate. In the week before the press conference, Obama appeared on Jay Leno's late-night talk show, gave an interview to the *New York Times*, participated in a forum on the Zillow.com online real estate site and on Amazon's Kindle Singles website, and gave several business speeches (Walsh 2013). That is, the variety of forms of presidential communication now extends beyond occasional chats on late-night talk shows. The Zillow and Amazon appearances reveal a more fragmented media landscape which draws on social media input from citizens, and it demonstrates a strategy by Obama to speak more directly to targeted audiences about particular issues, such as the housing market and mortgage rates. In addition, such appearances give the president greater opportunity to bypass the White House press corps.

The national and international authority of the president nonetheless continues to require forums, such as press conferences, where he attempts to influence the news agenda and is seen questioned by journalists who have correspondingly high authority within the journalistic field. Indeed, the conference hosted by President Obama was primarily about a struggle for power between the political and journalistic fields. We have noted that press conferences are called at the initiative of the politician, but this power is also countered by journalistic and public pressure for the hosting of a press conference. This particular event followed public criticism about the infrequency of Obama's press conferences and preceded his summer vacation. More substantively, much of the content of the press conference focused on his attempt to establish the political field as the appropriate site to address concerns over governmental surveillance after Edward Snowden's leaks of National Security Agency (NSA) activities.

This strategy was foregrounded in the president's opening statement, where he announced four measures to improve governmental oversight over surveillance activities, including proposed reforms to the Patriot Act and introducing an adversarial approach to Foreign Intelligence Surveillance Court (FISC) hearings. Obama also sought to reclaim the political initiative and public trust by establishing a consistent political narrative on the issue, referring both to his activities as a senator and to previous speeches, while also establishing a binary between the 'rational' and 'lawful' proposed reforms in the political field and the 'irrational' and 'emotional' tenor of public debate in the media. In his opening remarks he stated:

> As I said at the National Defense University back in May,...we have to strike the right balance between protecting our security and preserving our freedoms. And as part of this rebalancing, I called for a review of our surveillance programs. Unfortunately, rather than an orderly and lawful process to debate these issues and come up with appropriate reforms, repeated leaks of classified information have initiated the debate in a very passionate, but not always fully informed way.
>
> Now, keep in mind that as a senator, I expressed a healthy skepticism about these programs, and as President, I've taken steps to make sure they have strong oversight by all three branches of government and clear safeguards to prevent abuse and protect the rights of the American people. (Solo press conference 2013)

The president continued to defend the political process and criticize news media coverage of politics in later remarks on a delay to parts of the Affordable Care Act, known colloquially as 'Obamacare'. In his comments, he chastises journalists for their propensity to engage in 'gotcha' reportage, where changes from initial legislative plans are seen as faults or weaknesses rather than manifestations of complex political processes. In so doing, he invokes the topos of history, stating that future outcomes will likely parallel its precedents and, as such, we should expect problems in the implementation of the legislation:

> There is no doubt that in implementing the Affordable Care Act, a program of this significance, there are going to be some glitches. No doubt about it. There are going to be things where we say, you know what, we should have thought of that earlier. Or this would work a little bit better. Or this needs an adjustment. That was true of Social Security. That was true of Medicare.... That's true, by the way, of a car company rolling out a new car, it's true of Apple rolling out the new iPad. So you will be able to, whenever you want during the course of the next six months and probably the next year, find occasions where you say, ah-ha, you know what, that could have been done a little bit better. Or that thing, they're making an administrative change; that's not how it was originally thought this thing was going to work. Yes, exactly.... And I make no apologies for that. (Ibid.)

Obama's comments here perform the same function as Kevin Rudd's remarks in chapter 3, where there is a defence of the mechanics of the political process. The politician is seeking to protect himself from the journalistic scrutiny that highlights any deviance from previously declared positions on policy or strategy. Journalistic framing privileges political consistency, while politicians try to justify the complexities of policy-making and the exigencies of political machinations.

Obama must not only assert the viability of the political field and maintain its power over the journalistic field; he is also required to engage in a rhetorical construction of a national identity that has been threatened by the revelations of Snowden. The president mobilizes this vision of the nation through expressions of difference from other countries and the negotiation of domestic expressions of difference over security and freedom. Also, as we will see later in the analysis, he uses such lawful expressions of difference implicitly to exclude Edward Snowden from incorporation in the 'patriotism' that signifies membership of the nation. Obama concluded his opening remarks by saying:

It's true we have significant capabilities. What's also true is we show a restraint that many governments around the world don't even think to do, refuse to show – and that includes, by the way, some of America's most vocal critics.... And let me close with one additional thought. The men and women of our intelligence community work every single day to keep us safe because they love this country and believe in our values. They're patriots. And I believe that those who have lawfully raised their voices on behalf of privacy and civil liberties are also patriots who love our country and want it to live up to our highest ideals. So this is how we're going to resolve our differences in the United States – through vigorous public debate, guided by our Constitution, with reverence for our history as a nation of laws, and with respect for the facts. (Solo press conference 2013)

President Obama's opening remarks seek to frame the press conference agenda, but the event is, of course, defined primarily through the question and answer interaction between the president and journalists. We can note initially that there are not many questions: only eight journalists ask questions in a press conference of 52 minutes. This highlights how both the president's opening remarks and the length of his answers dominate the conference, which lacks the sharp focus and the more frequent interaction of a political interview, suggesting the control Obama exerts over the event. A US presidential press conference is also a more orderly affair than press conferences in many other countries, and there is considerable deference shown to the president by the journalists. President Obama works from a list of questioners, and so there is no jostling for position as journalists seek to be recognized by the political leader.

There are, nonetheless, power struggles between the questioners and the respondent, and Obama exerts his control over the process of questioning in an explicit manner over and above the selection of journalists. At one point he refuses to answer a question on drone strikes in Yemen, simply stating: 'I will not have a discussion about operational issues' (Solo press conference 2013). In another example he polices the rule that the journalists ask only one question, as we see in the following exchange involving Chuck Todd, the NBC news chief White House correspondent:

Obama: Chuck Todd.

Todd: Thank you, Mr. President. Given that you just announced a whole bunch of reforms based on essentially the leaks that Edward Snowden made on all of these surveillance programs, does that change – is your mindset changed about him? Is he now more a whistle-blower than he is a hacker, as you called him at one point, or somebody that shouldn't be filed charges? And should he be provided more protection? Is he a patriot? You just used those words. And then just to follow up on the personal – I want to follow up on a personal –

Obama: Okay, I want to make sure – everybody is asking one question it would be helpful.

Todd: No, I understand. It was a part of a question that you didn't answer. Can you get stuff done with Russia, big stuff done, without having a good personal relationship with Putin? (Solo press conference 2013)

The exchange reveals Obama establishing the parameters of the questioning process, but we also see that Todd is able to continue to ask the second question (and which Obama goes on to answer), although Todd must first assent to the rule and then justify his second question with an explanation. The narrative of the exchange, then, derives from the journalist acknowledging, and also exploiting, the conventions that determine the legitimacy of questions.

Obama exerts control over the questioning process in the press conference, but equally he seeks to establish cordial and, indeed, friendly relations with journalists. He jokes with them on occasion, and it is obvious from the exchanges that he knows the correspondents personally. The president shifts from a professional to a personal footing when he makes reference to the new baby of the *Wall Street Journal* correspondent Carol Lee:

Obama: Carol Lee. And, Carol, congratulations on Hudson.

Lee: Thank you, Mr. President.

Obama: Do you have pictures?

Lee: I do. I'll have to show you –

Obama: Okay, I'm going to have to see them.

Lee: I appreciate you making it a slow news week. I wanted to ask you about your evolution on the surveillance issues. (Solo press conference 2013)

Obama, then, exerts his control not in a domineering or disciplinary manner; instead, in a more productive expression of power, he establishes his authority over the process while attempting to defuse or downplay conflict and negativity that could be harmful to his own political fortunes, and he cultivates good relations with the journalists while allowing them to do their job.

All of the journalists show deference to President Obama – they all preface their questions with 'Thank you, Mr. President' – but equally the questions demonstrate the dimension of 'initiative' that Clayman and Heritage (2002b) have identified in modern press conferences, where questions are characterized by complexity, including preliminary statements, multiple questions and question cascades. We have already seen an example of this in Chuck Todd's intervention, and Major Garrett from CBS uses a question cascade in his inquiry about the appointment of the next chairperson of the Federal Reserve:

> *Garrett*: Thank you, Mr. President. I'd like to ask you about this debate that's playing itself out in editorial pages, in the blogosphere, even in the Senate Democratic caucus, about the choice you eventually will make for the next Federal Reserve chairman. There is a perception among Democrats that Larry Summers has the inside track, and perhaps you've made some assurances to him about that. Janet Yellen is the vice chair of the Federal Reserve. There are many women in the Senate who are Democrats who believe that breaking the glass ceiling there would be historic and important.
>
> *Obama*: Right.
>
> *Garrett*: Are you annoyed by this sort of roiling debate? Do you find it any way unseemly? And do you believe this will be one of the most important – if not the most important – economic decision you'll make in the remainder of your presidency? (Solo press conference 2013)

Garrett's preliminary statements provide context and justification for the subsequent questions. There is an implicit charge that Obama has already communicated with Summers, although this charge is softened by the low modality of 'perhaps', and it is not directly pursued. The potential conflict between perceptions that Summers is the president's preferred choice and the pressure to appoint a woman to the position is not, however, the focus of the questions. Instead, Garrett offers the president the opportunity to appear to be above the rumours and politics, and the final question cannot be classified as a tough question.

The journalistic challenging of Obama is most strongly expressed in follow-up questions – another indicator of initiative, given it usually conveys dissatisfaction with the supplied answer, and it infringes the convention of one question per person. Major Garrett, for example, follows up his question about the appointment of the next Federal Reserve chairperson with a more pointed question:

> *Garrett*: Can you see how the perception of you defending Larry Summers as vigorously as you just did and in other quarters lead some to believe you've already made up your mind?
>
> *Obama*: Well, except I just told you I haven't Major. I'd defend you if somebody was saying something that wasn't true about you [*laughter*]. I really would. In fact, I've done that in the White House sometimes [*laughter*]. (Solo press conference 2013)

As we can see from this exchange, the follow-up question is a more direct challenge to the president, although it is also softened by both the initial phrase 'Can you see...?', which is a form of indirectness known as an 'other-referencing question frame' (Clayman and Heritage 2002b) and the reference to unidentified others in the expression 'lead some to believe'. We also find here an example of Obama's use of humour to offset the imposition of his authority: the president at first directly refutes the basis of the question, but he then provides an explanation for his comments in the answer (Obama had explained he defended Summers publicly after criticisms) and extends this to Garrett in an amusing way that defuses the negativity of his disagreement with the question.

In contrast to the joint press conference, the solo press conference provides the incumbent freedom to express his or her views more candidly, and this applies in particular to other political leaders. The event in August 2013 occurred against the backdrop of deteriorating relations with Russia, and President Obama was forthright in his portrayal of the state of relations between the two countries. His discourse, nonetheless, also engages in a careful negotiation between policy and personalization frames. Contrasting his more productive relations with former President Medvedev during the earlier years of his presidency, Obama at one point observes:

> What's also true is, is that when President Putin – who was Prime Minister when Medvedev was president – came back into power I think we saw more rhetoric on the Russian side that was anti-American, that played into some of the old stereotypes about the Cold War contests between the United States and Russia. And I've encouraged Mr. Putin to think forward as opposed to backwards on those issues – with mixed success. (Solo press conference 2013)

In these comments Obama is direct in contrasting the two Russian leaders, but he softens his criticisms of Putin through his language use: his expression of persuasion – that he had 'encouraged' Mr. Putin – is a conventional diplomatic term that couches disagreement in a positive, projective way, as does the term 'mixed success'.

Obama's press conference discourse on Russia contains a mixture of abstract, diplomatic language that downplays conflict, while at other times there is direct acknowledgement of disagreement. One the one hand, he states it is 'probably appropriate for us to take a pause, reassess where it is that Russia is going', and that there is a need to 'calibrate the relationship', but alternatively he can explicitly declare on the issue of gay and lesbian rights that 'we have a strong disagreement on this issue'. While Obama seeks to derive a political advantage through personal criticism of Putin, he must also be careful not to further damage personal relations with the Russian leader, and he also attempts to shift framing of the issue away from personalities and towards more of a policy orientation. At one point, the president offers a strikingly negative description of Putin, but he softens the negative portrayal by referring to *journalistic* representations, and he does so in the context of a *defence* of the Russian leader, before shifting the footing of the discussion to policy issues:

> I don't have a bad personal relationship with Putin. When we have conversations, they're candid, they're blunt; oftentimes, they're constructive. I know the press likes to focus on body language and he's got that kind of slouch, looking like the bored kid in the back of the classroom. But the truth is, is that when we're in conversations together, oftentimes it's very productive. So the issue here really has to do with where do they want to take Russia – it's substantive on a policy front. (Solo press conference 2013)

In this way Obama is simply reporting on negative public perceptions of President Putin but nonetheless continuing to reinforce that perception in his restatement of that image.

The news media reportage of President Obama's press conference illustrated that journalists can be more aggressive in their critique afterwards, that they will seek a framing of personalization for their story, and that they will often employ a framing of political strategy as a means to report on issues. *The Economist*, for example, provided a critical commentary on Obama for both criticizing Snowden and announcing measures designed to address the problems Snowden had raised. The lead paragraph of the article stated: 'There was something surreal, in a Kafkaesque sort of way, about Barack Obama's press conference on August 9th. Aiming to ease concern over the government's surveillance programmes, the president announced reforms that seem both obvious and overdue. Then he criticized the man whose actions set those reforms in motion' ('The Snowden effect' 2013).

President Obama's solo press conference yielded much newswor-thy material – as we have seen, there were several comments on prominent individuals – but it was the president's unsurprising dec-laration that he did not consider Edward Snowden a 'patriot' that generated considerable news coverage. The lead paragraph in the *USA Today* story, for example, simply stated: 'President Obama said Friday that former National Security Agency contractor Edward Snowden is not a patriot for leaking details of previously secret US surveillance programs' (Madhani and Jackson 2013). In contrast, the *New York Times* focused on Obama's struggle to regain political control of the issue as it also provided detail of the president's announced reforms: 'President Obama on Friday sought to take control of the roiling debate over the National Security Agency's surveillance practices, releasing a more detailed legal justification for domestic spying and calling for more openness and scrutiny of the NSA's programs to reassure a skeptical public that its privacy is not being violated' (Savage and Shear 2013). Here we see a quality broad-sheet newspaper highlight the struggle between the political and media fields that we noted above, and a connection is made between a policy announcement and the political strategy informing such an announcement.

Joint Press Conference of Presidents Obama and Medvedev

We now turn to an analysis of the joint press conference with President Obama and Russia's President Dmitry Medvedev held in June 2010, some three years prior to the solo press conference we have just examined. It took place after President Medvedev's visit to Silicon Valley in California and some diplomatic talks between the two men and follows the convention of reporting on the substance of those talks. At this time American and Russian relations were improving, and so there is a positive tone to the encounter. The press conference features opening remarks by both presidents before ques-tions are fielded from American and Russian journalists. Our ability to analyse the language of the participants is affected by the fact that we receive a translation of the speech of Medvedev and the Russian journalists.

The presence of two leaders obviously introduces a different dynamic to that in a solo press conference. The *international* nature of the event highlights the extent to which the politicians are speaking not so much 'as individuals, but as representatives of their countries, governments and socio-political systems' (Bhatia 2006, p. 177). Joint press conferences are complicated by the presence of two national leaders, but such events usually do not feature substantive interaction between the two speakers. Each leader does, however, make references about the other leader and their role in the preceding talks. Unusually, then, the discourse in joint press conferences does not involve interaction, as we see in leaders' debates, but each speaker nonetheless positions the other through expressions of consensus and difference.

Each leader makes an opening statement that often begins with polite and pleasant remarks about the personal and informal features of their meeting. Such 'small talk' helps to establish the desired positive tone. In the Obama and Medvedev conference, President Obama starts his opening remarks by welcoming his 'friend and partner, President Medvedev' (Joint press conference 2010), recalls the hospitality he received on an earlier visit to Moscow, and makes reference to their meal earlier that day at a local Washington burger restaurant. The Russian leader, in turn, makes reference to the warm weather and invokes the visit to the burger restaurant with an attempt at humour: '...today I have managed to dine with President Barack Obama – an interesting place, which is typically American – probably it's not quite healthy, but it's very tasty, and you can feel the spirit of America' (ibid.). The substance of the opening statements involves each of the national leaders reporting on the talks they have just conducted. Obama offers a list of the agenda items of the talks and highlights the unity between the two leaders through repetition of 'together' and the first-person plural pronoun: 'Together, we negotiated and signed the historic new START Treaty.... Together, we've strengthened the global nonproliferation regime.... Together, our nations have deepened our cooperation against violent extremism.... Together, we've coordinated our efforts to strengthen the global economic recovery' (ibid.). The opening statements do not just report on the substance of the talks; they also attest to the communicative value of dialogue and diplomacy. In his opening remarks President Obama states of the Russian leader: 'in President Medvedev I've found a solid and reliable partner. We listen to one another and we speak candidly.' Later in his remarks he notes: 'I appreciated very much the opportunity to hear President Medvedev's vision for modernization in Russia' (ibid.).

As noted earlier, the primary function of joint press conferences is the projection of a united front where differences and conflict are downplayed. As such, these are highly formulaic events. The discourse of such encounters is often general and abstract and is characterized by a verbal narrative sequence where ongoing or future actions are noted, as in Obama's remark that 'we agreed to continue... to coordinate our diplomatic and humanitarian efforts' (Joint press conference 2010). As we can see, the dominant theme of joint press conferences is the projection of 'positivity', through expressions of praise, mutual understanding and common ground, and a promising future relationship (Bhatia 2006, p. 180). Joint press conferences in this sense are characterized as instances of politeness (Brown and Levinson 1990), where the function is to preserve the 'face' of the participants (Goffman 1967). The desire and political need to preserve face in the context of complex bilateral negotiations prompts the use of indirect discourse (Obeng 1997). Political leaders will also engage in strategies of evasion, such as minimizing or downplaying differences or deflecting moral and political blame (Bhatia 2006). Both Obama and Medvedev, for example, cited Georgia as an issue where there were policy differences, but each countered such acknowledgments quickly with positive statements:

> *Obama*: Our two countries continue to disagree on certain issues, such as Georgia, and we addressed those differences candidly. But by moving forward in areas where we do agree, we have succeeded in resetting our relationship...
>
> ...
>
> *Medvedev*: We have some differences – and Mr. President mentioned it – in terms of, for example, the after-effects of the conflict that was initiated by Georgia's leadership in 2008. But these differences do not prevent us from discussing future and launching new mechanisms of contacts. (Ibid.)

Expressions of power and delineations of difference are still articulated, even though such joint press conferences as the Obama–Medvedev event are characterized primarily by positivity. As we have noted, the expressions of power are often subtle but nonetheless work to position others. Obama's positive statements about Russia's membership of the WTO are also power statements that position the Russians, implicate them in the negotiation process and demand a sense of urgency, and Obama's opinion is strengthened through the use of modal verbs such as 'should': 'I told President Medvedev that our teams should accelerate their efforts to work together to complete this process in the very near future. Russia belongs in the WTO. That's good for Russia, it's good for America, and it's good for the world economy' (Joint press conference 2010). President Obama is keen to see an ongoing improvement in US and Russian relations, but he also derives political advantage by noting how poor the relationship was before he assumed power. He explicitly states early in his opening remarks:

> We just concluded some excellent discussions – discussions that would have been unlikely just 17 months ago. As we've both said before, when I came into office, the relationship between the United States and Russia had drifted – perhaps to the lowest point since the Cold War. There was too much distrust and too little real work on issues of common concern. (Ibid.)

In accord with diplomatic language, the agents who caused the poor relations – former presidents George W. Bush and Vladimir Putin – are not named, but the contrast enables Obama indirectly to attribute praise to himself and also to Medvedev. Obama's criticisms implicitly promote a positive self-portrayal emphasizing his moral character – his 'trust', his industry, doing 'real work' – and also his unifying leadership – addressing 'common concerns'.

There are no instances of strong disagreement in the press conference, apart from the noted differences on Georgia, but President Obama is also careful to attribute obligations to other parties where required: a question on the WTO from a Russian journalist enabled him to suggest that accession to membership will be dependent upon Russian domestic political process: 'A lot of the technical issues, the resolution of those technical issues, though, may be in the hands of the Russian government. We've already made progress on some issues like encryption, for example. There may certain international standards that require modifications in Russian law' (Joint press conference 2010). The discourse of the leaders, then, is positive and friendly, but nonetheless they use their authority to demonstrate and implement influence and power.

Joint press conferences are complex communicative events because they necessarily address different national audiences. In addition, the participating leaders use such events at least implicitly to address the leaders and publics of other nations. Obviously each of them is cognizant of addressing their own domestic audience, but joint press conferences are also opportunities to speak to other national audiences. That is, politicians are involved in instances of 'mediated public diplomacy', where there are short-term and targeted uses of *'mass communication (including the internet) to increase support of a country's specific foreign policies among audiences beyond that country's borders'* (Entman 2008, p. 88; original emphasis). President Obama makes references to the perceptions that Russian people have of Americans, and at one point he explicitly addresses them:

On the WTO, first of all, I emphasized to President Medvedev, I emphasized to his entire delegation, and I now want to emphasize to the Russian people, we think it is not only in the interests of the Russian Federation, but in the interests of the United States and in the interest of the world that Russia joins the WTO. (Joint press conference 2010)

The force of his comment is strengthened by the use of two tricolons, a classical rhetorical device often favored by the president, where a three-part list and repetition is deployed for emphasis. Of course, the use of the tricolons occurs not only for rhetorical effect but because they have the political effect of unifying the interests of the United States, Russia and a more global economic interest.

The influence and diplomacy of the national leaders extends to references to other countries, and this occurs in the press conference when a journalist asks a question about China's management of its currency, the Renminbi (RMB):

Thank you very much, Mr. President. I'd like to ask about the G20, since you are both heading to the summit. On China, you've already welcomed its decision on the yuan. Are you satisfied with how far the country has moved since that news? How will this influence your judgment on whether China is a currency manipulator? And when will you release your report to Congress on this matter? (Joint press conference 2010)

Obama picks up on the negative framing of the question – 'currency manipulator' – and exerts his authority on the subject, demonstrating his responsible leadership in acknowledgement of China's interests but ultimately seeking to determine the behaviour of others with an explicit directive:

I will say that we did not expect a complete 20-percent appreciation overnight, for example, simply because that would be extremely disruptive to world currency markets and to the Chinese economy. And ultimately, not surprisingly, China has got to make these decisions based on its sovereignty and its economic platform. But we have said consistently that we believe that the RMB is undervalued, that that provides China with an unfair trade advantage, and that we expect change. (Ibid.)

Obama, then, is using the platform of a joint press conference to convey the position of the United States on an issue that has been canvassed in other forums directly to the Chinese leadership. The force of his comments derives from his referencing of the historical repetition of the charge – 'we have said consistently' – the use of high modality – 'the RMB *is* undervalued' (although this is softened by the preceding 'we believe') – and the directive 'we expect change' (although this is softened by the deletion of the agent who will bring about the change).

Joint press conferences are usually characterized by comparatively fewer questions from journalists and less combative interactions. The Obama–Medvedev conference featured only four questions: two each from American and Russian journalists – only half the number posed in Obama's solo press conference – and there were no follow-up questions – apart from one instance where Obama asked to be reminded about part of a question he had not addressed. As such, the joint press conference is less of a dialogical encounter than most of the interrogative exchanges we are analysing in this volume. Both presidents address three out of the four questions, and this only lessens further the interactive quality of the event. Indeed, a question to a second political leader may not be answered for a couple of minutes after the first leader has addressed his question. The joint press conference, then, is a highly ritualistic encounter that allows for interactions between politicians and journalists, but the intensity of the interactions is subsumed by the extended discourse of the politicians, both in their opening statements and in their answers.

The questions in the Obama–Medvedev conference do, nonetheless, at times offer a challenge to the political leaders. The journalist from the ITAR-TASS news agency, for example, asked the following questions:

> My question to the President of the United States – you just mentioned that you discussed the issue of Russia joining the WTO during your talks. But I must admit that promises to facilitate Russia's entry have been heard by the Russian delegation for a decade. Could you more specifically name the time frame when you're referring to finalizing the process in the near future? And a question to Medvedev – yesterday you visited the Silicon Valley. How did your perceptions on future cooperation between Russia and the US in high-tech sphere change, and what indicators should be reached so that you can call the cooperation a successful one. Thank you. (Joint press conference 2010)

The adversarial question to President Obama contains a dimension of hostility, given the journalist indicates a skepticism in his prefatory statement regarding Obama's claims about Russia's WTO membership. This skepticism is also manifested in the actual question where accountability is sought from Obama over the time frame for Russia's WTO membership. In his answer Obama does not respond directly to the personal challenge of the questioner and instead offers a detailed and measured answer, outlining the reasons why he is confident that Russia will soon assume membership of the WTO.

In joint press conferences politicians often have the opportunity not to engage directly with the terms of the question. Their ability to evade questions and engage in obfuscation is partly facilitated by the more diplomatic tenor of the event. Political leaders also have more freedom to exert their agency in joint press conferences, given that, unlike the situation in political interviews, journalists do not engage in interruptions or extended challenges that discipline the responses of politicians and increase accountability. We see this here in the responses of the Russian president. The opening question of the press conference was from the journalist Carol Lee: 'And if I may, to President Medvedev, given your country's history and experience in Afghanistan, and your ability to talk candidly with President Obama, have you offered him any advice on the Afghan war? And do you believe that a foreign country can win in Afghanistan?' (Joint press conference 2010). This question cleverly draws on the leaders' own reports of their 'candid' rapport to encourage Medvedev to disclose details about Russia's judgement of the US involvement in Afghanistan. The president, however, resists the temptation to be as forthcoming on the 'front stage' of the press conference as he might be 'back stage' in the talks: 'You know, I hope that we have quite friendly relations with President Obama, but I try not to give pieces of advice that cannot be fulfilled. This is a hard topic, a difficult one' (ibid.). Medvedev completes his answer diplomatically by stating that he supported the US attempts to restore the functioning of the Afghanistan state, its civil society and economy. The greater initiative of political leaders in joint press conferences is also revealed when Medvedev decides to answer a question that was not directed to him. The Russian president also responded to the question that was posed to Obama about Russia's possible WTO membership, declaring: 'I will say a couple of words about the WTO because it's important for our country' (ibid.). While his subsequent comments do not add any substantive details to what had just been provided by the American president, his remarks have the effect of asserting Russia's agency in the negotiation process.

Beyond dealing with the specificity of questions, political leaders are conscious, through their performances and comments, of trying to convey an overall theme from a press conference that will be replicated in news media coverage. President Obama highlighted the positive state of relations between the two countries in his opening statement, alluding to the 'resetting' of the relationship, and this was reflected in the reportage of the event. The Associated Press story on the press conference began: 'President Barack Obama declared Thursday that he and Russian President Dmitry Medvedev have "succeeded in resetting" the relationship between the former Cold War adversaries that had dipped to a dangerous low in recent years' (Butler 2010). Not surprisingly, the visit to the burger restaurant was also used as the news hook in press conference reportage. The photo-op, of course, was a contrast to the formality of the conference, offering strong news images and good copy about lunch order details and reactions from other restaurant patrons. The lunchtime event, however, was not a frivolous distraction from the serious reportage of the press conference but, rather, a way of symbolizing the renewed relationship that Obama was keen to stress. Such symbolism was captured in the reportage of the *Washington Post*:

> During the Cold War, President Richard Nixon once gave Soviet leader Leonid Brezhnev a Lincoln Continental. The car fanatic and notoriously bad driver immediately took the startled president on a high-speed ride through the twisting mountain roads near Camp David, running a stop sign in the process.
>
> President Obama kept things simpler Thursday. He took visiting Russian President Dmitry Medvedev to his favorite hamburger joint, Ray's Hell Burger in Arlington County, and paid for Medvedev's order of a cheddar cheeseburger, piled high with onions, jalapeno peppers and mushrooms, shared fries and a Coke.
>
> Such symbols of high-level bonding have been important in the relationship between the two nuclear powers. For the Obama administration, the image of the two youthful leaders casually lunching on burgers serves as a useful counterpoint to superpower summitry and the high tensions at the end of George W. Bush's administration. (Kessler and Shear 2010)

Conclusion

We have noted in this chapter that press conferences differ from other interrogative encounters to the extent that they are held within the domain of the political field and politicians are able to exert greater control over their interactions with journalists, although the cumulative force of journalistic questioning can at times put politicians under considerable pressure. In the comments on the history of press conferences it was noted how they grew into more formal events and how the introduction of television rendered them forms of public spectacle. The differences between the two dominant types of press conference – the domestic, solo conference and the international joint conference – were initially highlighted, including the observation that, for US presidents in recent decades, the latter type has become more prevalent than the former.

The two case studies involving President Barack Obama further developed the differences between these two types of press conference. We saw in Obama's solo press conference the important functions of the opening statement, where the president sought to establish the framing of the event, where he tried to assert the legitimacy of the political field and political process over the more speculative media and public debate, and where he engaged in the rhetorical construction of national identity. The question and answer exchanges were then analysed, observing the deference of the journalists but also highlighting the power struggle between politician and journalist, where the president sought to establish control over the process of questioning and the journalists demonstrated initiative through complex and follow-up questions. The analysis also illustrated how subsequent news coverage of the press conference offered a more aggressive critique of the encounter. The analysis of the joint press conference of presidents Obama and Medvedev noted the comparative lack of interaction and different tempo of the event. It highlighted the positive nature of the diplomatic language that was employed and observed that, while there was little interaction between the two men, they nonetheless positioned the other, and the relationship between the two nations, through expressions of consensus and difference. The analysis further noted the plurality of audiences that were addressed through the press conference and the ways in which the speakers sought to exercise their influence over these audiences in different national contexts. The discussion about the media reportage emphasized the political management of the framing of the press conference and the way that such political management extended beyond the event itself to other related media events.

6

Current Affairs Forum Television

Introduction

A televisual genre such as current affairs forum television offers great promise in facilitating the complex dynamics of contemporary political communication and public life, given that it allows for the expression of a plurality of voices, including members of the public. In current affairs forum television, participating politicians encounter a range of views from other panelists and the audience, and the diversity of views that populate public opinion are on prominent display. Some have argued that the genre peaked in the 1980s and 1990s (Carpentier and Hannot 2009, p. 612), although McNair, Hibberd and Schlesinger could write in 2003 that 'there are more of those programmes on UK television and radio than ever before' (2003, p. 8). Current affairs forum television programmes may not have the same public prominence as other programmes that more regularly feature one-on-one political interviews, and they do not always completely capture public attention, as might be the case with leaders' debates in the heat of an election campaign, but they are a persistent feature of the televisual landscape, and they have an evolving identity through their enhanced ability to involve audience participation using Web 2.0 technologies.

The term 'current affairs forum television' is used here to distinguish such programmes from the broad range of the talk show genre, or audience-participation format television. I argue that other terms, such as 'TV forums' (Rushkoff 1996) or 'public participation broadcasting' (McNair et al. 2003) do not sufficiently capture the governmental or civic focus of current affairs forum television. As Haarman (1999, p. 1) notes, the fundamental components of a talk show are a host, a guest or panel of guests, a studio audience, and a focus on talk. Beyond this, the genre is open to a variety of manifestations and is itself characterized by an unsettling of generic conventions: 'audience discussion programmes challenge existing conceptions of genre, particularly the distinctions between entertainment and current affairs, ideas and emotions, argument and narrative' (Livingstone and Lunt 1994, p. 37). We can make a broad distinction between celebrity or public figure-type talk shows that involve more dyadic conversation and issue-type talk shows that actively involve the audience (Carbaugh 1988), noting that some programmes oscillate between such formats. Haarman (1999) identifies three basic formats of talk shows: the evening or celebrity format, the issue-oriented format and the audience discussion format. The issue-oriented format not only addresses particular political or social issues but also involves a separation of audience from panel guests, while still allowing an active role for the audience. This format encapsulates a broad range of programme types, from *The Jerry Springer Show* to the kind of current affairs forum television that is scrutinized in this chapter. According to Haarman's classificatory scheme, the audience discussion format identifies shows where the talk is conducted *entirely* by audience members.

The current affairs forum genre can be further differentiated into those programmes that have a more exclusive focus on parliamentary politics, such as *Q&A* in Australia and *Question Time* in the United Kingdom, and those that also deal more broadly with social issues, such as *Sunday Morning Live* in the UK and *Insight*, screened on the Special Broadcasting Service (SBS) in Australia. Popular current affairs forum television programmes in other countries include *Jan Publiek* in north Belgium (Carpentier and Hannot 2009). Of course, delineating current affairs television programmes with either a parliamentary or a social issues focus from other forms of talk shows is not to deny the political significance of those that deal with a range of personal and social issues in a more explicitly 'entertainment-based' format. Current affairs forum television is also distinguished from debate-style current affairs television, where a panel of participants argues for their respective positions on a more strictly defined topic. Such talk is more highly structured and controlled by the host, with careful monitoring of both the allotted time for speakers and the sequences of their interaction. Debate-style current affairs television is less conversational and more combative and usually involves little or no participation from a studio audience.

Current affairs forum television is informed by certain 'normative aspirations' (McNair et al. 2003, p. 34) that include an extended interactive talk format, the representation of the people in the public domain, the interrogation of political elites by the people, and the political engagement and mobilization of that citizenry. It can be seen as countering a political communication environment where access to, and interrogation of, political leaders is strictly controlled and political discourse is increasingly monological. McNair, Hibberd and Schlesinger's (2003) historical overview of the genre in the UK attests to the contribution the genre has made to the less deferential political culture in that country, although their claims that scrutiny of senior politicians is a distinctively British feature has been undermined in recent years by programmes such as *Q&A* in Australia, where prime ministers have made solo appearances and other leading government ministers regularly appear on panels.

Current affairs forum television is often involved in a scheduling televisual hierarchy with progressive degrees of textual 'openness': the more closed text of a conventional news story, focusing on factual reportage, gives way to a more open and extended treatment of an issue on an early-evening current affairs programme, which, in turn, pre-empts talk shows which are defined by their plurality of voice and debate. The genre of current affairs television has been in a state of decline in recent years (Turner 2005), and current affairs forum television programmes form a less prominent feature of television current affairs, often screening on public broadcasters, which themselves have long been in a state of crisis (Craig 2000). It is argued here, nonetheless, that these programmes are generating increased popularity because they are a means by which television can address the growing demand and need in a Web 2.0 media environment to facilitate greater public involvement and debate.

The chapter here focuses on the current affairs forum television programmes that deal more exclusively with parliamentary politics, such as *Question Time* and *Q&A*. *Question Time* is the longest-running current affairs forum television programme, having been started by the British Broadcasting Corporation (BBC) in 1979 and continuing to the present day. It was based on the popular radio programme *Any Questions?*, which started in 1948, and is still running. The veteran broadcaster Sir Robin Day presented *Question Time* for nearly ten years until June 1989, and David Dimbleby has presented the show since 1994. After Day's departure, the BBC adopted the current practice of hosting the programme each week in a different location within the UK. It regularly attracts over 2 million viewers but recorded its highest ratings of 7.9 million viewers in

2009, when Nick Griffin from the British National Party (BNP) was invited to take part.

Q&A was first screened by the Australian Broadcasting Corporation (ABC) in May 2008, replacing another experiment in the talk show format, *Difference of Opinion*, which featured a panel of experts but with less audience participation. *Q&A* is based upon the same format as the BBC's *Question Time* and also replicates the format of the popular and influential *Monday Conference* programme, which ran on the ABC from 1971 to 1978. *Q&A* has been a success for the ABC: the show regularly attracts over 600,000 viewers, a strong performance for a political discussion programme on Monday nights on the nation's public broadcaster (Simper 2011). Its most popular episode in the 2010 series, featuring the then prime minister Julia Gillard, attracted 840,000 viewers, which was more than for popular drama shows such as *Criminal Minds* and *CSI: Miami* but less than for the satirical news show *Good News Week* ('Q&A scores ratings record' 2010). *Q&A* has continued to attract political controversy and criticisms from government. In 2015, a contribution from a studio audience member, the former terrorism suspect Zaky Mallah, prompted outrage from Tony Abbott's government, a ban on frontbench ministers appearing on *Q&A*, and an inquiry into the programme.

Current affairs forum television programmes, and audience discussion programmes more broadly, have prompted a range of academic appraisals of their merit. Some studies (Carpignano et al. 1990; Livingstone and Lunt 1994; McNair et al. 2003) have praised audience discussion programmes, arguing they contribute to the democratization of the mass media. Such studies have highlighted the active role that ordinary people play in the shows, drawing on life experiences, expressions of emotion, and common sense in their contestation of expert knowledge. Carpignano, Andersen, Aronowitz and Difazio (1990, p. 35) argue that talk shows 'constitute a "contested space" in which new discursive practices are developed in contrast to the traditional modes of political and ideological representation.' Livingstone and Lunt (1994, p. 102) conclude that audience discussion programmes 'adopt an anti-elitist position...repudiating criticisms of the ordinary person as incompetent or ignorant, questioning the deference traditionally due to experts through their separation from the life-world and their incorporation into the system, and asserting instead the worth of the "common man".' Others have alternatively demonstrated how the modes of participation of ordinary people in audience discussion programmes are limited by the contexts of production (Carpentier 2001) and offer 'stereotypical expectations

regarding the communicative competence of "ordinary people"'
(Hamo 2006, p. 440), as well as the inability of the programmes to
initiate structural political change because of the dominant framing
of social problems through a perspective of personalization (McLaughlin 1993; Peck 1995).

This terrain of academic appraisal captures both the emancipatory
potential and the structural limitations of current affairs forum programmes, and specific conclusions need to be cognizant of the kind
of divisions within the talk show genre that have already been identified. Within Haarman's category of the issue-oriented format, for
example, some programmes employ a primarily therapeutic discourse
that individualizes audience participants, while those that are scrutinized here privilege more a subject position of citizen that usually
involves processes of self-abstraction. We will now build on this range
of evaluations with an exploration of the nature of the interactions
and the promotional strategies in current affairs forum television.

Hosts, Panelists and Audience Members

The hope that current affairs forum television offers a contemporary
media site where extended, rational discourse between political representatives and their constituents is not misguided, but it does require
qualification, as the roles and activities of the hosts, the panelists and
the audience members are investigated in more detail. Current affairs
forum television is still an institutional product, and, as such, the
topics under discussion, the nature of the discourse of individual
participants, including their timing, interactivity and modes of expression, along with the hierarchy of participants, all impose a regular
structure on the programme that not only disciplines and contains
the discourse but gives the show a recognizable unity and 'brand
image'.

The host is the public mechanism by which the programme's unity
and its successful management are realized. The centrality of the host
in television talk shows is emphasized when we consider how we can
summarize their identity and their functions. As Livingstone and Lunt
(1994, p. 56) asked: 'is he or she the chair of a debate, the adored
hero of a talk show, a referee, a conciliator, a judge, the compere of
a game show, a therapist, the host of a dinner-party conversation, a
manager or a spokesperson?' We can start by noting that the authority of the host does not reside simply in their individual personality,
media talent, journalistic skill or public appeal but in their embodiment and public manifestation of the controls that the production

process exerts over the structure and meaning potential of the programme. Features of the programmes, such as the discussion theme or themes, the selection of questions, the rules or guidelines for interaction and behaviour of participants, the timing, and forms of visual representations, are all either pre-determined by the production team or determined as the programme is produced, with vital input and direction by the host. The host is also the public face of the show, and here their authority is a complex composite of journalistic professionalism and public renown. Tony Jones, the host of *Q&A*, derives his journalistic authority from his previous hosting of the serious late-evening current affairs programme *Lateline*. There has also been, however, the cultivation of Jones's celebrity status: his personality is foregrounded in the programme promotion, and his catch-cry, 'I'll take that as a comment', when audience members fail to ask an actual question, has entered the political lexicon in Australia.

The host in current affairs forum programmes is also, of course, both a moderator and an interviewer, acting as a pivot between the studio audience and the panel of speakers and limiting and controlling the interaction between members of the public and the panel. Conventionally, the host will ask a member of the studio audience to pose their question and then often direct both particular panel members to speak and the subsequent discussion among the group. He or she may then return to the questioner to inquire if they are satisfied with the responses or simply move onto another question. The host can also interrupt the flow of contributions from panelists to interrogate particular individuals. There are, as such, constant changes in footing by the host and a fluidity of modes of interaction that occur in the narrative of the discussion, and hosts face the difficult task of knowing when to intervene to inquire further of a particular individual. Such interventions might be prompted by a need to clarify meaning or, in some circumstances, because the host is aware of the newsworthiness of a comment. In one episode of *Q&A* in the 2011 season, for example, Tony Jones twice initiated 'embedded interviews' with panel politicians Joe Hockey and Kate Ellis (*Q&A* 2011b). In response to Hockey's comments about his support for quotas on the minimum number of females on the boards of public companies, Jones quizzed the politician further, observing: 'It does seem that you are making news here.' While the host exerts great authority over the programme structure and flow, their authority is also frequently challenged, with panelists speaking without permission or themselves asking questions of other panelists. The plurality of panelists diffuses the possibility that there will be direct challenges to the host, as we saw in chapter 3 with the Rudd and

O'Brien interview, but there are nonetheless occasions when the host's subject position is foregrounded and problematized. In one episode of *Q&A* (*Q&A* 2011a), for example, a panel member interjected after a question had been posed about poor journalistic standards with the comment 'That sounds like a question for Tony Jones.'

The panelists of current affairs forum television programmes are figures of public authority, such as politicians, journalists or media commentators, academics, business people, celebrities, and leading figures in public bodies, think tanks, etc. It is only those who have been granted a position on the panel who are able to expound on issues, offering evidence to justify opinions, and given the extended time necessary to display and enact their knowledge and expertise. Not surprisingly, politicians always feature prominently: *Question Time*, for example, only expanded its panel in 1999 from four members, including three politicians and a political expert, to five members, allowing for non-political professionals, such as prominent business and entertainment figures (McNair et al. 2003, p. 66). Panelists on current affairs forum television programmes must not only have the requisite expertise but also be polished media performers. They must be able to distil their expertise into an appropriate media discourse and possess a personality that can be exploited profitably for the programme's appeal. While they must be able to engage constructively with others, they may be selected for their more idiosyncratic views and their potential to engender conflict and controversy.

The relatively direct interaction between an audience composed of 'ordinary citizens' and the host and panel members is obviously a primary feature of current affairs forum television. The sheer presence of a 'public' on television, and their voicing of direct, apparently unmediated or unedited discourse to political elites, still carries with it a sense of novelty, and a sense of anticipation of the potential for political 'frisson', that perhaps partly explains the appeal of such programmes. The 'involvement' of the audience is curtailed to the asking of questions, and there is little opportunity to initiate dialogue with panelists. Generally, current affairs forum television is informed by a structural logic that separates citizens from their political representatives and others with authority in the public realm. The studio audience is primarily positioned as just that: an *audience* that is observing the performance of the panelists and the host. Rarely is either the communicative competence or the social expertise of the questioner explicitly highlighted.

The audience is a differentiated entity, and it is becoming increasingly so with the introduction of online and social media technologies into the formats of such programmes. It is constituted both as a studio audience, where its members are programme participants, and as a viewing audience. The viewing audience, however, no longer necessarily assumes the traditional, more passive status of the home viewer, as the inclusion of Twitter feeds and online chat forums enable comment both on the host and panel members and on the studio audience itself.

Ordinary people increasingly feature in a variety of television genres, such as forms of lifestyle television, and Livingstone and Lunt (1994, p. 102) have called audience participation programmes 'a celebration of ordinary experience'. While the audience members of current affairs forum television are presented as 'ordinary' people, they often speak less as 'individuals', foregrounding their own subject position and life experience, and instead adopt a more generalized speaking position of 'citizen'. This is not to deny that speakers do regularly draw on personal experiences or display particular kinds of expertise, but it is noticeable how often questions echo conventional journalistic treatment of the issue. Current affairs forum television does not employ the kind of therapeutic discourse of many other audience participation programmes; rather, a current affairs or meta-political news discourse predominates. The latter term highlights that the questions and discussion of current affairs forum television often dissect the values that inform contemporary political issues, the strategies and negotiations that inform the political struggle over those issues, and the rules and conventions of the political field. Equally, the manner of enunciation does not foreground the individual personality of the audience member; questions are often read in a rather mechanical way. While one individual in a *Q&A* audience famously stood and threw a shoe at former prime minister John Howard, we are usually a long way from the antics of a *Jerry Springer* audience member.

It has also been noted that the audience members of current affairs forum television programmes possess and display a high degree of social capital. As McNair, Hibberd and Schlesinger (2003, p. 89) state, the various forms of 'public participation broadcasting [are] still the preserve of the already engaged citizen'. For this reason, some conservative political commentators have criticized the constitution of such audiences. As one commentator observed: 'What *Q&A* tends to draw for a crowd are the political junkies, the lobbyists, the pressure group flunkies, and those with intense single issue opinions' (Novak 2010). Similarly, it is argued that current affairs forum television audiences are overly represented by more progressive political views (Styles 2010).

Case Study: Interaction and Promotion in *Q&A*

We will now engage in an analysis of *Q&A*, exploring in more detail the communicative processes of interaction and promotion that occur in the popular Australian current affairs forum television programme. The analysed examples here are drawn from the 2011 series. The nature of the interactions that occur in the programme will be investigated, illustrating its more open and pluralistic discussion while also demonstrating the pleasures of textual closure that it provides. We will comment on the diverse types of enunciations and suggest that the audience's primary function is less that of interrogator and more that of witness, evaluating and validating the various discursive responses from the panel of experts. In this sense, the identity and different forms of the audience, together with the relationship between the plurality of individual performances and the more collective status of the audience as public, will be discussed. We will provide an investigation of the audience tweets and the meta-commentary that they provide. The analysis will conclude with scrutiny of how the genre of current affairs forum television operates as a promotional forum – how *Q&A* facilitates particular performances of the habitus of the journalistic and political participants. In addition, we will consider how the genre structures the journalistic and political fields, enabling particular negotiations of power between the different types of participants.

Episodes of *Q&A* start with a sweeping, tracking shot of a clapping audience before a transition to the host Tony Jones, who welcomes viewers and introduces the panelists with the line: 'Answering your questions tonight...' This opening provides visual and verbal cues to the programme's democratic promise and its power differentials. The audience is a central participant in *Q&A*, and the opening shot highlights its forum setting, promoting the promise of an active public. Jones's introduction confirms this promise that the audience will participate through the posing of questions, but the grammatical structure of his comment privileges the agency of the panelists, while the process of audience interrogation is rendered in the passive form. The hierarchy of the relationship between the 'questions' and the 'answers' that inform the very name and structure of the programmes is thus established.

Q&A mainly presents a disciplined posing of concise questions with limited opportunities for further interrogation. In this sense, its essence is not dialogue but the expression of a range of opinions. In managing exchanges between audience and panel members, and among the panel members, the host actively *prevents* opportunities for an elaborated dialogue in order to ensure that the flow of discussion is maintained and that a range of participants are able to address the issue. Manifested in Jones's catch-cry 'I'll take that as a comment', the *Q&A* host's function is to *police* the discursive parameters of the participants. When the publisher Louise Adler wanted to ask the then foreign minister Kevin Rudd a question, Jones interrupted her, stating: 'No, you don't get to ask questions, sorry about that. You can make a comment' (*Q&A* 2011c). Limited exchanges do nonetheless occur sometimes between audience members and panelists, despite this active curtailment of interaction. In the episode that featured the then prime minister, Julia Gillard, there was a relatively extended discussion between her and a teacher regarding the government's *My School* numeracy and literacy school performance website. The prime minister, after responding at length to a follow-up question from the teacher about the fairness of *My School* for ESL (English as a second language) and special education students, ended her answer by acknowledging the detail of the conversation and offering the possibility of extending the exchange at a later time (*Q&A* 2011d).

The panel discussion on *Q&A* primarily involves a sequence of individual answers to a posed question. Despite the programme's title, the discourse is not structured principally by an interrogative mode but by a mode of dissemination that is characterized by openness and plurality. Less so than other genres of talk show, such as confessional talk shows, the goal of current affairs forum television is not so much the resolution of particular political or social problems and the establishment of consensus as the production of what Carpignano, Andersen, Aronowitz and Difazio (1990, p. 51) call the 'ideology of public discourse', which maintains that, while 'agreement is not always attainable...communication is always possible, and television is the ultimate terrain of social consensus because it embodies the universality of communication.' This feature, nonetheless, represents a particular strength of the programme as the expression of a range of opinions, and the deployment of a range of discourse styles or 'registers' results in a more extended appraisal of issues with less discursive negotiation of an opposing point of view, as manifested in the direct challenges that occur in political interviews. This sequencing of comparatively 'independent' comments from a range of different types of panelists enhances the polysemic status of the programme, requiring a more active audience involvement in the text, and it also enhances *Q&A*'s democratic value.

We see an example of this in a discussion sequence on same-sex marriage that featured in the seventh episode of the 2011 series (*Q&A* 2011e). It was prompted by a video question from Josh Thomas, a young, gay celebrity comedian, who featured in a programme titled *Talking 'bout your Generation* on the commercial Ten Network. Thomas's question asked about the hypocrisy of comments by Julia Gillard – 'our atheist, "living in sin" prime minister' – arguing against same sex-marriage because 'it's against our culture and our heritage which... is based on the Bible.' Thomas completes his question, asking, 'WTF? Discuss.' The discussion that follows is largely the independent expression of opinions from panelists with host Tony Jones occasionally intervening to ask questions. Jones, for example, intervenes twice to ask panelists their personal views after they had addressed the politics of the same-sex marriage issue, sometimes to expose the tension inherent in their comments. Conservative commentator Miranda Devine, for example, had to acknowledge she agreed with Gillard after criticizing the prime minister for making the comments on same-sex marriage for political advantage, seeking to differentiate herself from the Greens in parliament.

As we have seen, panel contributions are often open but not totally independent utterances, but there are also other sequences where there is a greater degree of interrogation and panelists have to negotiate a narrative in a much more explicit manner. This 'narrativization' (Eriksson 2010) is less pronounced in current affairs forum television than in other talk show formats, but the discussion of an issue nonetheless assumes a degree of focus and coherence. In fact, particular interrogative sequences assume high levels of scrutiny because there is an opportunity for a more extended discussion than there is in conventional political interviews; there is usually more than one interrogator; and the audience's responses highlight evaluations of the exchanges, with an immediate rendering of public judgements about the quality of answers. Paradoxically, then, in addition to its noted openness and plurality, the programme provides moments of narrative closure through its panel exchanges.

We saw an example of this in the second episode of the 2011 series (*Q&A* 2011f), which featured an extended panel discussion about the Australian government's treatment of the WikiLeaks founder, Julian Assange. An initial question suggested a lack of consistency in the government's desire for greater democracy in the Middle East while also labelling Assange a criminal, despite the fact that he had not been charged with a crime. The Australian attorney general had previously said the government was investigating whether Assange's passport could be cancelled, and Julia Gillard had stated that the

WikiLeaks website was illegal, but a subsequent Australian Federal Police (AFP) investigation found Assange not guilty of any crime. The government's representative on the *Q&A* panel, the trade minister Craig Emerson, was the focus of a sustained interrogation. Emerson initially sought to impose a legal framing on the issue, separating Assange from the US soldier who was alleged to have released classified information and declaring that such a disclosure would be a crime. Jones then tries to shift the framing of the discourse while also reconnecting with the initial question that linked the government's response to WikiLeaks with democratic movements in the Middle East. Jones makes the point that it is the job of journalists to disclose secret information and that information made available by WikiLeaks was said to be influential in the initial democratic uprising in Tunisia. Emerson quickly acknowledges Jones's points but restates his legal framing of the WikiLeaks issue. As the minister elaborates his answer, a tweet is posted at the bottom of the screen: 'Craig Emerson public disclosure is not a crime.' Panelist John Pilger then interrupts Emerson and reframes the issue, following the results of the AFP investigation, as a political problem for the government. A sequence of accusations between Emerson and Pilger results in Jones again allowing Emerson to continue with his account before the host asks the following question: 'Given what you are saying and the fact that the investigation of the Federal Police had not even taken place when the attorney general said they were looking into whether they could cancel Assange's passport, do you think that was jumping the gun?' (ibid.). Emerson in his reply continues with his legal framing of the issue, avoiding the negative political associations that might be associated with a discussion about the government's handling of the affair. This fact is highlighted by amused murmurings from the audience that accompany another interruption by Pilger, who asks of Emerson: 'It's OK to withdraw an Australian's passport?' (ibid.). After another exchange between Pilger and Emerson, Jones intervenes and follows up on his question:

> *Jones*: The question I asked was whether it was jumping the gun to say 'we're looking at withdrawing his passport' before there was even an investigation.
>
> *Emerson*: Yes and I understand the question. And I'm saying that the investigation has then proceeded…He did not say. Robert McClelland did not say 'I am withdrawing his passport.' He did not say that.
>
> *Jones*: No, he said they were considering it.

Emerson: Well, he raised that issue. He did raise that issue. I concede that point. He did raise that issue.

Pilger: How would you feel if your Attorney General threatened to withdraw your passport? (Ibid.)

Emerson then draws on comments from the US ambassador to Australia that US concerns about WikiLeaks had not focused on Julian Assange. Jones responds: 'So are you saying that he had a more considered approach than our own attorney general?' (ibid.). The question is accompanied by laughter from the studio audience, and Pilger comments: 'Sounds like it' (ibid.), before there is a round of applause from the audience. Emerson then goes on to note that the ambassador's comments were made four days previously while McClelland's comment was made the preceding December, and he remarks: 'I suppose with the passage of three or four months, by definition there is a more considered basis of making those statements' (ibid.).

This exchange is offered in detail here to illustrate the discursive negotiations that can occur in current affairs forum television. Firstly, it is an extended interaction that unfolds over five minutes, and it is this length that enables the working through of the issue to its culmination in Emerson's admission. The length of the exchange can encompass some discursive 'skirmishes' between panelists while still facilitating the reorientation and progressive focusing of the narrative. Emerson's struggle to impose his framing of the issue is undermined not only by his own invocation of the US ambassador's comments but also by the persistent and the progressively sharper inquiry of Jones. Secondly, the interrogation in this exchange is structured by the different contributions of two questioners, Jones and Pilger, who together mobilize both rational and emotive responses to Emerson's answers. Jones's line of questioning drives the progressive focus on Emerson's answers, but Pilger's questions and comments serve several functions, highlighting the political controversy associated with the issue, adopting a more combative orientation to Emerson, foregrounding an emotional response, and validating the result of Jones's questioning. These types of contributions from the two questioners, working across different journalistic styles or registers, would not be possible from a single interviewer in a conventional one-on-one political interview. Thirdly, the active involvement of the studio audience, in responses to questions and answers, facilitates both the openness of the discourse *and also* a sense of discursive closure to interactions. The ability of politicians stubbornly to resist engaging with the substance of questions is undermined by the immediate and active responses of the studio audience. Equally, audience responses to interactions, manifested in applause, laughter and exclamations, are important markers of judgement that prompt an end to an exchange. The murmurings from the audience when Emerson restates his legal framing of the issue are an explicit signal from the public of the unsatisfactory nature of his reply, and their applause after Jones's final question (and before Emerson has a chance to reply) works with Pilger's comment to establish the conclusion of the exchange.

The *Q&A* audience is a differentiated entity, comprised of the studio audience, the viewing audience that participates through the posting of tweets, web and video questions, and the viewing audience, who do not actively participate. The different types of contributions from these audiences, and the subsequent production and performance of differentiated types of public subjectivity, are integral features of the discursive complexity of *Q&A*. Our focus here is on the studio audience and those who contribute to the programme through the Twitter feed. The identity of those in the studio audience who offer questions is defined partly through the kind of questions they ask and partly through their relational status to the rest of the studio audience and the panel members. As already noted, such questions are not usually marked by a high degree of individuality. They address important current affairs topics and, more often than not, are framed in a way that is in accord with what would be their presentation in other, more strictly journalistic contexts. As such, the questions facilitate the performance of 'citizenry', where the individual interests of questioners are usually subordinated to an orientation to a general interest.

The individuality of the questioners is not unimportant, however, and the simplicity and general nature of the questions belies a more complex process of public formation. The performance of citizenry in a programme such as *Q&A* is necessarily constituted through relations of difference: when people take part in *Q&A* they must engage in a process of self-abstraction in order to speak as citizen, but equally the existence and performance of the public needs individualized expressions of difference for it to assume a democratic status. As such, the posing of questions relating to current events facilitates the production of a 'we' with 'our' common concerns, but this unity can only be expressed cumulatively, through the proliferation of individual performances. The discursive construction of a public occurs, then, through a series of performances that map in a provisional way the concatenation of ideas and values that inform what it means to be a member of the Australian public. Indeed, much of the appeal of *Q&A* resides in the witnessing of the performance of this *civic* public.

The appeal, it is suggested, derives from the *absence* of the public from many forms of contemporary mass-mediated political communication, apart from the ubiquitous invocation of public opinion polls, and also the *transformation* of the public through their implication in issues of consumption and lifestyle in various forms of reality television.

We should not understate the importance of members of the public asking questions of their political representatives and other public figures, but we also need to highlight that the studio audience functions crucially as witness to the authority of the panelists. As the identity of the public is generated through relations of difference between questioners, so the identity of the panelists is established through their differentiation from members of the public. The interactions between questioners and panelists are often conducted in a civil and productive manner on *Q&A*; there is rarely the kind of rancour that often permeates political interviews. As we have noted, however, there is little sustained interaction between questioners and panelists, and the questions can be portrayed primarily as vehicles for the enunciations and performances of the high-profile panel members. As such, we do not have here the kind of transformation of witness/expert relations in Mehl's 'public sphere of exhibition' that characterizes forms of reality television, where the classical validation of the expert's authority by a witness has given way to occasions where 'the expert is invited to give general weight to the words of the individuals being examined' (2005, p. 24). *Q&A* panelists are usually sensitive to the interests and concerns of the people who pose questions, often alluding in passing to the questioner in the contexts of their extended answers, but the questions are primarily means for a panelist to demonstrate and validate their expertise. As such, an important function of the studio audience is to facilitate the production of what we might term a democratic spectacle. It is perhaps easily overlooked, given that *Q&A* is predominantly a form of 'talk television', that it is also a highly staged production, facilitating the dramatic presentation of a contemporary civic exercise.

Q&A incorporates Twitter responses from viewers into the body of the programme. While it is often popularly cast as a medium for the dissemination of multitudinous mundane quotidian notices, the reality is that Twitter is a powerful form of social conversation and collaboration that is increasingly harnessed by media corporations and social institutions. According to some early research (Kwak et al. 2010), more than 85 per cent of popular topics on Twitter relates to news stories. Twitter users, however, are conscious that their accounts simultaneously address multiple audiences in a process of 'context collapse' (Marwick and boyd 2010). As Marwick and boyd have noted, Twitter initiates a complex networked audience where, in some instances, the majority of followers can be known, but in other instances, particularly those users who have a 'micro-celebrity' status (Senft 2008), the followers of particular feeds assume a more traditional projected or imagined audience. The primary difference between the networked Twitter audience and the traditional mass media broadcast audience is that viewers are connected not only to the text producer but also to each other (ibid., p. 129).

The Twitter messages sent to the *Q&A* hashtag are incorporated into the broadcast logic of the programme and are screened by the producers before selected messages are broadcast. The individual selected message, then, while available in the Twitter sphere to all who subscribe to the hashtag, is disseminated to the 'traditional' television broadcast audience. It is significant that the tweets relate directly to the current programme discussion and rarely refer to preceding tweets. In this way, the use of Twitter messages in *Q&A* represents a transformation of the traditional broadcast audience because the audience is able to 'talk back' to the participants, but it also involves a restriction of the network potential of Twitter. Of course, while these tweets refer to the programme's discussion, they do not directly engage the participants, who are unaware of them. Rather, the messages are read by the viewing audience and, as such, complicate and enhance the process of viewing and represent a process of communication between audience members, independent of the involvement of the participants.

The tweets are a form of audience participation, but they function differently from the questions posed by the studio audience; they are predominantly observations and judgements on the responses from the panel participants and are usually expressed as statements. While the studio audience's questions are often framed in a way that downplays the individual's involvement in the issue and replicate a conventional journalistic treatment, the tweets are often individualized and strongly expressed opinions. They do, nonetheless, vary in tone and level of engagement with the discussion. Some tweets challenge comments from the panel, dissecting their logic, questioning facts, or interrogating the values that underlie statements. In one episode (*Q&A* 2011b), which included a discussion about the exorbitant level of executive salaries, Gail Kelly, the then CEO of Westpac Bank, declared that she could not defend the high level of salaries of corporate leaders but then proceeded to break down her remuneration into components, prompting the tweet: 'So it's $10 million but because it's in bits it's not really $10 million?' In another programme

(*Q&A* 2011c), featuring a discussion about the Afghanistan War, two consecutive tweets were posted that were critical of the panel discussion: 'Small steps? But it's already been 10 years! How long until some real progress is made??', and then, 'There's no debate on Afghanistan because both major parties have the same policy on it.' Other tweets are more flippant, emotional or comical and directed to the panel in a more personal manner. The episode (*Q&A* 2011e) previously discussed that featured the issue of same-sex marriage included a tweet about a panelist who was a former advisor to Prime Minister Kevin Rudd: 'I want to gay marry Lachlan Harris.'

The identity of the tweeters is also distinguished from the studio audience members, who are identified by name when they ask a question. The Twitter contributors, of course, are identified by their Twitter address, which sometimes includes a genuine name and sometimes is anonymous. The anonymous identity of tweeters and the mediated nature of their messages allow for a greater degree of openness to such contributions: it is easier for people to challenge, condemn and make fun of authority figures. The range of voices from the tweets is also more varied. While studio audience questions are always from 'ordinary' citizens, Twitter messages are from anonymous 'one-off' contributors, regular named individuals, and also sometimes high-profile journalists and public figures. Towards the end of the *Q&A* episode (*Q&A* 2011d) featuring Julia Gillard, the senior press gallery journalist Laurie Oakes tweeted: 'Agree with her or not, this is a pretty impressive performance.' In another episode (*Q&A* 2011g), the government minister Kate Ellis tweeted of the performance of her colleague Tanya Plibersek: 'I'm proud to be on Tanya's side.' The contributions from high-profile individuals are not limited to Twitter messages but also occur through video questions. In the episode (*Q&A* 2011d) featuring the prime minister, Gillard was confronted with a video question from Julian Assange. The occasional propensity of *Q&A* to have video questions from high-profile figures, in turn, feeds into comical tweets on the process of the programme. In an episode (*Q&A* 2011e) featuring a discussion about political change in Libya, one individual tweeted: 'Our next video question is from Col. Gaddafi.'

The studio questions, and also the video questions, assist in the development of the programme's narrative structure, but the tweets act more as a commentary on that narrative. As we have seen, the tweets offer a varied mix of styles: they can make formal political observations, they can use sarcasm and humour in critiques of comments, they can offer fulsome praise, they can be flippant, personal remarks about panelists, they can allude to the programme's structure and process, and they can refer to the tweeter's own private viewing practices. In this way, tweets realize more individualized responses, unlike the public questions of the studio audience, moving more freely between the public realm and the private domain. Their public status does not derive from their collective expression in the same manner as the studio audience questions. This variable mode of expression has attracted criticism from media commentators. Campbell (2011) wrote: 'The Twitter commentariat is possibly the worst thing about *Q&A*. What began as a well-meant gesture of inclusiveness has deteriorated into a scramble to be zingy enough for one's tweet to be displayed onscreen.' The tweets, however, also add to the discursive richness of the programme, allowing the emergence of a different type of public. Despite the criticism about the flippant nature of the Twitter messages, they by no means uniformly replicate a 'populist' response. In an episode (*Q&A* 2011h) where politicians are discussing the current everyday financial difficulties that Australians are facing, they encounter a number of tweets from those 'same' Australians, refusing the interpellation, and challenging the myth of the 'Aussie battler'. One explicitly states, 'The Aussie battler is a tired paradigm', while another directly addresses fellow viewers: 'We've never had it so good. Harden up Aussies.'

The coexistence of a political discourse from both panelists and the studio audience that is sometimes formal and sometimes more informal, together with the colloquial and succinct Twitter messages, video and Internet questions, takes us beyond now well-established observations about the 'conversationalization' (Fairclough 1995a) of political discourse to a recognition of the 'patchwork' character of contemporary mediated political language, where different media, discursive registers, performance styles, and modes of interaction can coexist within the one programme. *Q&A* does not offer us a Habermasian forum, despite its appeal as a site where there is a comparatively extended and informed public discussion of contemporary issues beyond the sound bites of the news and the heated, personal clashes of the political interview. Rather than a dialogical communicative encounter where there is rational, sustained scrutiny of issues with the deployment of a standardized discursive register, we have more of a plurality of modes of interaction, greater variability in performance styles and, in the tweets, the dissemination of a 'swift succession of isolated statements' (Carpenter 2001, p. 223). The tweets may not in themselves yield a sufficient territory for productive public discourse, but they do give the speeches of politicians and other public figures a certain abrasiveness, as that discourse encounters the sharp wit and myriad individual retorts that populate the quotidian contexts of reception of public discourse. An example of this clash between different registers deployed in both the panelists' comments and also in the accompanying tweets occurred in the episode (*Q&A* 2011e) where Josh Thomas posed a question about same-sex marriage. While the shadow education minister Christopher Pyne argued for the inclusion of the study of the Bible in the literature and history curricula of schools, declaring 'you cannot understand our attachment to pluralistic, liberal values if you don't understand our Judeo-Christian heritage', a dissenting tweet was posted, declaring simply that 'glee accepts gay marriage'. This exchange represents a clash between a conversational discourse that draws on contemporary popular culture and a discourse that emanates from the political field, drawing on the nation's historical and traditional moral and cultural framework. This is a real strength of *Q&A*: it has the potential to facilitate productive public discourse precisely through the ability to bring together incommensurate discourses.

We have seen in previous chapters how the production of political habitus is significantly generated through the particular interactions between the political and media fields. In *Q&A*, the noted discursive openness extends to the discourse and the performances of the politicians, who sometimes exploit this feature of the programme to foreground their individual character and personality, and also to signal political and policy positions that differ from those of their own political party. As we have noted, politicians must be more responsive to the immediate feedback from the studio audience and position themselves through reference to a greater number of opinions from both fellow panel members and a multiplicity of interrogators. Politicians themselves, however, also use the 'freedoms' of *Q&A* in a way that helps cast a different light on the practice of politics and the struggles inherent in the performance of individual political subjectivities. That is, we see a greater flexibility in the performances of a political habitus in a programme such as *Q&A*, and the strictures of the political field do not necessarily impose themselves on political performance as much as they might do in other contexts, such as political interviews. This is not to overstate such a feature of the programme; much of the political discourse remains disciplined and divides along conventional party lines, but there is also a more informal, conversational tone to the programme that is also regularly exploited by individual politicians.

In one episode (*Q&A* 2011a), the former Queensland premier Anna Bligh demonstrated particular aptitude both in negotiating an interrogation from a political opponent and in expressing in more personal terms an empathy for the Queensland people who had been affected by the floods earlier in the year. In response to questions from the then Queensland senator, Barnaby Joyce, Bligh outlined why the state did not have disaster insurance and explained that the government had self-insured through the setting aside of funds in the state's budget. She went on to add, in response to political conflict about the imposition of a flood levy:

> I guess what I would say to every federal politician, if you don't think this levy is worth it, come to my state, come and have a look at the people in Tully Heads, come and have a look at the people in Chinchilla and Dalby out in Barnaby's area, come and have a look in the suburbs of Brisbane, and what you'll find are people, just ordinary Australians, who need help, and they expect other Australians to say we are here for you. (Ibid.)

This is another example of successful political discourse where there is a demonstration of political competence in a way that distinguishes the politician within the contexts of the political field – being able to answer confidently and succinctly questions from a political opponent and demonstrate mastery of financial facts and figures – and then the ability to align themselves with the electorate in emotive terms, mobilizing the imagined community of 'ordinary Australians'. The demonstration of such political competence is partly facilitated by the more open interrogative process of *Q&A*, which sometimes allows politicians to be directly questioned by opponents.

Two other prominent examples of individual politicians who have used the more open forum of *Q&A* to differentiate themselves from colleagues in their own political parties are the former prime minister Kevin Rudd and the former opposition leader Malcolm Turnbull, who lost the leadership of the conservative Liberal Party partly over his support for an emissions trading scheme, before becoming prime minister in 2015. In addition, Turnbull distanced himself in his *Q&A* appearance (*Q&A* 2011j) from some comments by his colleagues, who were articulating a more conservative approach to multiculturalism and immigration in the week preceding this particular episode. After one speech, where Turnbull extolled the virtues of Islamic civilization throughout history, his fellow panelist Samah Hadid, Australia's UN youth representative, asked the former party leader: 'Malcolm, do you repeat this in the Coalition party room? Because I think it's necessary.'

Foreign minister Kevin Rudd's appearance (*Q&A* 2011c) on the programme became a major news story when he revealed details of divisions within cabinet when he was prime minister about the shelving of proposed climate change legislation. He stated there were some members of cabinet who had wanted to scrap the Emissions Trading Scheme completely, raising the suggestion that one of those people was the then current prime minister, Julia Gillard. Rudd also declared that the decision was wrong and that he took responsibility for it. His comments provoked an immediate and strong response from fellow panelists and host Tony Jones and prompted a string of Twitter messages. One tweet declared, 'Holy cow! Rudd just admitted he was "wrong" to scrap the ETS.' Another observed, 'This just became a rather large news story', and a third, from a senior television journalist, wryly observed, 'Now there's a yarn.' In his performance on *Q&A*, Rudd also attacked ALP factional leaders for intimidating others and holding back the party. As noted in chapter 3, Rudd's political power as prime minister derived largely from his popular public support, which counterbalanced his lack of a strong factional identity within the Labor Party, but his comments were nonetheless unusual for their frank criticism of the party structure.

Both Turnbull and Rudd have greater freedoms within the contexts of the political field as former party leaders, but the freedom to exercise their individual political habituses was also significantly facilitated by *Q&A*'s more open structure. Part of the appeal of *Q&A* derives from the opportunity for politicians and public figures to be more expansive in their replies, to show more of their personality, and to engage in interactive exchanges with a range of participants in a more relaxed manner. As has been noted, there is less emphasis than in conventional political interviews on the interrogative exchanges and more emphasis on the substantive content of the panelists' comments. Subsequently, there is also more opportunity for politicians to enact an individual political style (Pels 2003) informed by the demonstration of particular expressions of knowledge, character, wit, compassion and eloquence. Turnbull, well known prior to his political career as a high-profile lawyer and businessman, was able to refer to the history of Islamic scholarship during his response to the current debates about the use of foreign aid to fund schools in Indonesia. Rudd was able to demonstrate wit and humour as he outlined the circumstances surrounding the ETS decision in a way that compounded the sense of Rudd 'the individual', who wrestled with the political exigencies he encountered as prime minister. Even though contemporary political process imposes a disciplined and uniform restraint on politicians, Turnbull and Rudd's *Q&A* appearances nonetheless demonstrate the importance of the creation and performance of distinctive political habituses. Such habituses, of course, are not the expression of an independent subjectivity but the mobilization of particular resources of an individual subjectivity in the negotiation of the power relations that are encountered in the political field. These examples attest to the way in which the media field requirements for performance skills in *Q&A* mesh with an individual's political strategy within the political field.

Conclusion

In this chapter we have sought to delineate current affairs forum television from other forms of talk television while also noting the wide range of evaluations of the genre. Some have claimed, for example, that such programming provides a rare and valuable site where citizens can directly engage politicians, while others argue that, despite its promise, it in fact offers seriously circumscribed roles for ordinary people. We investigated the functions of the host, the panelists and the audience in current affairs forum television, noting the way the hosts control the interactions between participants, the performative requirements for panelists, and the differentiated nature of the audience. In the analysis, it was demonstrated how programmes such as *Q&A* offer a particular manifestation of political games. It was observed that the interactions between the studio audience and the panel members are carefully controlled and limited by the host, but *Q&A* nonetheless offers a representation of a civic public in a contemporary political environment where the public is often sidelined. We have argued that the ability of viewers to contribute to the discussion, most notably through the Twitter feed, lends a discursive richness to the programme, offering the means productively to critique the discourse of politicians and other public figures. The sheer flow of opinions in *Q&A* is a significant component of the show's appeal. The analysis has shown that the sense of openness to the discourse and the ability to mark a closure to the exchanges with the rendering of a judgement or the expression of consensus are important mechanisms in the production of the *pleasures* of the texts of current affairs forum television. The basis of the evaluation that occurs in such discursive closures was also noted. It may be that the judgement expressed in the evaluation of the studio audience relates to a particular value position, but equally it may be that the pleasure derives from more conventional expressions of 'gotcha' journalism, as we saw in the WikiLeaks exchange involving Craig Emerson. We have observed nonetheless that the discursive openness of current affairs forum television, together with expressions of collective judgement, is nonetheless in contrast to much televisual political discourse, where an individual opinion is articulated and receives singular jour-nalistic interrogation and scrutiny, often generating a more negative and combative representation of politics. While the conflict between the political and journalistic fields is not expressed as sharply in current affairs forum television as it is in political interviews, it is the 'freedoms' of a programme such as *Q&A* that allow individual politi-cians to negotiate the strictures of the political field and give greater expression to the specificity of their political habitus through their performances and interactions. Ultimately, it is arguable whether current affairs forum television fulfils the 'normative aspirations' of the genre, but it nonetheless offers a valuable media site where the evolving dynamics of contemporary political communication can be played out.

7

Political Celebrity Interviews

Introduction

Successful political leadership is now predicated on the ability of politicians to assume a general cultural appeal and to generate that appeal through performances across an increasingly differentiated media landscape. Political authority cannot derive solely from mastery of the political field, and to some extent it is now not even sufficient that political leaders are competent media performers; they must also exhibit a *character* that resonates with the public. Leaders vary in the degree to which they cultivate a general cultural appeal, but increasingly political authority stems from the ability of individuals to possess a personality and charisma that lends them something of a celebrity status. Such cultural appeal is based upon media and public scrutiny of the private and everyday life of the politician in addition to their public duties. The appeal of celebrity status stems partly from the apparent autonomy of that individual from the political system, although in reality leaders must engage in complex and subtle negotiations between such cultural appeal and authority within the political field. The cultivation of political celebrity is facilitated by the fact that politics increasingly escapes the confines of conventional news journalism. Political interviews and discussion are not limited to serious current affairs programmes but also appear across a range of so-called soft media, such as breakfast television, online discussion forums, chat shows and FM radio. In addition, politicians convey a particular character through their use of social media, most notably Twitter. The production of political celebrity within this post-broadcast media landscape (Prior 2006; Wilson 2011) poses particular challenges, as public desire for a coherent and authentic political subjectivity coexists uneasily with performances across a disparate media field.

Political celebrity interviews are prominent means by which leaders attempt to present a more humanized persona and cultivate the popularity associated with a celebrity status. Such media performances on chat shows and other entertainment-based media have ceased to be unusual or rare encounters and are now prevalent and important moments during election campaigns. It was something of a novelty when Bill Clinton played his saxophone on *The Arsenio Hall Show* and appeared on MTV in 1992, but now such appearances are commonplace: Barack Obama was interviewed on programmes such as *The Daily Show* and *The View* during the 2012 presidential campaign. Such appearances can enhance public perceptions of political leaders, given they can highlight an individual's authentic and charismatic personality, but, as with all mediated interrogative encounters, they can also backfire, as the British prime minister David Cameron discovered when he was unable to answer questions about British history on *The Late Show with David Letterman*. Of course, such media performances are not the only occasions where politicians cultivate their celebrity status. Leaders also demonstrate their charisma and their connection with the people through a range of public appearances, such as school and shopping mall visits and attendance at football matches. Such events 'ground' politicians in popular culture, allowing them to demonstrate their familiarity with the pleasures and stresses of everyday life, and they also provide a stage upon which leaders can display their particular personality. The former Australian prime minister Julia Gillard, for example, is a passionate supporter of the Western Bulldogs football club and was often filmed at matches.

The chapters in this book have so far illuminated the largely combative exchanges between politicians and journalists across interviews, debates and press conferences. In this final chapter, we investigate a different kind of interrogative encounter in political celebrity interviews, which is marked by greater degrees of collaboration between interviewers and interviewees in the construction of personalized narratives. Such interviews are not devoid of power struggles or active negotiations of the particular generic conventions, but here we see that the 'game' often involves a greater homology of interests between the political and media fields. Political celebrity interviews facilitate a different kind of subjectivity, rendering the interviewees more 'human', as the questioning extends beyond the confines of the machinations of the political field. Equally, they help us to reconsider the promotional and performative basis of all political interrogative encounters and prompt us to consider how 'celebrity' is now intrinsic to all political leadership. This chapter will discuss the nature of political celebrity, noting that its efficacy is founded on successful management of a representative gap between governors and the governed; the translation of popular appeal into authority within the political field; and negotiation of the tension that arises from the presentation of a coherent and authentic persona within a complex and fragmented mediated political environment. In this sense, we will demonstrate that political celebrity is not a singularly positive phenomenon but can also be the grounds for suspicion and criticism from the public and, most pointedly, political journalists. Finally, the features of political celebrity interviews will be highlighted through an analysis of Barack Obama's appearances on *The View* in 2012, once by himself and another time with his wife, Michelle. As has been stated previously, the choice of this case study for analysis has been prompted both by Obama's high-profile status as the US president and, in this particular case, as a result of his celebrity appeal. In this way, it is not necessarily representative of all such interviews, but the focus on Obama's performances on one popular and long-running programme allows for a greater depth of analysis.

The Contexts of Political Celebrity

While the articulation of 'celebrity' and 'politics' still carries with it a sense of novelty, political celebrity is a well-established historical phenomenon. As van Krieken (2012, p. 109) notes: 'Celebrity and politics are Siamese twins, for the simple reason that both are about visibility, recognition and esteem: where popular politics and any approximation of democracy was, there shall celebrity be.' Political celebrity predates the contemporary obsession with film stars, models, sports stars, singers and other types of celebrities (ibid., p. 99). Modern political celebrity can be traced back to the nineteenth and early twentieth century, when burgeoning democratic momentum coalesced with new forms of mass media, and particularly photographic media. These developments enabled (and indeed required) politicians and other prominent public figures, such as royalty, to present a mode of subjectivity, and to establish relationships with the public, that privileged notions of individuality, authenticity and familiarity. The political, cultural and media milieu of the latter part of the nineteenth century in the United States facilitated profound development in both the character of public identity and the relationship between the public and private spheres. As Ponce de Leon (2002) notes, this period saw public figures use media innovations, such as the interview, to cope with an increasingly assertive press and to exercise strategies of self-promotion that emphasized a natural and authentic identity grounded in a successful and harmonious private life.

The burgeoning modernization of the United States in the latter part of the nineteenth and the early part of twentieth century gave rise to a paradoxical orientation towards public identity that continues to animate and problematize contemporary celebrity status. On the one hand, the idea of an authentic, coherent public identity that captured the essence of an individual invoked a notion of the self expressed in secular Romanticism. This self was able to rise above social constraints and was characterized by the transparent expression of a constancy of behaviour across the boundaries of public and private life (King 2008, p. 118). On the other hand, economic and social opportunities provided people with greater freedom to fashion their own identity, and this 'aroused a profound suspicion of appearances – including a suspicion of the personas that public figures projected in the public sphere' (Ponce de Leon 2002, p. 41). As Ponce de Leon notes, the artifice of the public sphere meant that the real self of an individual could only be viewed in private, and this 'sparked a heightened interest in the private lives of public figures, and encouraged writers, reporters, and biographers to employ new techniques that made their subjects appear more realistic' (ibid.). This paradoxical orientation towards public identity was also manifested in the figure of the new modern politician. Increased dissatisfaction with partisan politics gave rise to a desire for 'real' individuals who could rise above party machinations and corruption while also possessing appropriate character, knowledge and skills:

> In the first quarter of the twentieth century, then, one can see in American politics the pursuit of a delicate balance between pragmatism and idealism, achieved only by a certain kind of individual character, with particular life experience, values and beliefs that needed to be demonstrated as being firm enough to withstand the corrosive effects of organized political life. (van Krieken 2012, p. 107)

Political celebrity not only derives from a particular historical context but is also an expression of intrinsic features of political subjectivity and political representation. Such an argument runs directly counter to common charges that political celebrity hinders a proper relationship of democratic representativeness (Crick 2002; Meyrowitz 1985; Postman 1987; Zolo 1992). Critiques of the prevalence of political celebrity argue that an undue emphasis on personal image and superficial matters marginalizes more substantive political issues that are of greater direct relevance to the concerns and welfare of the people. Equally, it is claimed that, while the individual distinctiveness of political celebrities may attract attention, it also invalidates their ability to be able to be true representatives of the people. As John Street (2004) has noted, acknowledging the historical precedents of political celebrity tempers, but does not necessarily undermine, such criticisms, and an argument must be marshalled to demonstrate that 'the celebrity politician is not in fact an exaggerated form or exceptional form of all political representation, but rather characteristic of the nature of political representation generally' (ibid., p. 449).

Such an argument is based upon an understanding of the necessarily symbolic and aesthetic dimensions of political representation that are always constituted through negotiations of both identification and distinction (see Ankersmit 2002, 2003; Pels 2003; Street 2004). There is always a substitutional basis to representation generally, and political representation specifically, that must incorporate judgements about the appearance or fit between the representative and the represented, even in accounts of political representation that foreground an understanding of representativeness based on the idea of 'acting for' instead of a more mimetic-based 'standing for' (see Pitkin 1967; Street 2004, pp. 442–3). As such, from the point of view of both those who are represented and their representatives, aesthetic judgements about political image and performance are legitimate features of any assessment of political representation. Street (ibid., p. 445) can then argue that 'Celebrity politics is a code for the performance of representations through the gestures and media available to those who wish to claim "representativeness".' The substitutional basis of political representation means that there will always be a representational gap, a negotiation of identification and distinction, which equates to the appeal and power of celebrities who are able to forge connections with their fans while also distinguishing themselves through their talent and/or appearance. Pels (2003, p. 49) argues with regard to celebrity politicians that: 'Political style is the concept that simultaneously marks this representative gap and bridges it in a novel fashion.' He further maintains that celebrity politicians negotiate the representative gap in a personalized democracy not by demonstrating that they are exactly the same as their constituents, but by exhibiting an *authenticity* that is consistently expressive of both the individuality of the politician and the will of the people they come to represent.

The negotiation of this representative gap is variously played out across the terrains of politics and popular media culture and manifested in a range of subject positions. We are familiar with those individuals from the entertainment industry, such as Bono and George Clooney, who use their celebrity status in political campaigning. The focus here is on those who have assumed political office, but there still remains a diversity of subject positions open to celebrity politicians, stemming both from the nature of their status and from their position within the political field. Liesbet van Zoonen's (2005, pp. 82–5) typology of the personae of celebrity politicians maps the range of such subject positions across axes of political insider/outsider and ordinary/special celebrity. Some conventional political leaders are obviously political insiders who assume celebrity status merely because of their leadership position. Other high-profile leaders, such as Barack Obama and Kevin Rudd, are conventional politicians, but they are attributed with a relative degree of autonomy from the strictures of the party political system and attract higher than normal levels of media and public attention because of their personality or charisma. It is difficult to derive status as a political celebrity as an outsider, but van Zoonen identifies the former US presidential candidate Ross Perot as one such figure. Finally, the former California governor Arnold Schwarzenegger is identified as the exemplar of a political outsider with special celebrity status.

The celebrity politician must also manage their political identity across the spectrum of the public and private spheres. While critics of the phenomenon of the celebrity politician may bemoan journalistic intrusions into the private lives of political leaders, the noted demand for the consistent expression of an authentic self is satisfied with the display of the politician across different 'spheres of action' (Corner 2003). John Corner (ibid., p. 73) has captured such a terrain, referring to the 'sphere of political institutions and processes', by which he means the internal processes of the political field, such as political party organization and administrative processes; the 'sphere of public and popular', which is the collection of mediated settings where politicians are publicly visible; and the 'private sphere', which is the politician's home life, friends, leisure activities and biographical history. Stanyer (2013, p. 15) has suggested that Corner's 'private sphere' would be better comprehended as the politician's 'personal sphere', and he has delineated the personal sphere into three overlapping domains: an individual politician's 'inner life' – their lifestyle choices, personal tastes and modes of behaviour, health and finances;

their 'domain of relationships' – those with family, friends and lovers; and their 'spatial domain' – not only their family home but also other spaces they inhabit in a private capacity, such as holiday destinations.

The performance of the celebrity politician, then, extends well beyond a stereotypical parade of talk shows, tabloid photo spreads, and 'meet and greets' with an adoring public, and instead traverses a complex terrain and web of relationships involving the sphere of institutional politics, a diversity of media settings, and the features and spaces that make up an individual's life story and everyday personal existence. We need to understand political celebrity in the ways that it is implicated in the exigencies of the political system, how it is variously exercised in an extraordinarily differentiated news, entertainment and social media landscape, and how individual resources of personality, knowledge and rhetoric are mobilized across such a diversity of institutional and communicative encounters.

The 'Celebrity-in-Chief'

Politicians may have always engaged to some degree with the popular culture of the time to enhance their electoral appeal, but we can also note that it is a relatively recent trend that politicians are now regularly interviewed on 'non-political' television programmes, such as late night, daytime talk shows and political satire programmes, as well as on social media sites. During the 2008 US presidential election campaign, both John McCain and Barack Obama appeared twice on *The Tonight Show with Jay Leno* and *The Late Show with David Letterman*. Such appearances are but a necessary part of a broader media campaign for political candidates which also includes a presence on the Internet and social media platforms. While a media hierarchy persists in the reportage of politics, the traditional news media are no longer the exclusive domain in which politics is discussed. Politics is always a cultural phenomenon, but, more so than ever before, politics mixes with celebrity culture, and entertainment media can set the political news agenda, as politicians seek out an increasingly disparate and politically disengaged public. As Jeffrey Jones (2005, p. 7) has noted: 'We have passed a point in which entertainment television would only occasionally dip into politics....Politics is now clearly an integral part of entertainment programming these days, and as such, its cultural location has broken the traditional bounded nature of programming assumptions about politics.'

Barack Obama, more so than any other US president, has actively cultivated such types of television media. Even though US presidents have a history of actively courting Hollywood and the entertainment media, the title of 'Celebrity-In-Chief' (Schroeder 2004) has been particularly employed as a criticism of Obama's political leadership (Herman 2012). Obama was the first sitting US president *outside* of an election campaign to appear on a late-night talk show when he was interviewed on *The Tonight Show with Jay Leno* in May 2009. He has appeared several times on *The Daily Show with Jon Stewart*, he has promoted science education on the *Mythbusters* programme, and he has even danced with Ellen DeGeneres on her daytime television programme. Obama has actively sought out online interview opportunities and has been interviewed by YouTube stars (McCarthy 2015). The president famously obtained the political support of Oprah Winfrey after participating in her programme during the 2008 presidential campaign, and he has appeared a number of times on the popular women's day-time talk show *The View*, both with and without his wife Michelle.

Barack Obama is the celebrity politician *par excellence*. Such is his fame that he has been described as a 'supercelebrity' (Kellner 2009, p. 717). Not even Vladimir Putin's bare-chested, tank-driving exploits match the global media and public fascination with Obama. Obama's celebrity status is based upon, but extends well beyond, the political capital that derives from his status as US president. It was, and continues to be, based upon his ability to communicate a particular political rhetoric, and it is also embodied in his habitus: his life history and family life, his looks and character, his personality and demeanour.

Obama has successfully employed this celebrity appeal for political effect, most famously in the 2008 presidential campaign, which was noted for its extraordinary online mobilization of public opinion and the use of the Internet to raise small donations from a multitude of citizens (Cornfield 2010; Gulati 2010). Obama had more than 2 million friends on Facebook, and the campaign compiled an email listserv of over 10 million addresses. His campaign was given impetus by support from professional musicians such as Will.i.am, who produced music videos, as well as videos of support from ordinary people (Kellner and Kim 2009). The most famous performance was the YouTube phenomenon 'Obama Girl', which featured a young woman singing of her love for Obama, interspersed with footage of the candidate. Obama's fame during the campaign spilled out of the media sphere and literally onto the streets, with graffiti, urban art, stickers and posters extolling the candidate not only in US cities but also in metropolises abroad (Linthicum 2008).

Obama's celebrity power at this time was difficult to counter, but the McCain campaign actually sought to distance Obama from the electorate by turning his celebrity status into a negative issue (Alexander 2010). After Obama's return from a triumphant visit to Europe, the McCain campaign ran a television advertisement that featured the punch line 'He's the biggest celebrity in the world, but is he ready to lead?' The advertisement generated controversy and criticism of the McCain campaign, but it also triggered questions about Obama's political experience and character. Mobilizing negative connotations associated with 'celebrity', and linking them to Obama, became a prominent feature of the McCain campaign prior to the Democratic convention. As Alexander (2010, p. 416) noted: 'If they can metaphorically frame Obama's acceptance speech as celebrity, none of his rhetorical skills will matter.' This underlines that there is no necessary meaning ascribed to celebrity status in politics and, instead, it is a site of struggle where values of popularity, authenticity, rhetoric and performance are contested and inflected for particular political interests.

The focus here is on Barack Obama's celebrity status and his political celebrity interviews, but the US president is not alone in a growing recognition of the political importance of courting entertainment media. Neveu (2005, p. 323) goes so far as to note that, in France, 'most politicians' appearances on the traditional analogue channels now tend to be on chat shows rather than on programmes specifically dedicated to the coverage of politics.' In Australia, when a leading political journalist criticized the then opposition leader, Kevin Rudd, about his strategy of targeting an unconventional section of the media, Rudd's reply was explicit: 'Guess what? There's a whole bunch of people out there who you may be surprised to know don't watch *Insiders* but do listen to FM radio. And my job as the alternative prime minister is to communicate with the entire country' (Hawthorne 2007). Politicians can be criticized for targeting 'soft media' interviews so that they are not subject to difficult interrogations, but equally we need to acknowledge the changing television and media environment, where there is a proliferation of viewing choices and where established social conventions of regularly watching nightly political programmes are a less common experience. In addition, as Rudd's comment indicates, soft media talk shows garner large audiences. This simple political reality is underlined when we consider not only that politicians are appearing on entertainment-based talk shows with greater frequency but also that substantial campaign advertising expenditure is targeted at such programmes (Baum 2005, p. 231).

There remains, however, considerable debate about the relative merits of 'hard news' and 'soft news' political programming. This debate is informed by broader concerns about the deleterious transformation of political journalism and the desiccation of the public sphere. For some, the trend of 'tabloidization' and greater infotainment in political reportage leads to less political content, greater public cynicism about politics, and a reduced focus on parliament (Bourdieu 1998; Sampson 1996). Others have maintained that transformations in political reportage have expanded our ideas of what constitutes politics beyond its traditional institutional manifestations and have contributed to a healthy scepticism towards political elites; politics now more directly addresses everyday public concerns and communicates to a broader range of the electorate (Hartley 1996; Jones 2005; McNair 2006). More specifically, with regard to television talk shows, it is difficult to determine the levels of political knowledge that viewers may gain from soft news programming and the kinds of effects produced by such shows (Baum 2003; Prior 2006). Some research demonstrates that, 'among low-awareness individuals', increased viewing of talk shows is linked to more 'likeability ratings' for politicians and, significantly in an increasingly polarized political environment, a greater probability of voting for candidates not previously preferred (Baum 2005, p. 228). It is also difficult to assess simply how much politics appears on entertainment-based talk shows. On the one hand, it is a common assumption that, when politicians conduct political celebrity interviews, there is less discussion of politics and more biographical and lifestyle talk (Neveu 2005). On the other hand, some research indicates a surprisingly high amount of political discussion on such programmes, despite subsequent news media reportage that focuses more on personal performance and disclosure (House 2011).

While we should not underestimate the overtly political content of programmes such as *The View*, it remains the case that 'the contrast between even the toughest of E-talk show interviews and typical traditional political interviews is stark' (Baum 2005, p. 230). As we will see, political celebrity interviewers usually have the priority of facilitating entertaining exchanges rather than engendering conflict through the thorough investigation of a subject. Political celebrity interviews in this sense allow politicians to be relatively freed from the constraints of the political field; they are spaces where political authenticity can be produced. We should not overlook the fact, however, that the *media field* imposes strictures on politicians in celebrity political interviews, which dictate a particular kind of 'performance' and circumscribe the discursive range of politics, making it harder to use and dissect the sometimes necessarily technical features of politics or to express conflict, anger, etc. As Neveu (2005, p. 332) notes: '... politics cannot simply be analysed as a game of identification with nice or smiling people. As an institutionalized realm of action affecting society, with its rules and imperatives and cognitive and normative dimensions, politics and professional politicians need other standards of evaluation than considerations based on psychology, lifestyle or emotional closeness.'

This discussion, oscillating between perceived strengths and weaknesses of political celebrity interviews, only highlights the multiple sites of politics in contemporary mediated society, with their accompanying requirements for politicians to possess a discursive and performative flexibility. Politics has been transformed by mediatization (Strömbäck 2008), and this has had significant ramifications for the operation of the public sphere. Any attempt to impose 'correct' places for the institutional practice and reportage of politics, or any representation that privileges the 'political' or 'media' contexts of contemporary politics, misses the substantive reality that political practice is necessarily rooted in specific institutions *and also* immersed in the swirling currents of media content and everyday life. The public meanings of politics will continue to arise from the negotiations between such institutional dictates and cultural contexts, and this occurs even in the frothy and friendly encounters of a programme such as *The View*.

Barack and Michelle Obama on *The View*

The View is an Emmy-award winning daytime talk television programme that featured veteran journalist Barbara Walters (before her retirement in 2014), comedian Whoopi Goldberg, and a panel of other co-hosts and was first screened in August 1997. By 2010 it was attracting 3.8 million viewers, slightly more than the leading Sunday political talk programme, NBC's *Meet the Press*, which attracts about 3.7 million viewers each week. The programme usually features an opening 'Hot Topics' segment where the panelists discuss current issues, before a celebrity interview and other segments on topics such as fashion and food, and then a segment titled 'Question of the Day', often prompted by contributions from the audience. Part of the appeal of *The View* derives from the interactions between the panel of co-hosts, whose generational, political, ethnic and professional background diversity contributes to its popularity among a broad range of viewers. Walters, who founded the programme with executive producer Bill Geddie, had been co-host from the outset, but there have been a number of different staff changes over the years, some of which were accompanied by controversy.

As a daytime talk programme, *The View* covers mainly light entertainment and celebrity news and issues, but the show has devoted more time to political interviews since the 2008 US presidential campaign. Hillary Clinton was the first candidate to take part in the programme, in October 2007, but it was Barack Obama's appearance in March 2008 that made a popular and political impact with favourable reviews. *The View* devoted the entire hour of the programme to Obama (now the norm with political interviewees) in contrast to the 20 minutes allotted to Clinton's appearance (House 2011, p. 39). As House notes:

> The political debates on the show became increasingly heated leading up to the election and cemented *The View's* status as a worthy contender in the political media game and potential as an agenda-setter. In the days following the election, *The View* devoted little attention to celebrity news and guests and instead, continued to keep the conversation geared toward the political. (Ibid., p. 41)

The programme attracted some criticism for its tough treatment of politicians and their spouses, most notably an interview with the Republican candidate Senator John McCain and his wife Cindy. After her appearance on the show, Cindy McCain was heard to have said on the campaign trail that Walters and the others had 'picked our bones clean' (Steinberg 2008).

The View, as such, is an exemplar of the immersion of politics in soft-news television programming, where it coexists in an increasingly naturalized manner with popular culture content. As Geddie has said of *The View*: 'We stray from serious to silly in a heartbeat. But I think it's a place where you get that interesting combination of where the candidates stand on the issues, and who they are as people' (Steinberg 2008). This plastic generic status gives rise to some interesting classifications, with one journalist describing *The View* as 'a halfway house in between a CNN interrogation and the razzing of *The Daily Show with Jon Stewart*' (Stanley 2008). There is a limit, however, to the show's coverage of politics. Walters has said daytime viewers 'don't want to be hit over the head with politics', and Rosie O'Donnell's attempt to steer the programme towards greater political content has been judged to have backfired (Chozick 2010).

As noted, *The View* has broad generational, ethnic and political appeal, reflecting the diversity of the panel, but the programme is defined primarily as for women: 79 per cent of the show's audience is female, with a median age of 59 (Chozick 2010). This particular gendered identity is, of course, signalled by the all-female panel, but also by the more informal discourse, where panelists often interrupt each other, laugh and add affirmations. As we will see, *The View* is not free of expressions of conflict, but its more consensually oriented exchanges distinguish it from those in many of the other interactive formats analysed in previous chapters. As such, of course, this distinction highlights the equally strongly gendered character of the other political talk formats that were examined, where men dominated as both interviewers and interviewees, and the discourse was strongly rule-governed, and conflict was foregrounded. The gendered identity of *The View* also stems from its scheduling in the daytime, which traditionally was a domain for programmes perceived to be popular with women, notably soap operas. As has just been noted, a virtue of *The View* is the way its particular generic identity allows it to engage with politics in a different way from other more strictly 'political' programmes, casting a different perspective on political leaders and issues. We will see this in the following analysis, where the gendered habitus and political appeal of Barack Obama is represented through his opportunity to appear, alongside his wife, as the only male on an all-female stage, where he talks of his family.

The political celebrity interview is flagged as a different kind of interrogative encounter from the very introduction of the interviewee(s). The esteem afforded to the interviewee is signalled by the familiar conventions of an extended introduction by the interviewer, followed by applause from the studio audience when the celebrity enters. This entry parallels introductory conventions for speeches and awards and other forms of address but is in contrast to political interviews, where an interviewee is already seated and the introduction and greeting is more perfunctory. The political celebrity interview, then, is immediately cast as a more explicitly *performative* encounter, where the *presentation* of the subject is foregrounded. The act of entering the communicative arena is also a feature of press conferences, where it is a means of expressing political authority, but press conferences do not conventionally feature active and positive responses from the assembled 'audience' of journalists, and the politician initiates and directs the interrogative encounter.

The entry of Barack and Michelle Obama on *The View* was striking, with the president and the first lady holding hands and the president also carrying a gift basket (*The View* 2012a). The Obamas displayed a smiling demeanour during their casual and leisurely entry, waving to acknowledge the standing ovation of the studio audience. Their appearance, as such, is immediately coded as highly personal and *social*, and this is reinforced by an extended greeting of the panel with kisses and embraces. In addition, President Obama surprisingly initiates the 'interview' with an explanation that the gift basket is for Barbara Walters, who is celebrating a birthday. He explains that Walters 'pilfers' White House souvenirs on her visits and so he is saving her the trouble in any subsequent visits, with the offering of White House napkins, playing cards, golf balls and beer. The humorous 'chiding' of Walters establishes an intimate and friendly rapport, and this is facilitated by the physical organization of the participants, with the Obamas seated in the middle of the lounge set and the panelists on either side of them. The 'layout' of the set, then, establishes an open, equal and personal relationship between interviewers and interviewees, quite unlike the political celebrity interviews of David Letterman, for example, where a desk or other furniture exacerbates the physical distance between the participants and signals their place in the hierarchy of roles. Before a question and answer exchange is even initiated, *The View* is able to convey the dynamics of political celebrity, which requires *both* an acknowledgement of difference through expressions of adulation *and* the formations of relations of equivalence through an intimate and casual discourse of friendship.

Obama's political celebrity status derives from a complex composite and performative balance of authority within the political field, ability in the media field, and the enactment of a particular habitus and display of charisma. Political celebrity is an amalgam of capacities: bodies of knowledge, communicative skills – ranging from persuasion to empathy, which can mobilize public opinion – physical looks and demeanour. It carries within it a distinctiveness that is tied to individual character, and it also exhibits a relative autonomy from the political field, deriving from an appeal or fame generated within the media field. Equally, political celebrity is intimately incorporated within notions of political competence: both require the ability to exhibit a sense of distinctiveness while also being attuned to specific demands of individual communicative encounters. As we saw in the chapter on political interviews, a pre-existing political authority and, in this case, celebrity status, provide an individual such as Obama with access to privileged spaces within the media field (such as *The View*), but that political celebrity status must continue to be animated and confirmed through performance. This performance is facilitated by the generic status of the programme, which prepares viewers with expectations about a political celebrity interview, and, as has just been noted, *The View* from its outset structures a subject position of political celebrity. But how is that identity realized through the interrogative processes of the interview? To what extent do the questions and answers address and make manifest the various bodies of knowledge, domains of action, and display and dissection of character?

The celebrity status of Obama derives partly from his mastery of the media field – in stark contrast to his predecessor, Obama is comfortable and proficient in the media spotlight – but throughout his interviews on *The View* there are surprisingly few explicit references to his fame or celebrity. Of course, his status *implicitly* informs discussion: as we will see, much of the talk about the president's domestic arrangements is informed by the negotiation between the confirmation of their ordinary and familiar dynamics and the fascination with the extraordinary status of the Obamas as the 'first family'. The interviews, however, do not dwell on his popularity or on acclamation of his performance in his (political) field, as we might see in celebrity interviews that feature an actor or a singer. Political celebrity, in this sense, is a more fraught and fragile phenomenon than other forms of celebrity where the mobilization of public unity engendered through their popularity is less problematic. One particular moment that does highlight the celebrity of Barack and Michelle Obama occurs early in their joint appearance, where the president recalls his first 'date' with Michelle. He tells the story of their purchasing ice cream and sitting in the street where they first kissed, the spot now commemorated with a plaque. This highlights, significantly, that Obama's political celebrity derives from his relationship with his wife, their romance, and their status as a 'power couple'.

The celebrity political interview often features more extended narrative responses from the interviewee, where there is an account of an incident or experience that discloses to the viewer something entertaining or telling about the person and their life. These extended answers, facilitated by more open questions from the interviewer, highlight how the content of discussion of celebrity interviews is not so much the interrogation of contestable issues but the presentation and promotion of the character of the interviewee. Often such stories provide detail about the 'back-stage' life of the celebrity, either from their personal life or from their activities. Such disclosures highlight the paradox of celebrityhood, where there is a desire for further, often more intimate, revelations from already highly exposed individuals in order to authenticate and deepen the image we have of them. One such example from *The View* interview with the Obamas involved the president telling a literally 'back-stage' story of his daughters' behaviour immediately before his appearance at the Democratic national convention. The account is offered in detail here.

> *Hasselbeck*: We were talking about the kids, the girls back stage. And, what, Malia is 14 and Sasha is 11? Is it true that before you spoke at the Democratic national convention that you had a kind of really special moment with them? Can you share?

> *Obama*: This is an example of how they make sure I don't take myself too seriously. So we're back stage and it's all covered up and people are whispering into their various headphones and this and that, and I'm about to go out on cue, and suddenly I see Malia and Sasha and they're like spinning around. And I said, 'What are you guys doing?', and they said, 'This is just like in the *Hannah Montana* movie, right before Hannah goes out and it's all enclosed like this, and then Billy Ray turns to her and says "Go get them baby".' And then they start performing the whole scene and cracking themselves up, and then suddenly there's: 'The President of the United States...', and I had to walk out [*pause*] thinking about Hannah Montana. That was what was on my mind at the convention, so...[*laughter*] (*The View* 2012a)

This apparently trivial story contains several features of a political celebrity interview and is a good example of how Obama performs his political character in such encounters. Firstly, the story *domesticates* politics: it grounds the drama and importance of a national convention in a sense of the ordinary, and it naturalizes or familiarizes the professional practice of politics through the articulation of Obama's performance of his political duties with his interactions with his daughters. Secondly, the story establishes a relation of equivalence between politics and *popular culture*. The invocation of *Hannah Montana* enables the political experience to assume something of the popularity of the movie through its shared narrative sequence of the 'back-stage moment'. In Obama's solo appearance on the programme, however, he was asked 'What do you know about popular culture?', and his answers in the following quiz (which included questions such as 'What is the controversial sex book that is on the bedside table of millions of women?') displayed a less than comprehensive knowledge. Thirdly, the performance of the narrative is an opportunity for the president of the United States to engage in a colloquial discourse. Obama is a skilled speaker, but here he deliberately adopts the register ('cracking themselves up') and rhythms and syntax of a conversational narrative ('and then Billy Ray...and then they start...and then suddenly'). He also pauses towards the end of his narrative to heighten the comic effect. Fourthly, the story is a way for Obama both to undercut his own seriousness and, by so doing, show a sense of humility and underline his political competence: he is at ease in such momentous occasions and he is able immediately and fluently to move from such back-stage distractions to an impressive performance of public oratory.

The celebrity status of politicians is often realized through expressions of self-deprecation, and this is a frequent strategy of Obama throughout his appearances on *The View*. The popularity and power of the celebrity politician is manifested in their freedom ironically to belittle or make fun of themselves, whether it be their appearance, their mannerisms or demeanour, or even their own political skills and performance. When talking about his use of Twitter, the president noted: 'I do it once in a while but, as Michelle says, I'm too long-winded for 140 characters' (*The View* 2012b). Similarly, when on the programme with his wife, Obama, surrounded by the women on the panel, declared: 'I told folks, I'm just supposed to be eye candy here for you guys' (*The View* 2012a). In contrast, a struggle in conventional political interviews revolves around the maintenance and enhancement of the reputation of the interviewee. Self-deprecation can be a useful strategy in political communication because it defuses conflict, the use of humour robbing an interrogator of the power of their charge. Such a strategy, however, is usually a resource only of those powerful enough to withstand such 'attacks' without damage to their argument or reputation, or of those who are already in a weak or marginal position and who seek favour or mercy from more powerful others.

The View interviews with the president of the United States may not focus substantially on Obama's fame and celebrity status, but they do nonetheless feature extended discussion about the *individual*, his character and everyday life. That is, they offer significant scrutiny of the *habitus* of Barack Obama. As was outlined in chapter 1, habitus refers to the ways in which structural factors and social conditions inform subjectivity, manifested in appearance, dress, accent, manners, deportment and interpersonal communicative capacities, and also how such 'individual' features are mobilized in the contexts of everyday and work life (Bourdieu 2002). Unlike conventional political interviews, where there is an exclusive interpellation of the professional identity of an interviewee, here in *The View* the panelists pepper the president with questions about his character, his likes and dislikes, his lifestyle and life history, his parenting skills, and his family and their domestic arrangements. Of course, the desire to know the individual is partly informed by the prestigious public office he holds, but across the two interviews analysed here there are very few questions about what it is like to be *president* and what it is like to work in the Oval Office. Instead, Obama is asked questions such as: 'Are you romantic?'; 'What will you be doing in five years from now?'; and 'I love the way you talk about the girls and the sports. What kind of rules do you have in parenting?' There is considerable discussion in the joint appearance about the dilemma of organizing everyday life and maintaining relationships, given the family's extraordinary status. The Obamas were asked, for example, about their evening dining routine.

> *Behar*: You want to have dinner when you can with the family. And I know that you're so busy.
>
> *Barack Obama*: Every night if we're home at 6.30 we have dinner.
>
> *Behar*: That's nice. But you don't bring your stuff to the table. Right? What happens to you during the day? So how do you know what his day is like? Do you pillow talk, or what goes on?
>
> *Michelle Obama*: We go over the broad aspects of all of our days – that's what we talk about, and he's usually last. The girls are like, 'So what did you do?', and then you get it, and then it's like, 'OK Dad that's enough'. Um, but it's usually after, because the girls take Beau out for a walk, and we usually get a little bit of time at the table just by ourselves, and then that's when we kinda catch up on serious stuff, but sometimes a lot of the things that Barack feels, like those moments with families, we want to talk to the girls about those things as well – you know, just let them understand first of all what their Dad is doing every day and what's going on in people's lives. So you know we're always having that lesson, 'You were blessed, you better understand this, I don't want to hear you complaining because there are people with real issues and understand that the world is complex and difficult in ways for people that you will never know, so you gotta, you've gotta know about these things and show empathy.' So it's really important to have those conversations. (*The View* 2012a)

As we see here, the appeal of celebrity political interviews derives partly from revelations about the management of the private and public realms and the coexistence of the extraordinary and the ordinary in everyday life. The interviews generate pleasures through disclosures about the 'back-stage' life of the political persona where we hear (if not in specific detail) about how their public lives impact on them personally, as well as pleasures associated with the confirmation of the domestic – the family dinner discourse, the walking of the dog, etc.

Part of Obama's public popularity and political success also stems from his personal communicative skills and his deportment, his apparent ease in his own body. His perceived ability to 'connect' with a broad range of Americans (notwithstanding his famous comments in the 2008 presidential campaign about people in small towns bitterly clinging to guns or religion or anti-immigrant sentiment) is seen to have derived partly from his diverse background and life history, and this facility is often literally embodied in gestures and other non-verbal communication, as one journalist noted in a report on Obama's appearance on *The View*:

> Mr. Obama used body language to bridge the gender gap. The candidate who is sometimes attacked by feminists as a golden youth passing over them on his way to the old boys' club reminded the co-hosts that he was 'surrounded by women' at home.
> He patted Ms. Behar's arm and whispered so intimately into Ms. Walters's ear that Ms. Hasselbeck accused them of 'canoodling.' Mr. Obama is an effective speaker, but he is just as smooth at wordless communication: he mixed a cool and somewhat princely demeanor with warm smiles and touches. (Stanley 2008)

Obama's effective non-verbal communication embodies both his confidence in his own political character and his ability to demonstrate a 'common touch', which is not only generically appropriate in such celebrity political interviews but expressive of a political *authenticity* that is crucial for any political leader. As van Leeuwen reminds us, 'authenticity', while a multifaceted term, can be traced to social semiotic understandings of modality. In this sense, authenticity ironically does not carry an 'objective' status: it is 'concerned more with the moral or artistic authority of the representation than with its truth or reality' (van Leeuwen 2001, p. 396). This, in turn, explains why authenticity is such an important currency in political leadership: it is less about the 'essence' of a particular political character and more about the expression of *public judgements* about the reality or truthfulness of a political habitus. This returns us to the comments earlier in this chapter about the necessarily symbolic and aesthetic dimensions of political representation.

While there may be much discussion on the character of Barack Obama, his family and some of the more trivial matters of his everyday life, as might be expected on a daytime chat show such as *The View*, there is also a surprisingly substantial discussion of politics across the two interviews. Both feature different narratives of serious and light-hearted discussion: the president's solo appearance starts with political discussion of issues, such as gay rights and the regulation of the financial system, while that featuring the couple commences with talk focusing more on their relationship and family before moving onto political issues, such as the attack on the American embassy in Libya. Barbara Walters flags such a shift in tone in the joint interview, throwing to the first advertisement break with the following comment to the president: 'We're going to come back, we're going to come back and ask you some questions yourself that are not as sweet and kind as these have been. We'll see. OK? [*Obama*: OK.] Alright? [*Obama*: Alright.] We'll be right back with the president and the first lady' (*The View* 2012a).

The interactional sequences in *The View* are generally characterized by greater interruptions of interviewees than occurs in conventional political interviews and are presented as more of an unstructured social chat, with interviewers often adding assents and throwaway comments. Such interjections do not usually interrogate or question the substance of the interviewee's narrative but function more generally as supportive devices. This feature of the programme is to some degree a function of the fact that there are several questioners on the panel. Despite this, the interviews with Barack Obama are characterized by a number of uninterrupted, lengthy responses by the president when he is addressing substantive political issues. The unusual nature of these replies is flagged at one point by Walters, who, after a number of lengthy answers by Obama on the subject of financial regulations, observes: 'Mr President, I have been on this show for sixteen years, and so has Joy. This is the first time we have all sat and not done crosstalk.' Obama responds: 'I know. I am very impressed. I'm a little nervous about it. You're so well behaved' (*The View* 2012b).

In this sense, the president's appearances on *The View* are characterized by a relative absence of conflict. As we have seen in preceding chapters, conflict is the motor for many interrogative exchanges across political interviews, debates and media conferences, but the celebrity political interview is characterized predominantly by a friendly, supportive context. The respect afforded to the president is partly informed by his unique political office, but beyond this the generic status of the celebrity political interview dictates that the interrogative exchanges yield a certain entertainment value that is generated by a cooperative relationship between interviewer and interviewee. That said, the interviews are not without disagreement, but such differences do not carry the intensity found in more conventional political interviews. At one point, for example, Obama disagrees with a contention of Elisabeth Hasselbeck:

> *Hasselbeck*: Mr President, um, I agree [*applause for Obama's previous answer*]. I mean you and I share the view, um, in terms of rights for gay couples and gay marriage. Um, you know, after hearing your position, um, one that you held for your entire presidency up until – what – maybe five days ago, you and Mitt Romney, um, actually agreed personally on the definition of marriage. Now that you have a new personal definition of it, um, practically speaking, how will you move things forward any more than Mitt Romney in terms of leaving it to the states, because at this point you have both said 'We'll leave it to the states to decide.' Will that be your plan moving forward...?
>
> *Obama*: Elisabeth, that's not actually true. I mean Mitt Romney has said he wants a constitutional amendment. That's not a state issue. That federalizes the whole issue and that's a major difference...(*The View* 2012b)

Throughout the interviews, the president seeks to manage carefully all expressions of conflict and consensus: highlighting in a reasonable way the differences within the political field between himself and his political opponent; promoting his administration's achievements while acknowledging the ongoing economic difficulties and their impact on ordinary Americans; and endorsing the merits of democratic process, and by so doing aligning himself with the people and the US democratic imaginary. Obama is assisted in this process by the 'soft' questions he receives, which highlight political differences in a way that allows him to appear magnanimous and extol the virtues of the US democratic process, as the following extended excerpt illustrates:.

> *Obama*: ...we've still got work to do, um, what I can tell you is, because of the steps we took, the economy is much stronger than it was when I came into office. Basically we have seen, er, two and a half years of consecutive jobs growth, economic growth, and, you know, we still have some head winds out there. Er, Europe is still weak and that ends up creating uncertainty for the business community here, er, gas prices were high, they're starting to come down a little bit, but a lot of families who have to drive 40 to 50 miles, you know, to get to work, they're still feeling the pinch, and, as I said, the housing market is probably the area where you're still seeing the biggest drag on the economy. So, er, but you know, as I – we were talking about Joe Biden – er, Joe has a, er, has a favourite expression, he says, er, 'Don't compare me to the Almighty, compare me to the alternative', and I think what you'll see in this campaign is two very different visions

about how we move the country forward. I believe we've got to invest in education, er, making college affordable, science and technology, rebuilding our roads, rebuilding the country, er, that all those things can be done in a sensible way while we're bringing our deficit down in a balanced way. I think that everyone sitting on this couch is probably going to have to pay a little bit more in taxes so we don't have to raise taxes for middle-class families [*applause*]. And that's a different view from what Mr Romney believes. And that's a legitimate debate to have. I think, er, this is going to be a really important election, and an eye-opening election.

Walters: There are some critics who say that, er, Mr Romney is a rich man who is out of touch. Is that accurate?

Obama: You know, er, my sense is that he loves his family. I think he's been successful, and we should applaud success in this country. Um, but he has a different vision about how to move the country forward. His theory is that, if you if you slash taxes even further, if you, er, leave business, banks, whoever, to do whatever it is they want, then everything will be OK...

Behar: But that didn't work last time, right?

Obama: Well...

Behar: What makes him think it is going to work this time?

Obama: That's my argument...

Behar: Yeah...

Obama: ...and the great thing is that, ultimately, the American people are going to settle it, right? [*applause*]

Behar: That's right. (*The View* 2012b)

From this excerpt we see the way in which political celebrity interviews can function to bring together, in a harmonious and productive way, the interests of the political and the media fields and also facilitate their respective courting and mobilizing of the public, as manifested in the studio audience. More so than in current affairs forum television programmes, the studio audience of political celebrity interviews is a unified entity. Unlike in the former, where the public audience is a differentiated entity with individuals asking questions of the panel of speakers, members of *The View* studio audience do not speak or ask questions and express themselves only through applause, even though it is likely that they possess a range of political views and opinions. This audience, then, is cast less as a group of citizens viewing their elected public representative and more as fans of a celebrity who also happens to be the holder of the highest political office in the nation. To the extent that they do participate as citizens, it is through their acceptance of the unified interpellation of the 'American people' rather than as a differentiated and agonistic entity.

The function of programmes such as *The View* in the president's political strategy management, and the symbiotic relationship between the political and media fields created by such interviews, was highlighted during the opening of Obama's solo appearance. The president had planned to announce his support for gay marriage on the programme, but Vice President Joe Biden's unexpected pre-emptory comments on the subject prompted Obama to announce the decision in an earlier interview, on ABC's *Good Morning America*. This prompted the following exchange at the start of Obama's appearance on *The View*:

> *Behar*: Is it true that you were going to announce the gay marriage thing on this show?
>
> *Obama*: It was a possibility. It was. We had been discussing it for, er, for a few weeks, and we thought, what are formats where we can talk about it not just as a policy issue but as a personal issue?...
>
> *Behar*: Right.
>
> *Obama*: ...and, er, all of you came to mind.
>
> *Behar*: Vice-President Biden jumped the gun a little bit. That was, you know, he sort of... You were planning to say it but he seemed to kind of jump the gun. Were you OK with that? Because...
>
> *Obama*: I was OK with it because it came out of a generosity of spirit. You know, when you get to know Joe Biden, he is the most honest, straightforward guy. He's warm, he tells you what he thinks, er, and...
>
> *Walters*: Did you tell him what you thought about his doing that?
>
> *Obama*: You know, what we talked about it and what I said was, I am never going to blame anyone for telling what they believe because I think it's important, er, for everyone in my administration to feel like, we want to be disciplined, we want to make sure we get our message out there but, at the same time on issues of principle, I always admire people who go out and speak their minds.
>
> *Walters*: Well, we're happy that you did it with our colleagues on GMA, but we sort of would have liked it [*laughter*].
>
> *Obama*: What can I tell ya?
>
> *Walters*: The next time you're gonna announce something huge, just call us, anyone one of us... (*The View* 2012b)

This exchange is relatively unusual because the machinations of the political and media fields are discussed quite explicitly. The president reveals the political planning that informs such announcements, as well as the alignment of the public framing of the announcement with an appropriate media outlet: Obama wants to cast the issue of gay marriage not just as a policy announcement but as a personal response, and this is fulfilled in his subsequent discussion on *The View*. Talk shows are thus ideal vehicles for the public dissemination of such policy announcements, given the contemporary diversified media landscape, where politics is increasingly cast through the more personalized perspectives of party leaders. The discussion also exemplifies the *exchange value* of such interviews and the homology between the promotional requirements of the politician and the media professionals: the president's announcement had a particular newsworthiness, and such an exclusive story would have been a valuable asset for *The View*. This discussion of the breakdown in the internal management of the political field is also manifested in different levels of discourse: Obama's attempt to rationalize Biden's gaffe, in order to minimize damage both to himself and to his administration's standing, is undermined by Walters's interruption, which ironically echoes Obama's discourse and alludes to the 'back stage' of the political field ('Did you tell him what you thought about his doing that?'). Equally, Obama alludes to the disparity between his public defence of Biden and the reality of Biden's political mistake in his joking comment: 'What can I tell ya?' While such a comment may seem a trivial aside in the exchange, it is indicative of the more open interrogative dynamics in political celebrity interviews rather than the combative and tightly controlled discourse of conventional political interviews.

Conclusion

In this chapter it has been noted that political celebrity interviews are now a more common feature of the political communication landscape, and yet they are relatively distinct from other forms of interrogative encounters because there is often a less combative relationship between interviewers and interviewees. Not all political leaders can be considered celebrities, but all must nonetheless convey a character that resonates with the public and involves the promotion of their personal narratives and their private lives. We have noted that the necessarily symbolic and aesthetic dimensions of political representation require politicians to express identification with the electorate through a political style that is often enacted in political celebrity interviews. The merits of 'soft news' political programming were discussed, and the importance of a cultivation of celebrity in the political ascension of Barack Obama was noted. In our analysis of Barack and Michelle Obama's appearances on *The View*, we noted the narrative structures of political celebrity interviews, which contain more open questions and extended answers and investigate the 'backstage' life of their subjects. We highlighted how much of the discussion focused on the habitus of Obama, captured both in his actual bodily performance and in the personal questions that are posed by the panel members. The analysis also revealed the particular blending in political celebrity interviews between questions about the character and everyday life of politicians and more substantive questions on conventional political issues. The chapter further demonstrated that, while they are less combative than other exchanges we have analysed, political celebrity interviews nonetheless still require a careful negotiation of conflict and consensus. We also discussed how the audience in *The View* is cast more as a unified group of fans unlike the studio audience of current affairs forum television programmes.

Conclusion

The success of political leadership is crucially dependent upon the ability to perform successfully in media-based interrogative encounters. The preceding analyses have highlighted the performative flexibility that is required of political leaders: we have seen President Barack Obama, for example, negotiate the diplomacy of a joint press conference, tackle a political opponent in the presidential debates, and chat amiably on the sofa on daytime television. Contemporary political performance is not limited to such encounters – politicians must now manage a social media presence and engage in niche targeting of constituencies through online appearances – but the interviews, debates and press conferences that we have examined here continue to be prominent means by which leaders present themselves publicly and, in turn, are publicly judged. The diversity of types of interaction that we have scrutinized in this book attests to the need for politicians to be sensitive to generic specificity across interactions: they can engage directly with a questioner in a political celebrity interview, where the celebrity status of the host enables the more personal expression of views, in contrast to a political interview, where the journalist may be merely the animator of the opposing views of others. The performative flexibility of politicians must also be expressed within particular interrogative encounters; regardless of the kind of media encounter, a politician must be able to move appropriately between expressions of political authority and demonstrations of their individual character and personality.

The different forms of interaction influenced the discursive strategies of the politicians: both David Cameron and Kevin Rudd were required to engage more sharply in the combative exchanges of political interviews, where conflict with opponents and colleagues were foregrounded, in contrast to the more consensus-oriented discussion of *The View*, which required Barack Obama to be more forthcoming and personal. Despite these different forms of interaction, all of the featured politicians negotiated both the internal and external relational logics of political discourse that were identified in chapter 2. In all of the exchanges we analysed, politicians defined themselves within the political field through a contrast with their opponents, and they also sought to distinguish themselves through relations external to the political field, including figures from other fields – most notably, the public. This was obvious in the leaders' debates in chapter 4, where other political leaders and the public were present in the communicative exchange (although, as we saw, Nick Clegg sought to distinguish himself from the leaders of the major parties while Gordon Brown tried to forge common ground with Clegg), but, even in his political celebrity interview on *The View*, President Obama politely but firmly contrasted his economic policy direction from that of Mitt Romney, while also extolling the virtues of American democracy in a way that garnered support from the studio audience.

These points underline the centrality, importance and legitimacy of political performance in media interviews, leaders' debates and press conferences. Politicians are not the simple repository of policies but embodied subjects, grounded in particular cultural and social contexts, who discipline themselves in accord with the strictures of the political field and adapt to and exploit the variety of media environments they encounter in order to engage with constituencies. It has been argued in this book that the pre-existing institutional authority of political leaders must be made manifest on an ongoing basis in media performances in order to obtain and sustain that authority. Politics is ultimately a communicative and performative phenomenon that requires the successful implementation of rhetoric to generate trust in others who can then grant their support. Aptitude in political performance is a substantive skill that incorporates bodily and discursive competence. This understanding works against separations of political 'substance' from 'image' and instead, following Pels (2003), sees political style as a necessary fusion of argument and manner.

We noted in chapter 1 that both political and journalistic bodies are integral to the expression of speech acts, and yet the bodily performance of both are not usually foregrounded, precisely because they involve highly conventional and disciplined forms of performance. These forms of performance are nonetheless expressions of the power of each of the respective fields: the journalist must embody a negotiation between neutralism and interrogation, and the politician must convey their authority through rational argument while also engaging the public. Crucially, our emphasis on interrogative exchanges highlights that performances are not solitary acts but always instances of corporeal intersubjective relations (Crossley 1995): the creation and meanings of performances are always produced through their orientation towards others. It follows that an important feature of media-based interrogative exchanges is the reading of the performative bodies of politicians and journalists. We saw an example of this in the analysis in chapter 6, where the unsatisfactory explanation by the Australian politician Craig Emerson was marked by active murmurings from the studio audience. Equally, in chapter 7 we noted the effectiveness of President Obama's non-verbal communication skills in his performances on *The View*.

In this book there has been a focus on politics as an 'expressive' phenomenon (Washbourne 2010, p. 43), and in particular the analyses have highlighted the deployment of emotional discourse by politicians. These expressions of emotion, or affect, are important means by which politicians seek to demonstrate their 'human side' and establish connections with the electorate. We have seen that the use of a discourse of affect is often not an exclusive attempt by a political leader to demonstrate their 'non-political' character but, rather, a means by which they seek to convey the relevance and the importance of the political issue to the everyday lives of people. This was revealed in the analysis of prime minister David Cameron's discussion about Internet regulation, where he exhibited his own emotional investment in the issue as a parent together with an explanation of its legality and politics. Similarly, in chapter 4, it was noted that one of the primary reasons why Liberal Democrat leader Nick Clegg performed so well in the debates was his emotional identification with the concerns raised by questioners. This point, in turn, emphasizes that the 'political games' that occur in mediated political interrogative exchanges are not just about the expression and management of conflict but also revolve around the ability of politicians to facilitate forms of consensus around particular issues; this consensus often arises through forms of emotional identification.

The theoretical discussion around performance and the analyses across different types of interrogative exchanges have revealed that the *character* of individual politicians, and their ability to harness that character in particular communicative encounters, is integral to their success. Evaluations of contemporary politics have often bemoaned the undue significance given to individual political leaders, their personalities and their media performance skills, and such criticisms are certainly not without merit. However, this book has sought to counterbalance such concerns by reminding us that the practice of politics necessarily requires individuals who can harness their particular character, intelligence, personality and rhetorical skills to articulate political goals and bring about change. We need, then, to acknowledge more substantively the subject position of the politician, illuminating how individuals are always and variously an extraordinary condensation of processes of socialization, life narratives, bodily attributes and performative skills that are exercised in specific institutional and interpersonal communicative contexts.

This point, in turn, highlights that the emphasis on the particular character of performing politicians needs to move beyond the specificity of the individual performance to a focus on the more structural constitution of their subjectivity, captured in Bourdieu's concept of habitus. One negative consequence of the 'presidentialization' of modern politics is that it tends to foster a view that the charismatic and authoritative personality of a political leader derives relatively autonomously from their individual character, deracinated from complex processes of socialization and engagements with the structures and conventions of the political field. The way that politicians speak, the confidence and poise with which they present themselves and interact with others, is so much more than the simple product of media training and practice. The concept of habitus shifts our attention from the individual to the way that social contexts and values are embedded in, and realized through, the practices and discourse of subjects. This is not, however, a deterministic account of subjectivity; socially constituted individuals also use the resources and skills that stem from such a background in their particular engagements with contemporary social contexts and interactions, and this can be done with varying degrees of success. The former Australian prime minister Kevin Rudd drew on his humble upbringing as well as his elite diplomatic background in his political practice, and he often drew attention to himself with his sometimes clumsy and obvious use of Australian slang in a bid to align himself with 'ordinary' Australians.

We have canvassed a broad range of interactions between politicians and journalists in the preceding chapters: from the direct confrontations of political interviews to the friendly banter of the political celebrity interviews. There are important differences across the programmes we have analysed, but we should also reflect here on the significance of the common process of interaction between journalists and politicians. Discussion about political communication often revolves around evaluations of who has dominance in exchanges:

who leads the 'tango' in political source relations or to what degree the adroit skills of spin doctors neuter the probing power of journalists. These are important questions, but sometimes we glide too easily over the fundamental significance of interactions between journalists and politicians. The simple question and answer exchange, in all its forms, represents an integral site of political knowledge production, and it is a distillation of a crucial democratic process whereby those in power must account for themselves.

The simple question and answer exchange is also a site of struggle between the political and journalistic fields for authority. Journalists and politicians seek to establish the priority of their particular framing and interpretation of issues, and ultimately authority is claimed through the ability to speak for, or identify with, the public. It was outlined in chapter 2 both how the concept of field highlights the way in which the interests of particular social and occupational institutional sites are realized through conventions of practice and discursive competence and how the political and journalistic fields, in particular, are dependent upon forging connections with public opinion. The political and journalistic fields have separate institutional interests that influence how individual politicians and journalists act and speak, but the mediated nature of public life, which dictates that the public practice of politics occurs on and through the media, brings these powerful social actors together onto the same stage, where they must engage in discursive battles in order to establish, maintain and enhance their power. The analyses in the preceding chapters have demonstrated how much of the interrogative exchanges involves both journalists and politicians explicitly and implicitly challenging not only the individual other but also the authority of their respective field, and equally how much of the exchanges also involves participants outlining and attempting to legitimize why, as members of a particular field, they act and speak as they do. In this sense, contemporary political communication is substantially concerned with this struggle for ascendency between the political and journalistic fields.

Throughout this book we have examined the roles of journalists in their interactions with politicians, and we have noted the varying degrees of prominence and influence they have across a range of interrogative encounters. Andrew Marr, Barrie Cassidy and Kerry O'Brien were active and critical questioners in the political interviews that were analysed in chapter 3, whereas the moderators in the UK leaders' debates in chapter 4 were limited to facilitating the question and answer exchange between the studio audience and the politicians. In chapter 6 it was noted how *Q&A* host Tony Jones performed a more complex role in current affairs forum television, shifting footing between facilitating the question and answer exchange and assuming the more direct role of interviewer. In the political interviews there was the direct and sustained interaction between a single interviewer and interviewee, while the joint press conferences in chapter 5 saw a more diffuse array of questioners interacting with more than one political leader, and the political celebrity interviews of *The View* involved a panel of five questioners.

The case studies highlighted not only the various formats of inquiry but also the differing identity and status of those who posed questions to the politicians. The political interviews in chapter 3 featured interviewers who are senior political journalists possessing authority within their field. Similarly, the press conferences in chapter 5 featured questions from elite national political correspondents representing major news organizations. Here there were direct and detailed challenges to the politicians, manifested in both a performative authority and an engagement with the complexities of policy and strategy. In contrast, the panelists of *The View* possess an authority that derives from the broader media field: the host Barbara Walters had a distinguished career as a news broadcaster but others, such as Whoopi Goldberg and Rosie O'Donnell, are television personalities with backgrounds in comedy and acting who have also cultivated an activist status for a variety of causes. These case studies, then, suggest the breadth of the media field and the way that the journalistic field is implicated in broader contexts of entertainment media and subject to forces of commercialization. Alternatively, we can note that a programme such as *The View* seeks to gain authority within the media field through the appearances of senior political leaders on the show.

In addition to media professionals, members of the public question politicians in some of the case studies, notably the televised leaders' debates and current affairs forum television. Significantly, the media field imposes its authority on such public interrogations, with debate moderators and programme hosts facilitating the interaction. Nonetheless, the case studies in chapters 4 and 6 highlight those opportunities when citizens can engage relatively directly with their political representatives. We see here active, articulate and differentiated political subjects, in contrast to the audience of *The View*, who are limited to collective cheering and applause. We have also noted, however, in both the UK leaders' debates and *Q&A*, that most questions are constrained and posed in a formal manner, usually not highlighting individual circumstances and often replicating the news agenda and performative style of the journalistic field. Indeed, watching the UK leaders' debates, it becomes strongly apparent that this is a forum in which politicians, not the public, perform. The public, then, when its members do have the opportunity in media-based interrogative encounters to be participants, is very much cast as a highly disciplined entity.

We noted in chapter 1 a trend away from more monological, authoritative forms of broadcasting to looser, more interactive and entertainment-oriented programming, and this was evident in most of our case studies. All of the interrogative encounters that were analysed, with the exception of press conferences in chapter 5, occurred within the media field and can be characterized as highly stylized and foregrounding the performative skills of the presenters. It can be concluded that this is a generalized contemporary television phenomenon given that most of our case studies were from public service broadcasting programmes. The programme structure and style, together with the performative emphasis, derives partly from scheduling: the post-news, weekday, early-evening scheduling of *The 7.30 Report* replicates a more traditional current affairs format, in contrast to the Sunday morning political talk programmes such as *The Andrew Marr Show*, where authoritative political and weekly news discussion and interviews comingle with film and theatre reviews and musical performances in more of a magazine-style format. Such points highlight how the authoritative political talk we have analysed in the case studies is often embedded in a more general media environment.

Such points also attest to the need for a balanced and nuanced understanding of journalistic performance in televisual interrogative encounters with politicians. The practices of journalism occur through embodied performances, and there is a need to retrieve and elucidate the significance of journalistic bodies in the meaning-making processes of mediated political interrogative exchanges, while also highlighting how such performances are partly motivated by industry and commercial imperatives to manufacture an engaging journalistic persona and programme. As was initially outlined in chapter 1, journalistic performances are the complex composite of responses to the performative demands of the televisual medium itself, the particular broadcasting outlet and programme genre, generalized journalistic principles, and the marshalling of individual attributes. We see this kind of complex negotiation, for example, in the figure of *Q&A* host Tony Jones, who tries to cultivate and give coherent expression to a journalistic persona who is a lively, intelligent and engaging character who is also grounded in the cultural and journalistic authority of the national public broadcaster.

The variety of the case studies we examined cumulatively demon-strates that an important function of journalism, and public inter-rogation more generally, is to keep the political open. People may have complaints about what questions are asked by journalists and the manner of the interactions, but the generalized process of ques-tioning perpetually renders particular issues, and society as a whole, problematic. We can explain the significance of this process simply by noting that it is the job of the journalist always to test the veracity and substance of politicians' ideas, policies and practices. Interview-ers are fulfilling the fourth-estate function of journalism by critiquing those who hold power in society and explaining the exercise of that power to the populace. As was argued in chapter 2, we can also base an understanding of the journalistic function more substantively on the agonistic character of democracy, which recognizes that democ-racy itself is animated by ongoing contestation. This feature of democracy arises partly out of its temporal unfolding: the articulation of promises about future actions and scenarios is interrogated in order to generate trust and allocate power, and subsequently there are evaluations and defences of past actions and outcomes. There are of course truths that journalism must investigate and seek to prove – whether a politician lied or broke the law – but the idea that politi-cal and journalistic machinations hide some underlying truth or sin-gular conclusion is blind to the reality that politics necessarily involves the ongoing exercise of power in the struggle to impose a particular vision of the common good. It is, of course, not only journalists that keep the political open: while the public is often a disciplined entity in the political talk formats we have examined, there are also forums where a more robust and provocative public discourse occurs, as we saw in current affairs forum television in chapter 6. In that analysis it was revealed how the Twitter feed and video questions from members of the public critique the discourse of the politicians and offer challenges to political orthodoxy.

Throughout this book we have focused in close detail on the dis-cursive exchanges between politicians and journalists, but we have also sought to broaden the scope of analysis to consider public involvement in the programmes and the public reception and report-age of the interrogative exchanges. As the analysis of the US presi-dential debates revealed, the usage of social media is resulting in a highly differentiated public consumption of the debates between those who encounter them solely through television and those who incorporate Twitter in their reception. The analyses of the leaders' debates and current affairs forum television highlighted how televi-sual political talk is now an increasingly porous textual entity with greater public involvement in the programme itself; the instantaneous feedback on the programme in turn influences public and journalistic reception of the unfolding event. It was noted how the discussion in the interrogative exchanges is always located in the flow of broader current political debate, and hence an understanding of the political and news contexts of the discussion can assist us in our analysis. The dynamics and meanings of the communicative events are very much informed by 'extra-textual' events – the leaders' debates are, for example, by their campaign context. We also saw in chapter 5 how the photo opportunity of Obama and Medvedev at the burger restaurant was a significant factor in the framing of the meanings of the press conference, and those references to the event were subsequently picked up in the news reportage of the conference.

Throughout this book the nature of the interactions that occur in media interviews, leaders' debates, press conferences, current affairs forum television and political celebrity interviews have been highlighted and scrutinized. The analysis has been informed by a dialogic understanding of language that emphasizes the inherent contestability of words. Language, in this sense, cannot be singularly 'owned' by speakers; the meanings of words cannot be limited to the intentions of the users of those words. Language also does not have a simple referential function; rather, it works in its social deployment. A focus on the utterance as the basic unit of analysis highlights its necessary orientation to others. This is always the case, but it is particularly pertinent to the interrogative exchanges that have been the subject of our attention. The struggles that occur between politicians and journalists in interrogative exchanges stem, then, from attempts to impose a singular understanding or meaning on words that perpetually refuse such capture because of their socially charged life. We can be critical of politicians who deliberately do not disclose all details, or seek to misrepresent an event or the words they or others have previously uttered, but we need to understand that, ultimately, politicians can only but seek to bend words to their will. It is this nature of language that lends the media-based interrogations we have examined their *political* character.

The contestable nature of language and the complex nature of the interactions between politicians and journalists have been highlighted across the case studies that have been examined in the book. We have revealed the dimensions of aggressive questioning by journalists that have challenged the claims and authority of the interviewees. We have also seen politicians engage in expressions of modality where they carefully calculate and modulate the probability of outcomes, and we have drawn attention to the argumentative strategies that leaders have deployed in their attempts to persuade the journalist and the viewing public about the legitimacy of their position. In chapter 3 the discursive struggle that occurred between Andrew Marr and David Cameron over whether the prime minister had 'talked' to political consultant Lynton Crosby was scrutinized. We revealed how the use, or non-use, of such a simple word had broader political ramifications, and this fact drove the combative interaction between interviewer and interviewee with an ultimate disagreement about whether the prime minister had answered the question. In chapter 5 we saw how a significant feature of Barack Obama's solo press conference was the president's attempt to manage the rhetorical construction of national identity through his invocation of 'patriotism' and the delegation of that identity to particular groups while excluding the actions of Edward Snowden.

These discursive struggles are not simply between interviewer and interviewee but represent a broader confrontation between the political and journalistic fields. The increasingly mediated nature of public life has meant that the practices and public significance of politics occur within and arise from mediated contexts, and this in turn has meant that there is now both greater convergence and sharper confrontations between the political and the journalistic fields. There is now greater fluidity of staffing across the two fields, as individuals move between journalistic and political positions, as press secretaries, politicians and political commentators. This has been accompanied in recent decades by greater expertise and proficiency in media management and a foregrounding and awareness of the everyday information management practices and discursive strategies of practitioners in both fields. As such, media interviews, leaders' debates and press conferences have been increasingly dominated by what we have called 'political games', where politicians and journalists are acutely aware of the positioning and defences of the other and each individual seeks to exploit their own resources and advantages to further the interests of their own professional position. These 'games' occur because the public interactions between politicians and journalists address important political matters and public policy issues that crucially involve the exercise of *power*.

Both the political and journalistic fields are powerful institutional sites in themselves, but both also depend crucially on external recognition and support to enable their authority to be realized. It is ironic that the intense struggles between the two that we have outlined sometimes result in each of the institutions being judged as not sufficiently representing the interests of that entity which is crucial to their power: the public. Nonetheless, as we have seen, the public is a major site of struggle in the interrogative exchanges: Kevin Rudd challenged interviewer Kerry O'Brien by indicating he was closer to the Australian public than the journalist; Queensland premier Anna Bligh identified with the suffering of flood victims; and David Cameron was at pains to identify with the concerns of British parents over online access to pornography, while the journalist Andrew Marr taunted him by stating that the polls suggested the public was deserting his party. These struggles between politicians and journalists, where each seeks to invoke and speak for the public, highlights the extent to which the mass public is a product of discourse, 'unknowable' in any singular, definitive way (Craig 2004). This, in turn, is a major contributing factor to the openness and perpetual contestation of public discourse that has been emphasized throughout the book. Of course, this point needs to be contrasted with recognition that, across different forms of mediated political interaction, members of the public are now themselves speaking and contributing to debate through social media. This does not render public opinion suddenly 'knowable', and indeed it can further highlight the heterogeneous nature of public opinion, but it does complicate the respective powers of the political and journalistic fields, and it influences the nature of the interactions between politicians and journalists.

This book has been prompted by recognition that there is public consternation over the nature of the relationships between politicians and journalists and also the quality of contemporary political discourse, encapsulated in particular forms of interactions in interviews, debates and press conferences. Throughout I have sought to explain both why we have got ourselves into this perceived predicament and how we should perceive the current state of affairs. In essence, I have argued that, beyond our immediate frustrations about boring politicians or shouting matches where no one learns anything, we need to acknowledge the necessary play of politics that occurs in such encounters. There is much at stake in these interviews, debates and press conferences, and we should expect political performances to be calculated and highly disciplined. It has been argued therefore that the performances in these interrogative events are vital in the production of meaning, and we need to have a greater understanding of the discursive strategies that are employed by both politicians and journalists. We have seen that such performances and discursive strategies vary considerably across a diverse range of events and media programming; politicians must negotiate a range of televisual genres, where they encounter varying degrees of scrutiny from different kinds and amounts of participants. The discussion has also compelled us to consider the contestable nature of public discourse and the primacy of trust over truth in political interrogative exchanges. This perhaps involves a reorientation of the evaluative frameworks of many who are dismissive of the lack of truthfulness in contemporary political talk. I have argued in response that, ultimately, truth is not the goal of political communication; rather, it is the battleground upon which political communication occurs.

References

Alexander, J. (2010) 'Barack Obama meets celebrity metaphor', *Society*, 47: 410–18.

Alway, J. (1999) 'No body there: Habermas and feminism', *Current Perspectives in Social Theory*, 19: 117–41.

Ampofo, L., Anstead, N., and O'Loughlin, B. (2011) 'Trust, confidence, and credibility: citizen responses on Twitter to opinion polls during the 2010 UK general election', *Information, Communication & Society*, 14(6): 850–71.

An, C., and Pfau, M. (2004) 'The efficacy of inoculation in televised political debates', *Journal of Communication*, 54(3): 421–35.

Anderson, R., Baxter, L. A., and Cissna, C. N. (eds) (2004) *Dialogue: theorizing difference in communication studies*. Thousand Oaks, CA: Sage.

Ankersmit, F. (2002) *Political representation*. Stanford, CA: Stanford University Press.

Ankersmit, F. (2003) 'Democracy's inner voice: political style as unintended consequence of political action', in J. Corner and D. Pels (eds), *Media and the restyling of politics*. London: Sage.

Anstead, N., and O'Loughlin, B. (2011) 'The emerging viewertariat and BBC *Question Time*: television debate and real-time commenting online', *International Journal of Press/Politics*, 16(4): 440–62.

Arendt, H. (1958) *The human condition*. Chicago: University of Chicago Press.

Aristotle (1981) *The politics*. Rev. edn, trans. T. A. Sinclair, rev. T. J. Saunders, Harmondsworth: Penguin.

Atkinson, P., and Silverman, D. (1997) 'Kundera's immortality: the interview society and the invention of the self', *Qualitative Inquiry*, 3(3): 304–25.

Austin, J. L. (1975) *How to do things with words*. 2nd edn, Oxford: Oxford University Press.

Bai, M. (2012) 'Obama's enthusiasm gap', *New York Times*, 4 October, http://thecaucus.blogs.nytimes.com/2012/10/04/obamas-enthusiasm-gap/?_php=true&_type=blogs&_php=true&_type=blogs&_r=1.

Bakhtin, M. (1981) *The dialogic imagination: four essays*, trans. C. Emerson and M. Holquist, ed. M. Holquist. Austin: University of Texas Press.

Bakhtin, M. (1986) *Speech genres and other late essays*, trans. V. W. McGhee, ed. C. Emerson and M. Holquist. Austin: University of Texas Press.

Banning, S. A., and Billingsley, S. (2007) 'Journalistic aggressiveness in joint versus solo presidential press conferences', *Mass Communication and Society*, 10(4): 461–78.

Barnett, C. (2003) *Culture and democracy: media, space and representation*. Edinburgh: Edinburgh University Press.

Baum, M. (2003) 'Soft news and political knowledge: evidence of absence or absence of evidence?', *Political Communication*, 20(2): 173–90.

Baum, M. (2005) 'Talking the vote: why presidential candidates hit the talk show circuit', *American Journal of Political Science*, 49(2): 213–34.

Beck, U., and Beck-Gernsheim, E. (2002) *Individualization: institutionalized individualism and its social and political consequences*, trans. P. Camiller. London: Sage.

Bell, A. (1991) *The language of news media*. Oxford: Blackwell.

Bell, P., and van Leeuwen, T. (1994) *The media interview: confession, contest, conversation*. Kensington: University of New South Wales Press.

Bennett, D. (2012) 'Twitter won the presidential debate', *The Wire*, 4 October, www.thewire.com/politics/2012/10/twitter-won-presidential-debate/57593/.

Bennett, W. L., and Entman, R. M. (eds) (2001) *Mediated politics: communication in the future of democracy*. Cambridge: Cambridge University Press.

Ben-Porath, E. N. (2007) 'Internal fragmentation of the news', *Journalism Studies*, 8(3): 414–31.

Benson, R. (1999) 'Field theory in comparative context: a new paradigm for media studies', *Theory and Society*, 28(3): 463–98.

Benson, R., and Neveu, E. (eds) (2005) *Bourdieu and the journalistic field*. Cambridge: Polity.

Bhatia, A. (2006) 'Critical discourse analysis of political press conferences', *Discourse & Society*, 17(2): 173–203.

Birdsell, D. S., et al. (2002) 'White paper on televised political campaign debates', *Argumentation & Advocacy*, 38(4): 199–218.

Booth, R. (2013) 'David Cameron's "Team Nigella" quotes could have sunk Saatchi PAs' trial', *The Guardian*, 20 December, www.theguardian.com/politics/2013/dec/20/david-cameron-team-nigella-lawson-quote-trial.

Bourdieu, P. (1977) *Outline of a theory of practice*. Cambridge: Cambridge University Press.

Bourdieu, P. (1990) *The logic of practice*, trans. R. Nice. Cambridge: Polity.

Bourdieu, P. (1991) *Language and symbolic power*. Cambridge: Polity.

Bourdieu, P. (1998) *On television*. New York: New Press.

Bourdieu, P. (2002) 'Habitus', in J. Hillier and E. Rooksby (eds), *Habitus: a sense of place*. Aldershot: Ashgate.

Bourdieu, P. (2005) 'The political field, the social science field, and the journalistic field', in R. Benson and E. Neveu (eds), *Bourdieu and the journalistic field*. Cambridge: Polity.

Bourdieu, P., and Wacquant, L. (1992) *An invitation to reflexive sociology*. Cambridge: Polity.

Boussofara-Omar, N. (2006) 'Learning the "linguistic habitus" of a politician: a presidential authoritative voice in the making', *Journal of Language and Politics*, 5(3): 325–58.

Brants, K. (2013) 'Trust, cynicism, and responsiveness: the uneasy situation of journalism in democracy', in C. Peters and M. Broersma (eds), *Rethinking journalism: trust and participation in a transformed news landscape*. Abingdon: Routledge.

Broersma, M. (2010) 'Journalism as performative discourse: the importance of form and style in journalism', in V. Rupar (ed.), *Journalism and meaning making: reading the newspaper*. Cresskill, NJ: Hampton Press.

Brown, P., and Levinson, S. C. (1990) *Politeness: some universals in language usage*. Cambridge: Cambridge University Press.

Bruns, A. (2008) 'Life beyond the public sphere: towards a networked model for political deliberation', *Information Polity*, 13: 65–79.

Butler, D. (2010) 'Obama: U.S. has "reset" relations with Russia', *Associated Press*, 24 June, www.nbcnews.com/id/37892671/ns/politics-white_house/t/obama-us-has-reset-relations-russia/#.VAl_x6VvcYV.

Butler, J. (1990) *Gender trouble*. New York: Routledge.

Butler, J. (1999) 'Performativity's social magic', in R. Shusterman (ed.), *Bourdieu: a critical reader*. Oxford: Blackwell.

Byrnes, S. (2010) 'Who's posher: Clegg or Cameron?', *The Guardian*, 20 April, www.theguardian.com/commentisfree/2010/apr/20/clegg-cameron-posher.

Calhoun, C. (1995) *Critical social theory*. Cambridge: Polity.

Campbell, M. (2011) 'Actual intellectuals with passionate arguments = best Q&A ever!' *Crikey.com*, 4 October, www.crikey.com.au/2011/10/04/actual-intellectuals-with-passionate-arguments-best-qa-ever/#comments.

Cappella, J. N., and Jamieson, K. H. (1997) *Spiral of cynicism: the press and the public good*. New York: Oxford University Press.

Carbaugh, D. (1988) *Talking American: cultural discourses on Donahue*. Princeton, NJ: Ablex.

Carlin, D. B., Vigil, T., Buehler, S., and McDonald, K. (2009) *The third agenda in U.S. presidential debates: debatewatch and viewer reactions, 1996–2004*. Westport, CT: Praeger.

Carlson, M. (2004) *Performance: a critical introduction*. 2nd edn, New York: Routledge.

Carpentier, N. (2001) 'Managing audience participation: the construction of participation in an audience discussion programme', *European Journal of Communication*, 16(2): 209–32.

Carpentier, N., and Hannot, W. (2009) 'To be a common hero: the uneasy balance between the ordinary and ordinariness in the subject position of mediated ordinary people in the talk show *Jan Publiek*', *International Journal of Cultural Studies*, 12(6): 597–616.

Carpignano, P., Andersen, R., Aronowitz, S., and Difazio, W. (1990) 'Chatter in the age of electronic reproduction: talk television and the "public mind"', *Social Text*, 25/26: 33–55.

Chadwick, A. (2011) 'Britain's first live televised party leaders' debate: from the news cycle to the political information cycle', *Parliamentary Affairs*, 64(1): 24–44.

Chadwick, A. (2013) *The hybrid media system: politics and power*. Oxford: Oxford University Press.

Chaney, D. (1993) *Fictions of collective life: public drama in late modern culture*. London: Routledge.

Charteris-Black, J. (2005) *Politicians and rhetoric: the persuasive power of metaphor*. Basingstoke: Palgrave Macmillan.

Chau, B. H. (ed.) (2007) *Elections as popular culture in Asia*. London: Routledge.

Chilton, P., and Schaffner, C. (eds) (2002) *Politics as text and talk: analytic approaches to political discourse*. Amsterdam: John Benjamins.

Chouliaraki, L., and Fairclough, N. (1999) *Discourse in late modernity: rethinking critical discourse analysis*. Edinburgh: Edinburgh University Press.

Chozick, A. (2010) 'A little gab, a little politics', *Wall Street Journal*, 10 June, http://online.wsj.com/article/SB1000142405274870457530457529 6371206044884.html.

Cissna, K. N., and Anderson, R. (1994) 'Communication and the ground of dialogue', in *The reach of dialogue: confirmation, voice, and community*. Cresskill, NJ: Hampton Press.

Clayman, S. (2004) 'Arenas of interaction in the mediated public sphere', *Poetics*, 32: 29–49.

Clayman, S., and Heritage, J. (2002a) *The news interview: journalists and public figures on the air*. Cambridge: Cambridge University Press.

Clayman, S., and Heritage, J. (2002b) 'Questioning presidents: journalistic deference and adversarialness in the press conferences of US presidents Eisenhower and Reagan', *Journal of Communication*, 52: 749–75.

Clayman, S., Elliott, M. N., Heritage, J., and Beckett, M. K. (2010) 'A watershed in White House journalism: explaining the post-1968 rise of aggressive presidential news', *Political Communication*, 27(3): 229–47.

Clayman, S., Elliott, M. N., Heritage, J., and Beckett, M. K. (2012) 'The president's questioners: consequential attributes of the White House press corps', *International Journal of Press/Politics*, 17(1): 100–21.

Clayman, S., Elliott, M. N., Heritage, J., and McDonald, L. L. (2006) 'Historical trends in questioning presidents, 1953–2000', *Presidential Studies Quarterly*, 36(4): 561–83.

Coleman, S. (2000) 'Meaningful political debate in the age of the soundbite', in S. Coleman (ed.), *Televised election debates: international perspectives*. London: Macmillan.

Coleman, S., and Ross, K. (2010) *The media and the public: 'them' and 'us' in media discourse*. Chichester: Wiley-Blackwell.

Conley, D., and Lamble, S. (2006) *The daily miracle: an introduction to journalism*. Oxford: Oxford University Press.

Corner, J. (1995) *Television form and public address*. London: Edward Arnold.

Corner, J. (2003) 'Mediated persona and political culture', in J. Corner and D. Pels (eds), *Media and the restyling of politics*. London: Sage.

Corner, J., and Pels, D. (eds) (2003) *Media and the restyling of politics*. London: Sage.

Cornfield, M. (2010) 'Game-changers: new technologies and the 2008 presidential election', in L. Sabato (ed.), *The year of Obama: how Barack Obama won the White House*. New York: Longman.

Couldry, N. (2004) 'Liveness, "reality" and the mediated habitus from television to the mobile phone', *Communication Review*, 7: 353–61.

Craig, G. (1999) 'Plastic vision: an analysis of Reuters financial television', *UTS Review*, 5(1): 111–25.

Craig, G. (2000) 'Perpetual crisis: the politics of saving the ABC', *Media International Australia*, no. 94: 105–16.

Craig, G. (2004) *The media, politics and public life*. Sydney: Allen & Unwin.

Craig, G. (2007) 'Moving through discourses: an assessment of the New Zealand 2005 election televised leaders' debates', *Media International Australia*, no. 123: 18–32.

Craig, G. (2008) 'Kevin Rudd and the framing of politics and political leadership in news media interviews', *Communication, Politics and Culture*, 41(2): 84–99.

Craig, G. (2009) 'Leaders' debates and news media interviews', in C. Rudd, J. Hayward and G. Craig (eds), *Informing voters? Politics, media and the New Zealand election 2008*. Auckland: Pearson.

Craig, G. (2010a) 'Dialogue and dissemination in news media interviews', *Journalism: Theory, Practice & Criticism*, 11(1): 75–90.

Craig, G. (2010b) 'Media interviews and debates', *Australian Cultural History*, 28(1): 39–46.

Crick, B. (2002) *Democracy: a very short introduction*. Oxford: Oxford University Press.

Crossley, N. (1995) 'Body techniques, agency and intercorporeality: on Goffman's *Relations in Public*', *Sociology*, 29(1): 133–49.

Crossley, N. (1997) 'Corporeality and communicative action: embodying the renewal of critical theory', *Body & Society*, 3(1): 17–46.

Crossley, N. (2001) 'The phenomenological habitus and its construction', *Theory and Society*, 30(1): 81–120.

Crossley, N., and Roberts, J. M. (eds) (2004) *After Habermas: new perspectives on the public sphere*. Oxford: Blackwell.

D'Angelo, P., and Lombard, M. (2008) 'The power of the press: the effects of press frames in political campaign news on media perceptions', *Atlantic Journal of Communication*, 16(1): 1–32.

D'Angelo, P., Calderone, M., and Territola, A. (2005) 'Strategy and issue framing: an exploratory analysis of topics and frames in campaign 2004 print news', *Atlantic Journal of Communication*, 13(4): 199–219.

Darras, E. (2005) 'Media consecration of the political order', in R. Benson and E. Neveu (eds), *Bourdieu and the journalistic field*. Cambridge: Polity.

Davis, A., and Seymour, E. (2010) 'Generating forms of media capital inside and outside a field: the strange case of David Cameron in the UK political field', *Media, Culture & Society*, 32(5): 739–59.

Dayan, D., and Katz, E. (1994) *Media events: the live broadcasting of history*. Cambridge, MA: Harvard University Press.

DeLuca, K. M., and Peeples, J. (2002) 'From public sphere to public screen: democracy, activism and the "violence of Seattle"', *Critical Studies in Media Communication*, 19(2): 125–51.

Drew, P., and Heritage, J. (eds) (1992) *Talk at work: interaction in institutional settings*. Cambridge: Cambridge University Press.

Drucker, S. J., and Hunold, J. P. (1987) 'The debating game', *Critical Studies in Mass Communication*, 4(2): 202–7.

Eaton, G. (2013) 'What happened to Cameron's monthly press conferences?', *New Statesman*, 1 July, www.newstatesman.com/politics/2013/07/what-happened-camerons-monthly-press-conferences.

Eldridge, L. (1997) 'Drama in a dramaturgical society', in J. Wallace, R. Jones and S. Nield (eds), *Raymond Williams now: knowledge, limits and the future*. London: Macmillan.

Entman, R. M. (2008) 'Theorizing mediated public diplomacy: the US case', *International Journal of Press/Politics*, 13(2): 87–102.

Eriksson, G. (2010) 'Politicians in celebrity talk show interviews: the narrativization of personal experiences', *Text & Talk*, 30(5): 529–51.

Eriksson, G. (2011) 'Follow-up questions in political press conferences', *Journal of Pragmatics*, 43: 3331–44.

Eriksson, G., and Östman, J. (2013) 'Cooperative or adversarial? Journalists' enactment of the watchdog function in political news production', *International Journal of Press/Politics*, 18(3): 304–24.

Eshbaugh-Soha, M. (2013) 'Presidential influence of the news media: the case of the press conference', *Political Communication*, 30(4): 548–64.

Esser, F., and D'Angelo, P. (2003) 'Framing the press and publicity process: a content analysis of meta-coverage in campaign 2000 network news', *American Behavioral Scientist*, 46(5): 617–41.

Esser, F., Reinemann, C., and Fan, D. (2001) 'Spin doctors in the United States, Great Britain, and Germany: metacommunication about media manipulation', *Harvard International Journal of Press/Politics*, 6(1): 16–45.

Fairclough, N. (1992) *Discourse and social change*. Cambridge: Polity.

Fairclough, N. (1995a) *Media discourse*. London: Edward Arnold.

Fairclough, N. (1995b) *Critical discourse analysis: the critical study of language*. London: Longman.

Fairclough, N. (2000) *New Labour, new language?* London: Routledge.

Farrell, D. M., and Schmitt-Beck, R. (eds) (2002) *Do political campaigns matter? Campaign effects in elections and referendums*. London: Routledge.

Farrell, P. (2014) 'Without press briefings, how can journalists hold Morrison to account?' *The Guardian*, 15 January, www.theguardian.com/commentisfree/2014/jan/15/without-press-briefings-how-can-journalists-hold-morrison-to-account?CMP=fb_gu.

Foucault, M. (1972) *The archaeology of knowledge*. London: Routledge.

Foucault, M. (1988) 'The political technology of individuals', in L. H. Martin, H. Gutman and P. H. Hutton (eds), *Technologies of the self: a seminar with Michel Foucault*. Amherst: University of Massachusetts Press.

Foucault, M. (1991) *Discipline and punish: the birth of the prison*, trans. A. Sheridan. London: Penguin.

Gardiner, M. E. (2004) 'Wild publics and grotesque symposiums: Habermas and Bakhtin on dialogue, everyday life and the public sphere', in N. Crossley and J. M. Roberts (eds), *After Habermas: new perspectives on the public sphere*. Oxford: Blackwell.

Giddens, A. (1990) *The consequences of modernity*. Cambridge: Polity.

'Gillard in marathon press conference over Slater and Gordon' (2012) Australianpolitics.com, 23 August, http://australianpolitics.com/2012/08/23/gillard-marathon-press-conference-slater-gordon.html.

Goffman, E. (1959) *The presentation of self in everyday life*. New York: Anchor Books.

Goffman, E. (1967) *Interaction ritual: essays on face-to-face behaviour*. London: Allen Lane.

Goffman, E. (1981) *Forms of talk*. Philadelphia: University of Pennsylvania Press.

Gulati, G. J. (2010) 'No laughing matter: the role of new media in the 2008 election', in L. Sabato (ed.), *The year of Obama: how Barack Obama won the White House*. New York: Longman.

Haarman, L. (1999) 'Performing talk', in L. Haarman (ed.), *Talk about shows: la parola e lo spettacolo*. Bologna: CLUEB.

Habermas, J. (1984) *The theory of communicative action*, Vol. 1: Reason and the rationalization of society, trans. T. Docherty. Boston: Beacon Press.

Habermas, J. (1987) *The theory of communicative action*, Vol. 2: Lifeworld and system: the critique of functionalist reason, trans. T. Docherty. Boston: Beacon Press.

Habermas, J. (1989) *The structural transformation of the public sphere: an inquiry into a category of bourgeois society*, trans. T. Docherty with F. Lawrence. Cambridge: Polity.

Habermas, J. (1992) 'Further reflections on the public sphere', in C. Calhoun (ed.), *Habermas and the public sphere*. Cambridge, MA: MIT Press.

Hamo, M. (2006) 'Caught between freedom and control: "ordinary" people's discursive positioning on an Israeli prime-time talk show', *Discourse & Society*, 17(4): 427–45.

Hardt, M., and Negri, A. (2004) *Multitude: war and democracy in the age of empire*. New York: Penguin.

Hartley, J. (1992) *The politics of pictures: the creation of the public in the age of popular media*. London: Routledge.

Hartley, J. (1996) *Popular reality: journalism, modernity, popular culture*. London: Edward Arnold.

Hawthorne, J., Houston, J. B., and McKinney, M. S. (2013) 'Live-tweeting a presidential primary debate: exploring new political conversations', *Social Science Computer Review*, 31(5): 552–62.

Hawthorne, M. (2007) 'Rudd gatecrashes toddler's party', *Sydney Morning Herald*, 17 November, http://news.smh.com.au/national/rudd-gatecrashes-toddlersparty-20071117-1axi.html.

Herman, A. (2012) 'If only celebrity in chief Obama had been asked about his iPod in debate', *Fox News*, 5 October, www.foxnews.com/opinion/2012/10/05/if-only-celebrity-in-chief-obama-had-been-asked-about-his-ipod-in-debate/.

Hesmondhalgh, D. (2006) 'Bourdieu, the media and cultural production', *Media, Culture & Society*, 28(2): 211–31.

Himelboim, I., McCreery, S., and Smith, M. (2013) 'Birds of a feather tweet together: integrating network and content analyses to examine cross-ideology exposure on Twitter', *Journal of Computer-Mediated Communication*, 18: 154–74.

House, K. (2011) '*The View* from the Oval Office: the audience effects of presidential appearances on entertainment talk shows', masters' thesis, Georgetown University.

Houston, J. B., McKinney, M. S., Hawthorne, J., and Spialek, M. L. (2013) 'Frequency of tweeting during presidential debates: effect on debate attitudes and knowledge', *Communication Studies*, 64(5): 548–60.

Hutchby, I. (2011) 'Doing non-neutral: belligerent interaction in the hybrid political interview', in M. Ekström and M. Patrona (eds), *Talking politics in broadcast media: cross-cultural perspectives on political interviewing, journalism and accountability*. Amsterdam: John Benjamins.

Ipsos MORI (2010) 'The leaders' debates: the worms' final verdict – lessons to be learned', 30 April, www.ipsos-mori.com/Assets/Docs/News/The_Leaders_Debates_-_Summary.pdf.

Isotalus, P., and Aarnio, E. (2006) 'A model of televised election discussion: the Finnish multi-party system perspective', *Javnost – The Public*, 13: 61–71.

Jacobs, G. (2011) 'Press conferences on the Internet: technology, mediation and access in the news', *Journal of Pragmatics*, 43: 1900–11.

Jones, J. (2005) *Entertaining politics: new political television and civic culture*. Lanham, MD: Rowman & Littlefield.

Jørgensen, M., and Phillips, L. (2002) *Discourse analysis as theory and method*. London: Sage.

Keane, B. (2012) 'Gillard uses her luck to confront smear campaign', Crikey.com, 24 August, www.crikey.com.au/2012/08/24/gillard-uses-her-luck-to-confront-smear-campaign/?wpmp_switcher=mobile.

Keane, J. (2010) *The life and death of democracy*. London: Pocket Books.

Kellner, D. (2009) 'Barack Obama and celebrity spectacle', *International Journal of Communication*, 3: 715–41.

Kellner, D., and Kim, G. (2009) 'YouTube, politics and pedagogy: some critical reflections', in R. Hammer and D. Kellner (eds), *Media/cultural studies: critical approaches*. New York: Peter Lang.

Kerbel, M. R. (1999) *Remote & controlled: media politics in a cynical age*. 2nd edn, Boulder, CO: Westview Press.

Kershaw, B. (1999) *The politics of performance: between Brecht and Baudrillard*. London: Routledge.

Kessler, G., and Shear, M. D. (2010) 'Presidents Obama and Medvedev bond at Ray's Hell Burger', *Washington Post*, 25 June, www.washingtonpost.com/wp-dyn/content/article/2010/06/24/AR2010062402479.html.

King, B. (2008) 'Stardom, celebrity and the para-confession', *Social Semiotics*, 18(2): 115–32.

Kirk, R., and Schill, D. (2011) 'A digital agora: citizen participation in the 2008 presidential debates', *American Behavioral Scientist*, 55(3): 325–47.

Kraus, S. (2011) *Televised presidential debates and public policy*. 2nd edn, New York: Routledge.

van Krieken, R. (2012) *Celebrity society*. London: Routledge.

Kumar, K. (1977) 'Holding the middle ground: the BBC, the public and the professional broadcaster', in J. Curran, M. Gurevitch and J. Woollacott (eds), *Mass Communication and Society*. London: Edward Arnold.

Kumar, M. J. (2003) '"Does this constitute a press conference?" Defining and tabulating modern presidential press conferences', *Presidential Studies Quarterly*, 33(1): 221–37.

Kumar, M. J. (2005) 'Presidential press conferences: the importance and evolution of an enduring forum', *Presidential Studies Quarterly*, 35(1): 166–92.

Kwak, H., Lee, C., Park, H., and Moon, S. (2010) 'What Is Twitter, a social network or a news media?', *Proceedings of the 19th International Conference on World Wide Web*. New York: ACM.

Laclau, E., and Mouffe, C. (1985) *Hegemony and socialist strategy: towards a radical democratic politics*. London: Verso.

Lakoff, R. T. (1990) *Talking power: the politics of language*. New York: Basic Books.

Lang, G. E. (1987) 'Still seeking answers', *Critical Studies in Mass Communication*, 4: 211–14.

Lawrence, R. G. (2000) 'Game-framing the issues: tracking the strategy frame in public policy issues', *Political Communication*, 17: 93–114.

van Leeuwen, T. (2001) 'What is authenticity?', *Discourse Studies*, 3: 392–7.

Lefort, C. (1986) *The political forms of modern society: bureaucracy, democracy, totalitarianism*. Oxford: Blackwell.

Lefort, C. (1988) *Democracy and political theory*, trans. D. Macey. Minneapolis: University of Minnesota Press.

Liebes, T., and Kampf, Z. (2009) 'Performance journalism: the case of media's coverage of war and terror', *Communication Review*, 12(3): 239–49.

Linthicum, K. (2008) 'Tagged, he's it election becomes their turf', *Los Angeles Times*, 23 August, http://articles.latimes.com/2008/aug/23/entertainment/et-streetart23.

Livingstone, S., and Lunt, P. (1994) *Talk on television: audience participation and public debate*. London: Routledge.

Luginbühl, M. (2007) 'Conversational violence in political TV debates: forms and functions', *Journal of Pragmatics*, 39: 1371–87.

McCarthy, T. (2015) 'Obama courts YouTube generation in interviews with online stars', *The Guardian*, 23 January, www.theguardian.com/us-news/2015/jan/22/obama-courts-youtube-generation-interviews-stars.

McKinney, M. S., Houston, B., and Hawthorne, J. (2014) 'Social watching a 2012 Republican presidential primary debate', *American Behavioral Scientist*, 58(4): 556–73.

McLaughlin, L. (1993) 'Chastity criminals in the age of electronic reproduction: re-viewing talk television and the public sphere', *Journal of Communication Inquiry*, 17(1): 41–55.

McNair, B. (2000) *Journalism and democracy: an evaluation of the political public sphere*. London: Routledge.

McNair, B. (2006) *Cultural chaos: journalism, news and power in a globalized world*. London: Routledge.

McNair, B., Hibberd, M., and Schlesinger, P. (2003) *Mediated access: broadcasting and democratic participation in the age of mediated politics*. Luton: University of Luton Press.

Madhani, A., and Jackson, D. (2013) 'Obama: I don't see Snowden as a patriot', *USA Today*, 9 August, www.usatoday.com/story/news/politics/2013/08/09/obama-news-conference/2636191/.

Martin, J. R., and White, P. R. R. (2005) *The language of evaluation: appraisal in English*. Basingstoke: Palgrave Macmillan.

Martinson, J. (2013) 'Julia Gillard is right: women's body parts are not for public consumption', *The Guardian*, 12 June, www.theguardian.com/commentisfree/2013/jun/12/julia-gillard-women-body-parts-meat.

Marwick, A. E., and boyd, d. (2010) 'I tweet honestly, I tweet passionately: Twitter users, context collapse, and the imagined audience', *New Media & Society*, 13(1): 114–33.

Mason, R. (2013) 'David Cameron: the price of a loaf of bread? No idea, I have a breadmaker', *The Guardian*, 1 October, www.theguardian.com/politics/2013/oct/01/david-cameron-price-of-bread.

May, A. L. (2008) 'Campaign 2008: it's on YouTube', *Nieman Reports*, summer: 24–8.

Maybin, J. (2001) 'Language, struggle and voice: the Bakhtin/Volosinov writings', in M. Wetherell, S. Taylor and S. Yates (eds), *Discourse theory and practice: a reader*. London: Sage.

Mehl, D. (2005) 'The public on the television screen: towards a public sphere of exhibition', *Journal of Media Practice*, 6(1): 19–28.

Merleau-Ponty, M. (1962) *The phenomenology of perception*. New York: Routledge.

Meyrowitz, J. (1985) *No sense of place*. Oxford: Oxford University Press.

Mills, S. (2012) 'How Twitter is winning the 2012 US election', *The Guardian*, 16 October, www.theguardian.com/commentisfree/2012/oct/16/twitter-winning-2012-us-election.

Minow, N. N., and LaMay, C. L. (2008) *Inside the presidential debates: their improbable past and promising future*. Chicago: University of Chicago Press.

Mitchell, A., and Hitlin, P. (2013) 'Twitter reaction to events often at odds with overall public opinion', *Pew Research Center*, 4 March, www.pewresearch.org/2013/03/04/twitter-reaction-to-events-often-at-odds-with-overall-public-opinion/.

Montgomery, M. (2008) 'The discourse of the broadcast news interview', *Journalism Studies*, 9(2): 260–77.

Montgomery, M. (2011) 'The accountability interview, politics and change in UK public service broadcasting', in M. Ekström and M. Patrona (eds), *Talking politics in broadcast media: cross-cultural perspectives on political interviewing, journalism and accountability*. Amsterdam: John Benjamins.

Morgan, M. (2012) 'The politics of Twitter: presidential debate is most tweeted political event in history', *Deseret News*, 3 October, www.deseretnews.com/article/865563737/The-politics-of-Twitter-Presidential-debate-is-most-tweeted-political-event-in-history.html?pg=all.

Mouffe, C. (1993) *The return of the political*. London: Verso.

Mouffe, C. (2000) *The democratic paradox*. London: Verso.

Mughan, A. (2000) *Media and the presidentialization of parliamentary elections*. Basingstoke: Palgrave.

Murse, T. (2012) 'How many people watch presidential debates', *About. com*, 5 October.

Neveu, E. (2005) 'Politicians without politics, a polity without citizens: the politics of the chat show in contemporary France', *Modern & Contemporary France*, 13(3): 323–35.

Ngak, C. (2012) 'Big Bird to KitchenAid: social media hits and misses from the presidential debate', *CBS News*, 4 October, www.cbsnews.com/news/big-bird-to-kitchenaid-social-media-hits-and-misses-from-the-presidential-debate/.

Norris, P. (2000) 'The evolution of campaign communications', in Norris, *A virtuous circle: political communications in postindustrial societies*. Cambridge: Cambridge University Press.

Novak, M. (2010) 'It's better to take *Q&A* as a comment, not democracy', *The Punch*, 26 October, www.ipa.org.au/news/2226/it-s-better-to-take-q-a-as-a-comment-not-democracy.

'Obama' (2012) *Otago Daily Times*, 8 November, p. 1.

'Obama–Romney debate draws bigger TV audience than 2008' (2012) *Reuters*, 4 October, www.reuters.com/article/2012/10/04/usa-campaign-tvratings-idUSL1E8L4I2720121004.

Obeng, S. G. (1997) 'Language and politics: indirectness in political discourse', *Discourse & Society*, 8(1): 49–83.

Olanoff, D. (2012) 'First 2012 presidential debate saw 10.3m tweets and gave politics a new dimension', *TechCrunch*, 4 October, http://techcrunch.com/2012/10/04/first-2012-presidential-debate-saw-10-3m-tweets-and-gave-politics-a-new-dimension/.

Papacharissi, Z. (2015) *Affective publics: sentiment, technology and politics.* Oxford: Oxford University Press.

Patterson, T. E. (1993) *Out of order.* New York: Knopf.

Pattie, C., and Johnston, R. (2011) 'A tale of sound and fury, signifying something? The impact of the leaders' debates in the 2010 UK general election', *Journal of Elections, Public Opinion & Parties*, 21(2): 147–77.

Pauly, J. J. (2004) 'Media studies and the dialogue of democracy', in R. Anderson, L. A. Baxter and K. N. Cissna (eds), *Dialogue: theorizing difference in communication studies.* Thousand Oaks, CA: Sage.

Peck, J. (1995) 'TV talk shows as therapeutic discourse: the ideological labor of the televised talking cure', *Communication Theory*, 5(1): 58–81.

Pels, D. (2003) 'Aesthetic representation and political style: re-balancing identity and difference in media democracy', in J. Corner and D. Pels (eds), *Media and the restyling of politics.* London: Sage.

Peterson, J. (2012) 'Presidential debate most tweeted political event in US history', *Daily Caller*, 4 October, http://dailycaller.com/2012/10/04/presidential-debate-most-tweeted-political-event-in-us-history/.

Pfau, M. (2002) 'The subtle nature of presidential debate influence', *Argumentation & Advocacy*, 38: 251–61.

Pitkin, H. F. (1967) *The concept of representation.* Berkeley: University of California Press.

Poguntke, T., and Webb, P. (2005) *The presidentialization of politics: a comparative study of modern democracies.* Oxford: Oxford University Press.

Ponce de Leon, C. (2002) *Self-exposure: human-interest journalism and the emergence of celebrity in America, 1890–1940.* Chapel Hill: University of North Carolina Press.

Postman, N. (1987) *Amusing ourselves to death.* London: Methuen.

Prior, M. (2006) *Post-broadcast democracy: how media choice increases inequality in political involvement and polarizes elections.* Cambridge: Cambridge University Press.

'Q&A scores ratings record' (2010) *ABC News*, 10 August, updated 13 December, www.abc.net.au/news/2010-08-10/q-and-a-scores-ratings-record/939262.

Reisigl, M. (2008) 'Rhetoric of political speeches', in R. Wodak and V. Koller (eds), *Handbook of communication in the public sphere*. Berlin: Mouton de Gruyter.

Richardson, J. (2007) *Analysing newspapers: an approach from critical discourse analysis*. Basingstoke: Palgrave.

Roper, J. (1998) *When the worm turns: an infotainment format for televised election debates which set a political agenda in New Zealand*. Hamilton: University of Waikato.

Rottinghaus, B. (2009) 'Strategic leaders: determining successful presidential opinion leadership tactics through public appeals', *Political Communication*, 26: 296–316.

Rowland, R. C. (2013) 'The first 2012 presidential campaign debate: the decline of reason in presidential debates', *Communication Studies*, 64(5): 528–47.

Rudd, C., Hayward, J., and Craig, G. (eds) (2009) *Informing voters? Politics, media and the New Zealand election 2008*. Auckland: Pearson.

Rushkoff, D. (1996) *Media virus! Hidden agendas in popular culture*. New York: Ballantine Books.

Sampson, A. (1996) 'The crisis at the heart of our media', *British Journalism Review*, 17(3): 42–51.

Sanders, K. (2009) 'Campaign effects: is anyone ever persuaded?', in Sanders, *Communicating politics in the twenty-first century*. Basingstoke: Palgrave Macmillan.

Savage, C., and Shear, M. D. (2013) 'President moves to ease worries on surveillance', *New York Times*, 9 August, www.nytimes.com/2013/08/10/us/politics/obama-news-conference.html.

Scannell, P. (ed.) (1991) *Broadcast talk*. London: Sage.

Schroeder, A. (2000) *Presidential debates: forty years of high-risk TV*. New York: Columbia University Press.

Schroeder, A. (2004) *Celebrity-in-chief: how show business took over the White House*. Boulder, CO: Westview Press.

Schudson, M. (1994) 'Question authority: a history of the news interview in American journalism, 1860s–1930s', *Media, Culture & Society*, 16: 565–87.

Schudson, M. (2005) 'Autonomy from what?', in R. Benson and E. Neveu (eds), *Bourdieu and the journalistic field*. Cambridge: Polity.

Searle, J. (1969) *Speech acts: an essay in the philosophy of language*. Cambridge: Cambridge University Press.

Sedorkin, G. (2011) *Interviewing: a guide for journalists and writers*. 2nd edn, Sydney: Allen & Unwin.

Senft, T. (2008) *Camgirls: celebrity and community in the age of social networks*. New York: Peter Lang.

Senior, P. (2008) 'Electoral impact of televised leaders' debates on Australian federal elections', *Australian Journal of Political Science*, 43(3): 443–64.

Seymour-Ure, C. (2003) *Prime ministers and the media: issues of power and control*. Oxford: Blackwell.

Simper, E. (2011) 'Just quietly, Aunty has a success story', *The Australian*, 11 April, www.theaustralian.com.au/business/opinion/just-quietly-aunty-has-a-success-story/story-e6frg9to-1226036877118.

Simpson, P. (1993) *Language, ideology and point of view*. London: Routledge.

Smith, C. (1990) *Presidential press conferences: a critical approach*. New York: Praeger.

'The Snowden effect' (2013) *The Economist*, 10 August, www.economist.com/blogs/democracyinamerica/2013/08/american-surveillance.

'Social media weighs in on 2012 presidential debate' (2012) *Associated Press*, 4 October, www.foxnews.com/tech/2012/10/04/social-media-weighs-in-on-2012-presidential-debate/.

Sparrow, A. (2009) 'Cameron "desperately embarrassed" over Bullingdon Club days', *The Guardian*, 4 October, www.theguardian.com/politics/2009/oct/04/david-cameron-bullingdon-club.

Stanley, A. (2008) 'Michelle Obama shows her warmer side on "The View"', *New York Times*, 19 June, www.nytimes.com/2008/06/19/us/politics/19watch.html?_r=0.

Stanyer, J. (2013) *Intimate politics: publicity, privacy and the personal lives of politicians in media-saturated democracies*. Cambridge: Polity.

Steinberg, J. (2008) '"The View" has its eye on politics this year', *New York Times*, 23 September, http://query.nytimes.com/gst/fullpage.html?res=9A01E4DF1439F930A1575AC0A96E9C8B63.

Street, J. (2003) 'The celebrity politician: political style and popular culture', in J. Corner and D. Pels (eds), *Media and the restyling of politics*. London: Sage.

Street, J. (2004) 'Celebrity politicians: popular culture and political representation', *British Journal of Politics & International Relations*, 6(4): 435–52.

Strömbäck, J. (2008) 'Four phases of mediatization: an analysis of the mediatization of politics', *International Journal of Press/Politics*, 13(3): 228–46.

Styles, J. (2010) 'This "adventure in democracy" is unfair and unbalanced', *Spectator Australia*, 3 March, www.spectator.co.uk/australia/5813678/this-adventure-in-democracy-is-unfair-and-unbalanced/.

Thompson, J. (1991) 'Editor's introduction', in P. Bourdieu, *Language & symbolic power*. Cambridge, MA: Harvard University Press.

Thompson, J. (1995) *The media and modernity: a social theory of the media*. Cambridge: Polity.

Thompson, J. (2000) *Political scandal: power and visibility in the media age*. Cambridge: Polity.

Thussu, D. K. (2007) *News as entertainment: the rise of global infotainment*. Los Angeles: Sage.

Tolson, A. (2006) *Media talk: spoken discourse on TV and radio*. Edinburgh: Edinburgh University Press.

Tryon, C. (2007) 'Is Internet politics better off than it was four years ago?', *Flow TV*, 6(8), http://flowtv.org/?p=797.

Turner, G. (2005) *Ending the affair: the decline of television current affairs in Australia*. Sydney: University of South Wales Press.

Valentino, N. A., Buhr, T. A., and Beckmann, M. N. (2001) 'When the frame is the game: revisiting the impact of "strategic" campaign coverage on citizens' information retention', *Journalism and Mass Communication Quarterly*, 78(1): 93–112.

Van Aelst, P., Sheafer, T., and Stanyer, J. (2012) 'The personalization of mediated political communication: a review of concepts, operationalizations and key findings' *Journalism*, 13(2): 203–20.

de Vreese, C. H. (2004) 'The effects of strategic news on political cynicism, issue evaluations and policy support: a two-wave experiment', *Mass Communication and Society*, 7(2): 191–215.

de Vreese, C., and Elenbaas, M. (2008) 'Media in the game of politics: effects of strategic metacoverage on political cynicism', *International Journal of Press/Politics*, 13(3): 285–309.

Walsh, K. T. (2013) 'Obama: press conference, then vacation', *US News & World Report*, 9 August, www.usnews.com/news/blogs/ken-walshs-washington/2013/08/09/obama-press-conference-then-vacation.

Washbourne, N. (2010) *Mediating politics: newspapers, radio, television and the Internet*. Maidenhead: Open University Press.

Webb, J., Schirato, T., and Danaher, G. (2002) *Understanding Bourdieu*. Crows Nest, NSW: Allen & Unwin.

Wierzbicka, A. (2006) 'The concept of "dialogue" in cross-linguistic and cross-cultural perspective', *Discourse Studies*, 8(5): 675–703.

Williams, R. (1975) *Drama in a dramatized society: an inaugural lecture*. Cambridge: Cambridge University Press.

Wilson, J. (2011) '*Sunrise* to sunset: Kevin Rudd as celebrity in Australia's post-broadcast democracy', *Celebrity Studies*, 2(1): 97–9.

Wintour, P. (2013) 'How David Cameron and Nick Clegg turned into 24-hour news machines', *The Guardian*, 8 August, www.theguardian.com/politics/2013/aug/08/david-cameron-nick-clegg-24-hour-news-machines.

Wodak, R. (2011) *The discourse of politics in action: politics as usual*. Basingstoke: Palgrave Macmillan.

Wodak, R., Kwon, W., and Clarke, I. (2011) '"Getting people on board": discursive leadership for consensus building in team meetings', *Discourse & Society*, 22(5): 592–644.

Woolf, N. (2012) 'US presidential debate liveblog', *New Statesman*, 3 October, www.newstatesman.com/blogs/politics/2012/10/us-presidential-debate-liveblog.

Wring, D., and Ward, S. (2010) 'The media and the 2010 campaign: the television election?', *Parliamentary Affairs*, 63(4): 802–17.

Wynne, D., and O'Connor, J. (1998) 'Consumption and the postmodern city', *Urban Studies*, 35(5/6): 841–64.

Younane Brookes, S. (2011) 'Unscripted and unpredictable: communication and connection in "televised town halls": Australian federal election 2010', *Communication, Politics & Culture*, 44(2): 57–74.
Young, I. (1987) 'Impartiality and the civic public: some implications of feminist critiques of moral and political theory', in S. Benhabib and D. Cornell (eds), *Feminism as critique*. Cambridge: Polity.
Zolo, D. (1992) *Democracy and Complexity*. Cambridge: Polity.
van Zoonen, L. (2005) *Entertaining the citizen: when politics and popular culture converge*. Lanham, MD: Rowman & Littlefield.

Programme References

The Andrew Marr Show (2013a) 'Interview: David Cameron, MP, prime minister', 21 July, transcript, http://news.bbc.co.uk/1/shared/bsp/hi/pdfs/210713.pdf.
The Andrew Marr Show (2013b) 'Interview with David Cameron, prime minister, leader, Conservative Party', 29 September, transcript, http://news.bbc.co.uk/1/shared/bsp/hi/pdfs/99999.pdf.
The Andrew Marr Show (2014) 'Interview with prime minister, David Cameron', 5 January, transcript, http://news.bbc.co.uk/1/shared/bsp/hi/pdfs/05011401.pdf.
BBC debate (2010) 'Final prime ministerial debate, 29 April', transcript, http://news.bbc.co.uk/1/shared/bsp/hi/pdfs/30_04_10_finaldebate.pdf.
Insiders (2010) 'Rudd backs Combet over Garrett's old job', 28 February, transcript, www.abc.net.au/insiders/content/2010/s2832260.htm.
ITV debate (2010) 'First prime ministerial debate, 15 April', transcript, http://news.bbc.co.uk/1/shared/bsp/hi/pdfs/16_04_10_firstdebate.pdf.
Joint press conference (2010) 'Remarks by President Obama and President Medvedev of Russia at joint press conference', June 24, transcript, www.whitehouse.gov/the-press-office/remarks-president-obama-and-president-medvedev-russia-joint-press-conference.
Q&A (2011a) 'Q and A goes to Brisbane', 21 February, transcript, www.abc.net.au/tv/qanda/txt/s3138582.htm.
Q&A (2011b) 'The gender divide', 7 March, transcript, www.abc.net.au/tv/qanda/txt/s3151089.htm.
Q&A (2011c) 'Confessions of Kevin', 4 April, transcript, www.abc.net.au/tv/qanda/txt/s3176092.htm.
Q&A (2011d) 'Julia Gillard meets the people', 14 March, transcript, www.abc.net.au/tv/qanda/txt/s3157403.htm.
Q&A (2011e) 'The Q and A century', 21 March, transcript, www.abc.net.au/tv/qanda/txt/s3163803.htm.
Q&A (2011f) 'Revolution, revelations and romance', 14 February, transcript, www.abc.net.au/tv/qanda/txt/s3132359.htm.
Q&A (2011g) 'After the massacre', 28 March, transcript, www.abc.net.au/tv/qanda/txt/s3169816.htm.

Q&A (2011h) 'Cate's carbon controversy', 30 May, transcript, www. abc.net.au/tv/qanda/txt/s3224649.htm.

Q&A (2011j) 'The carbon curse', 28 February, transcript, www.abc.net.au/ tv/qanda/txt/s3144701.htm.

7.30 Report (2010) 'Angry Rudd defends ETS backflip', 12 May, transcript, www.abc.net.au/7.30/content/2010/s2897846.htm.

Sky debate (2010) 'Second prime ministerial debate, 22 April', transcript, http://news.bbc.co.uk/1/shared/bsp/hi/pdfs/23_04_10_seconddebate.pdf.

Solo press conference (2013) 'Remarks by the president in a press conference', 9 August, transcript, www.whitehouse.gov/the-press-office/ 2013/08/09/remarks-president-press-conference.

US debate (2012) 'Full 2012 first US presidential debate', 3 October, https:// www.youtube.com/watch?v=6g6Vj058tXQ.

The View (2012a) 'Barack and Michelle Obama on "The View"', 25 September, https://www.youtube.com/watch?v=Hdn1iX1a528.

The View (2012b) 'President Obama on "The View"', 15 May, https:// www.youtube.com/watch?v=RoUKmP55Uww.

Index